TSUBAKI·CHOU Lonely Planet

3

MIKA
YAMAMORI

CONTENTS

THE STORY SO FAR...

Stuck with her father's debts and forcefully evicted from her home, high schooler Fumi Ohno finds a job as the housekeeper for the novelist Akatsuki Kibikino. Despite a rocky first encounter, the two soon figure out how to live and work together. When Fumi's father strains his back, Akatsuki gives her the money she needs without batting an eye. Touched by his kindness and comforting words, Fumi admits to herself that she's fallen for her employer, but right after she does, a bookstore employee at Akatsuki's book signing issues an abrupt declaration of war!

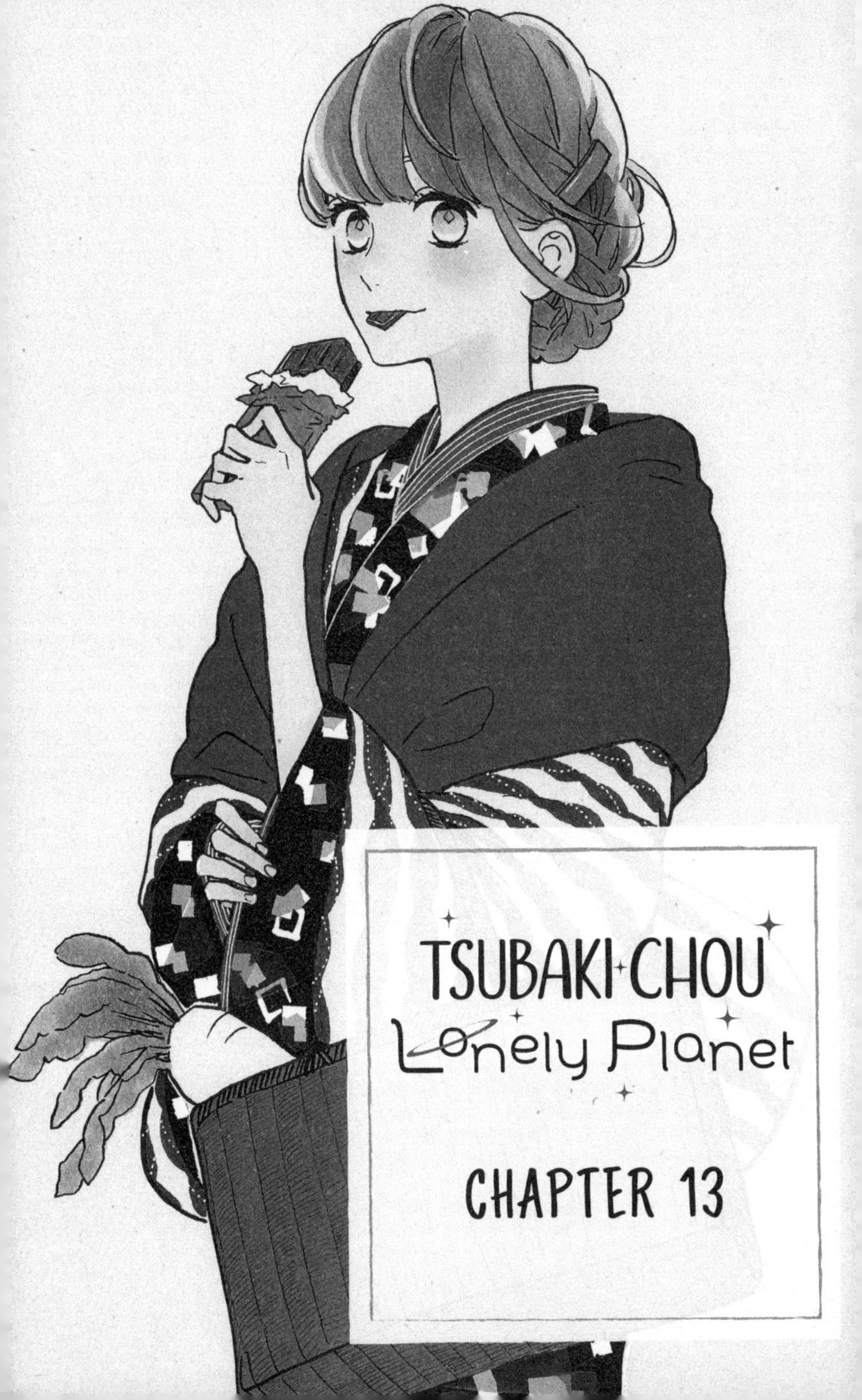
TSUBAKI-CHOU
Lonely Planet
CHAPTER 13

And so...

Tsubaki-chou Lonely Planet is on Volume 3 already!! S-so fast...

My assistant Kame-chan moved to Osaka this year, and I'm really happy about it!

Yaaay!

I'll keep working like crazy, so please stick with me!

If you enjoy *Tsubaki-chou* even a little, I'll be thrilled!

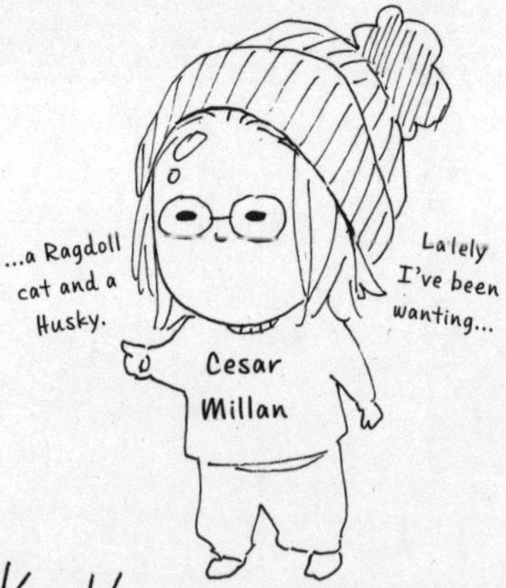
Lately I've been wanting...
...a Ragdoll cat and a Husky.
Cesar Millan

February 2016

Mika!!

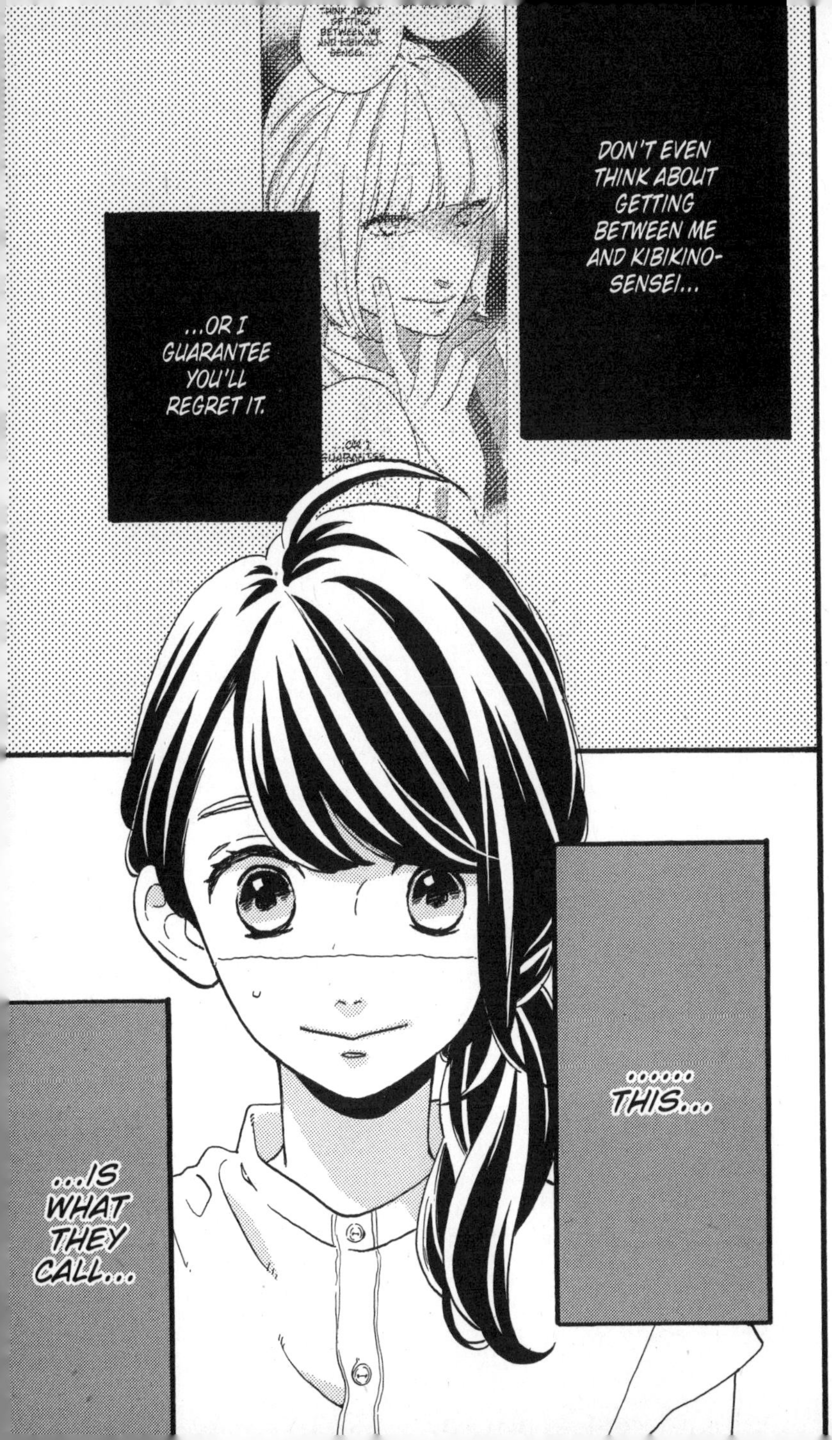
DON'T EVEN THINK ABOUT GETTING BETWEEN ME AND KIBIKINO-SENSEI...
...OR I GUARANTEE YOU'LL REGRET IT.
......THIS...
...IS WHAT THEY CALL...

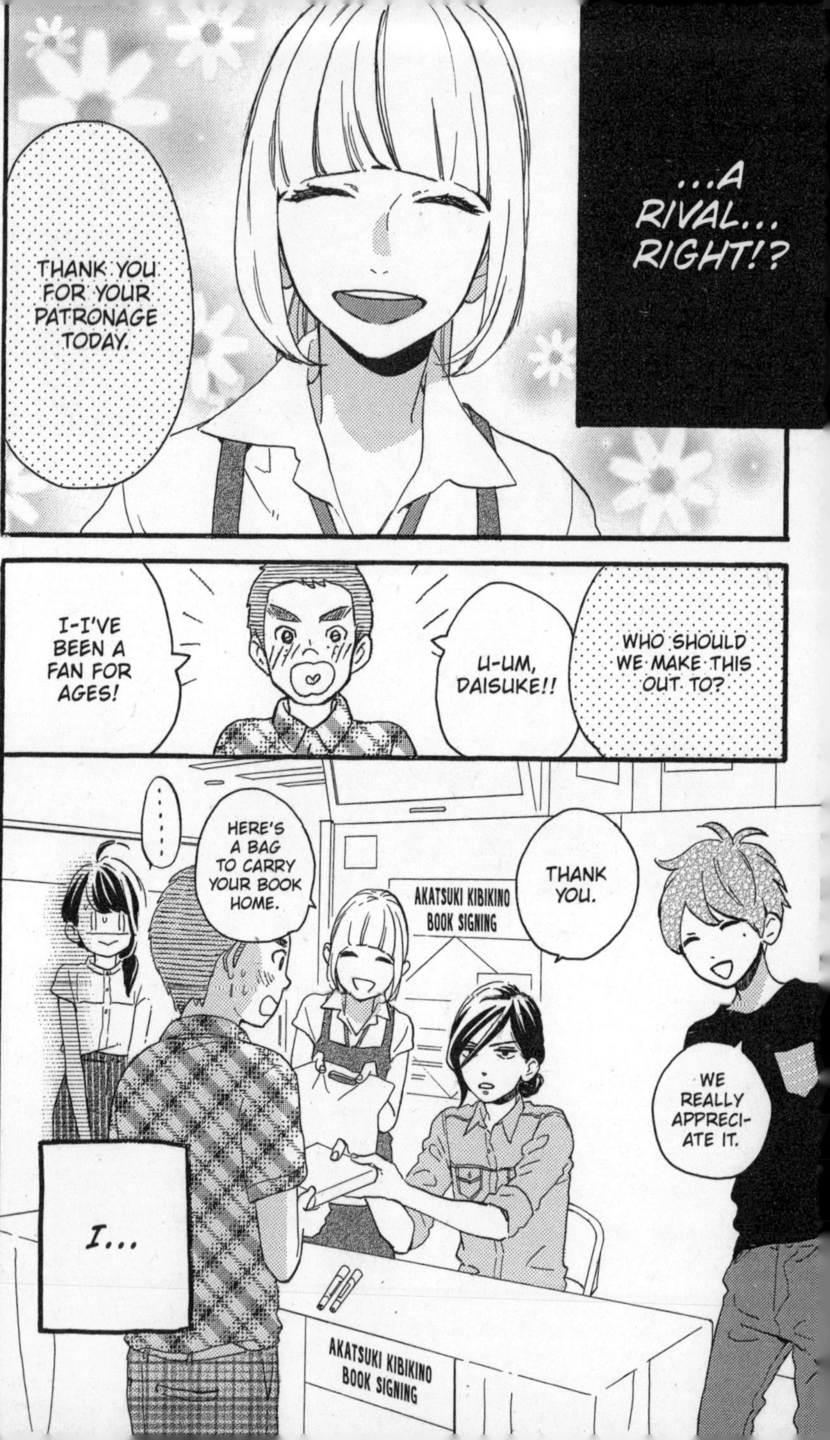
...A RIVAL... RIGHT!?
THANK YOU FOR YOUR PATRONAGE TODAY.
WHO SHOULD WE MAKE THIS OUT TO?
U-UM, DAISUKE!!
I-I'VE BEEN A FAN FOR AGES!
THANK YOU.
WE REALLY APPRECI-ATE IT.
AKATSUKI KIBIKINO BOOK SIGNING
HERE'S A BAG TO CARRY YOUR BOOK HOME.
......
I...
AKATSUKI KIBIKINO BOOK SIGNING

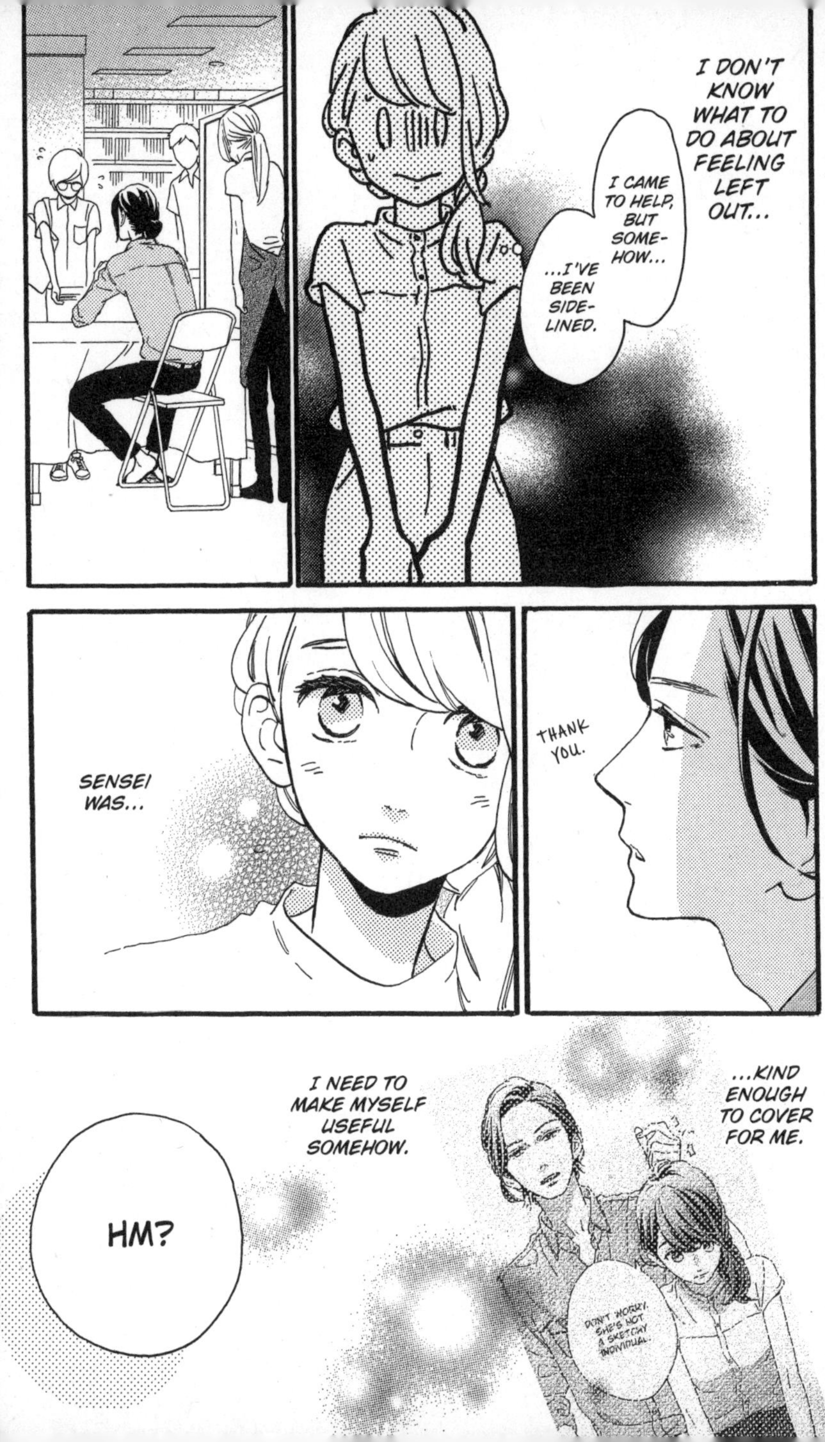
I DON'T KNOW WHAT TO DO ABOUT FEELING LEFT OUT...
I CAME TO HELP, BUT SOMEHOW...
...I'VE BEEN SIDELINED.
THANK YOU.
SENSEI WAS...
...KIND ENOUGH TO COVER FOR ME.
DON'T WORRY. SHE'S NOT A SKETCHY INDIVIDUAL.
I NEED TO MAKE MYSELF USEFUL SOMEHOW.
HM?

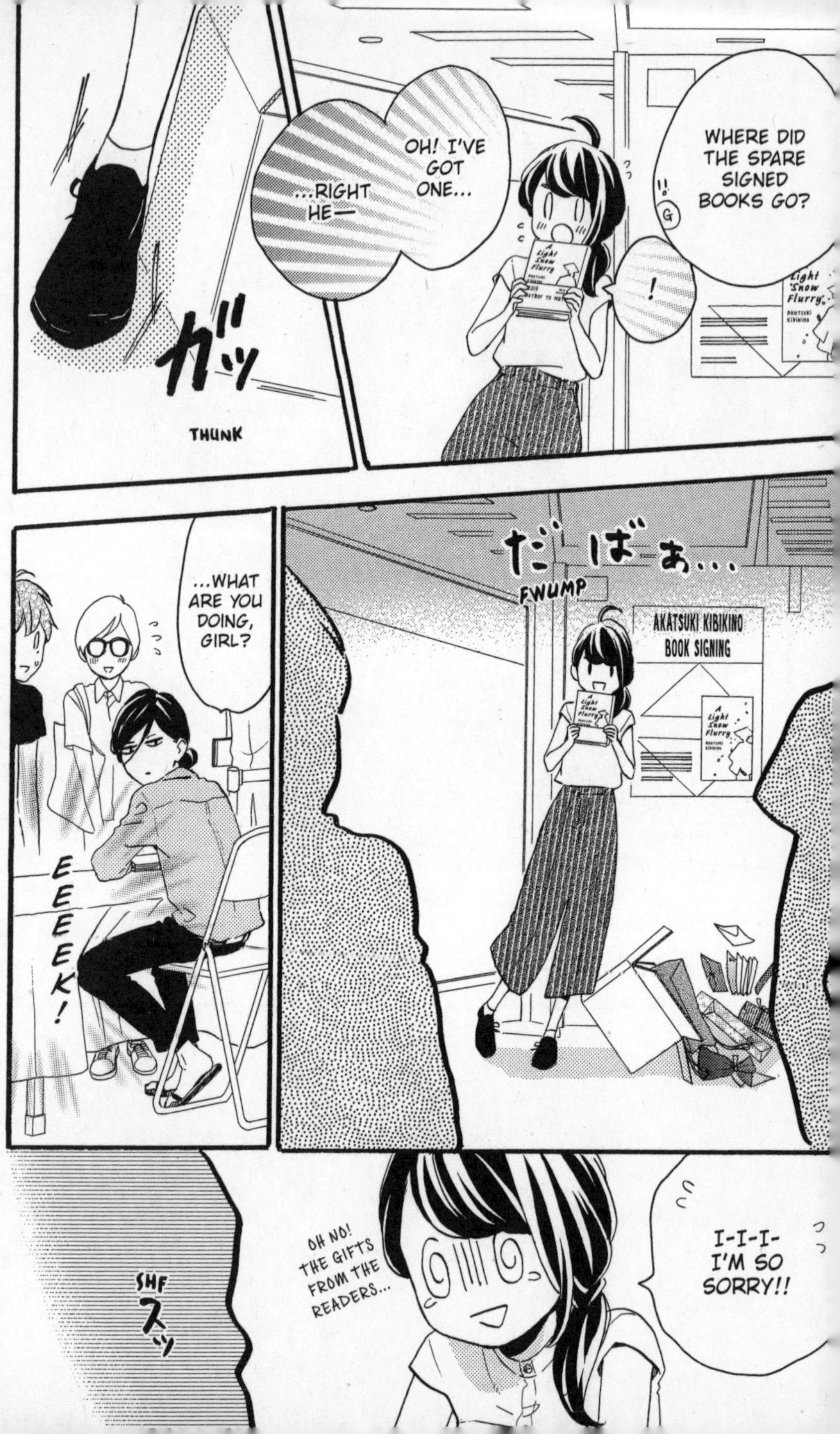
WHERE DID THE SPARE SIGNED BOOKS GO?
!
OH! I'VE GOT ONE...
...RIGHT HE—
A Light Snow Flurry
ガッ
THUNK
だばぁ...
FWUMP
AKATSUKI KIBIKINO BOOK SIGNING
A Light Snow Flurry
...WHAT ARE YOU DOING, GIRL?
EEEEEK!
I-I-I- I'M SO SORRY!!
OH NO! THE GIFTS FROM THE READERS...
SHF
スッ

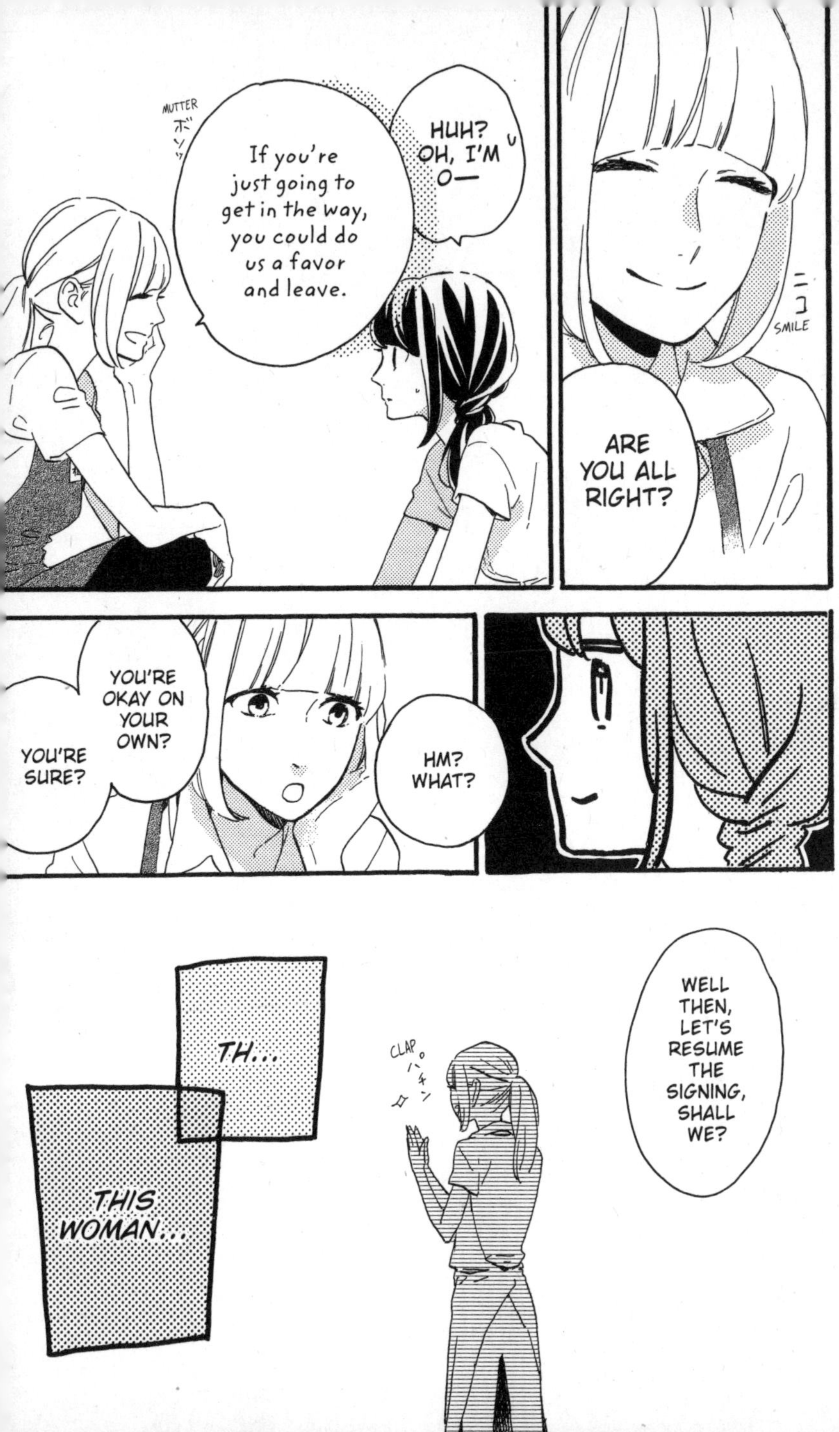
SMILE
ARE YOU ALL RIGHT?
HUH? OH, I'M O—
If you're just going to get in the way, you could do us a favor and leave.
MUTTER
HM? WHAT?
YOU'RE OKAY ON YOUR OWN?
YOU'RE SURE?
WELL THEN, LET'S RESUME THE SIGNING, SHALL WE?
CLAP
TH...
THIS WOMAN...

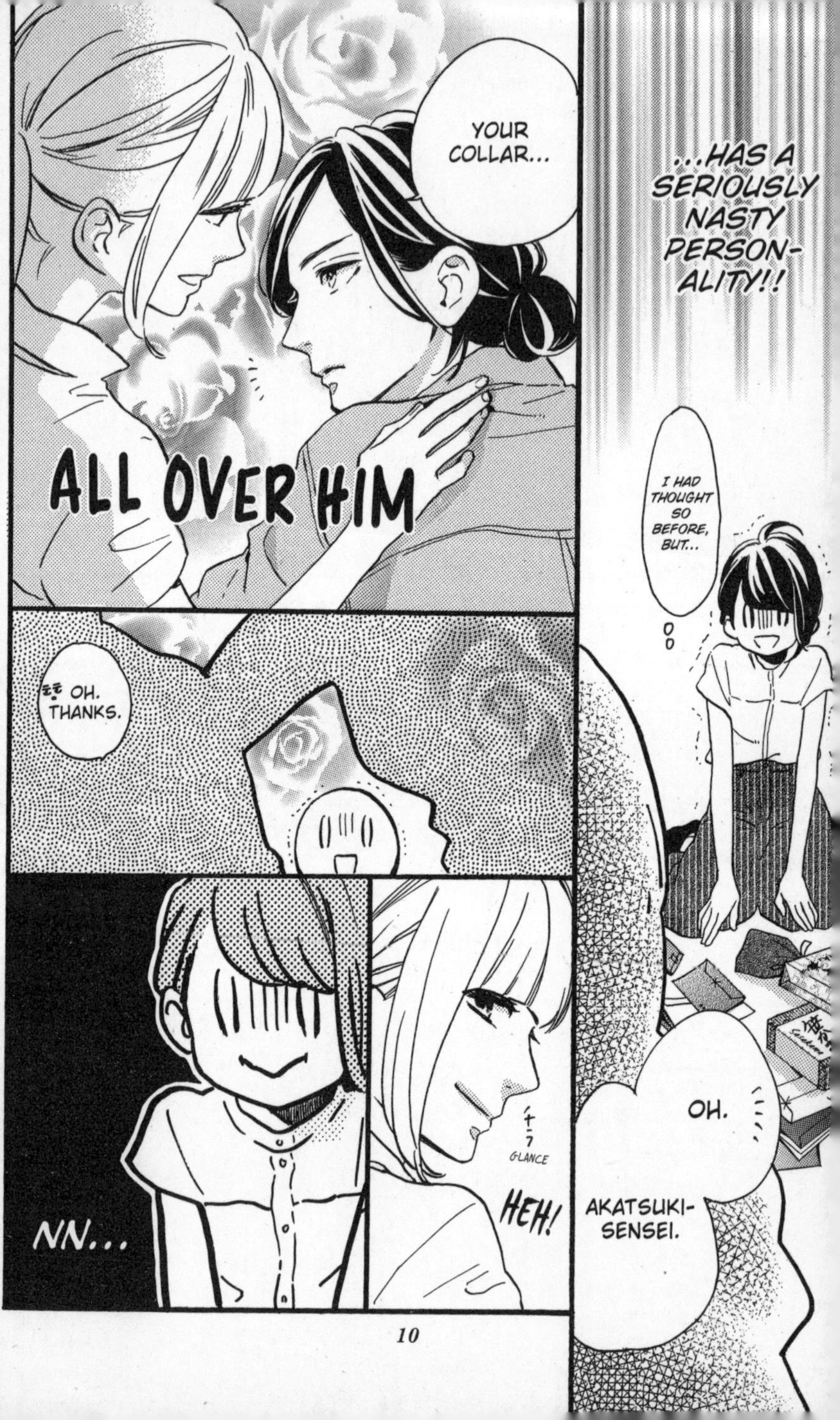
...HAS A SERIOUSLY NASTY PERSON-ALITY!!
I HAD THOUGHT SO BEFORE, BUT...
OH.
AKATSUKI-SENSEI.
YOUR COLLAR...
ALL OVER HIM
OH. THANKS.
GLANCE
HEH!
NN...

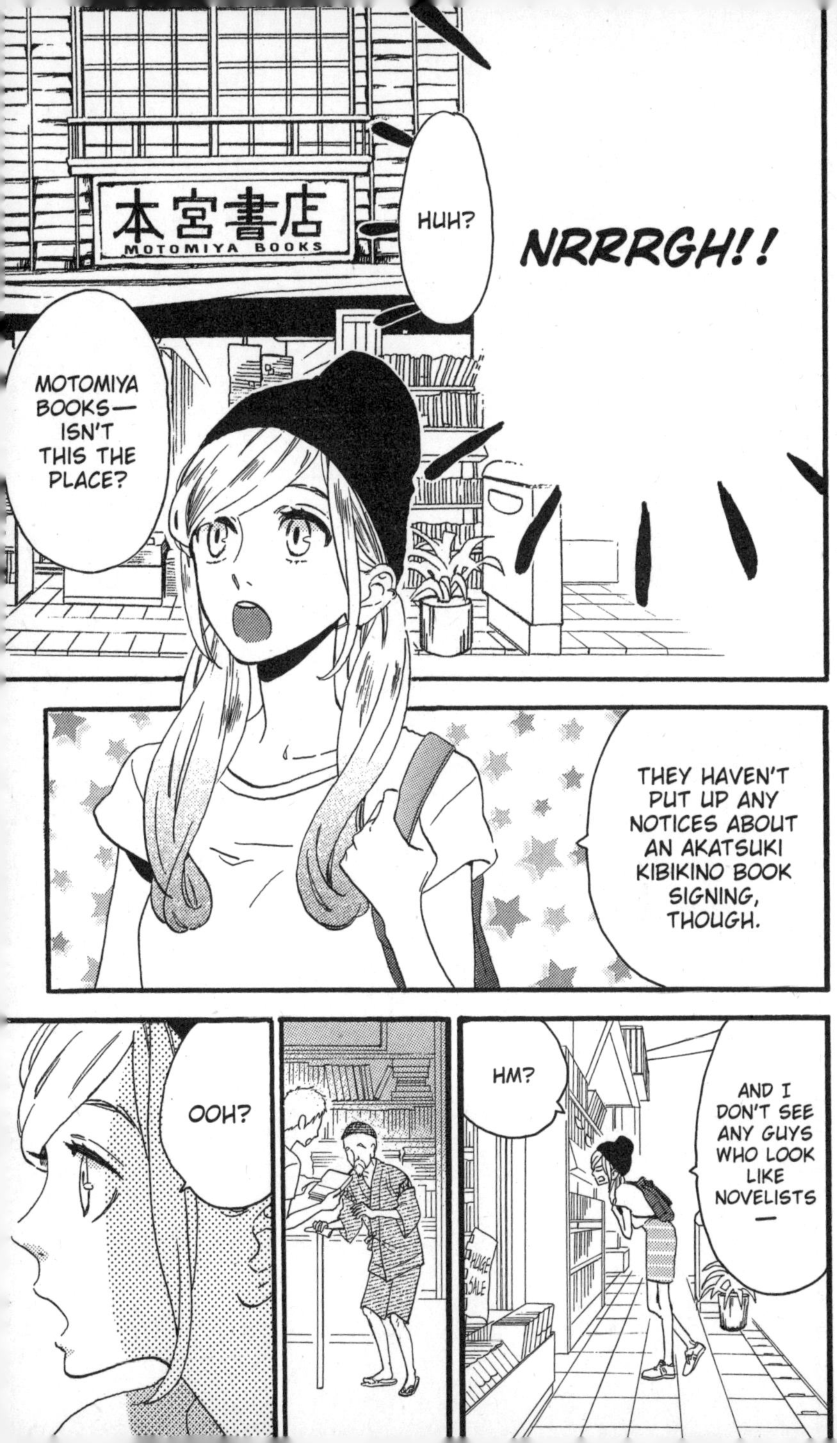
NRRRGH!!
HUH?
本宮書店
MOTOMIYA BOOKS
MOTOMIYA BOOKS—ISN'T THIS THE PLACE?
THEY HAVEN'T PUT UP ANY NOTICES ABOUT AN AKATSUKI KIBIKINO BOOK SIGNING, THOUGH.
AND I DON'T SEE ANY GUYS WHO LOOK LIKE NOVELISTS—
HM?
HUGE SALE
OOH?

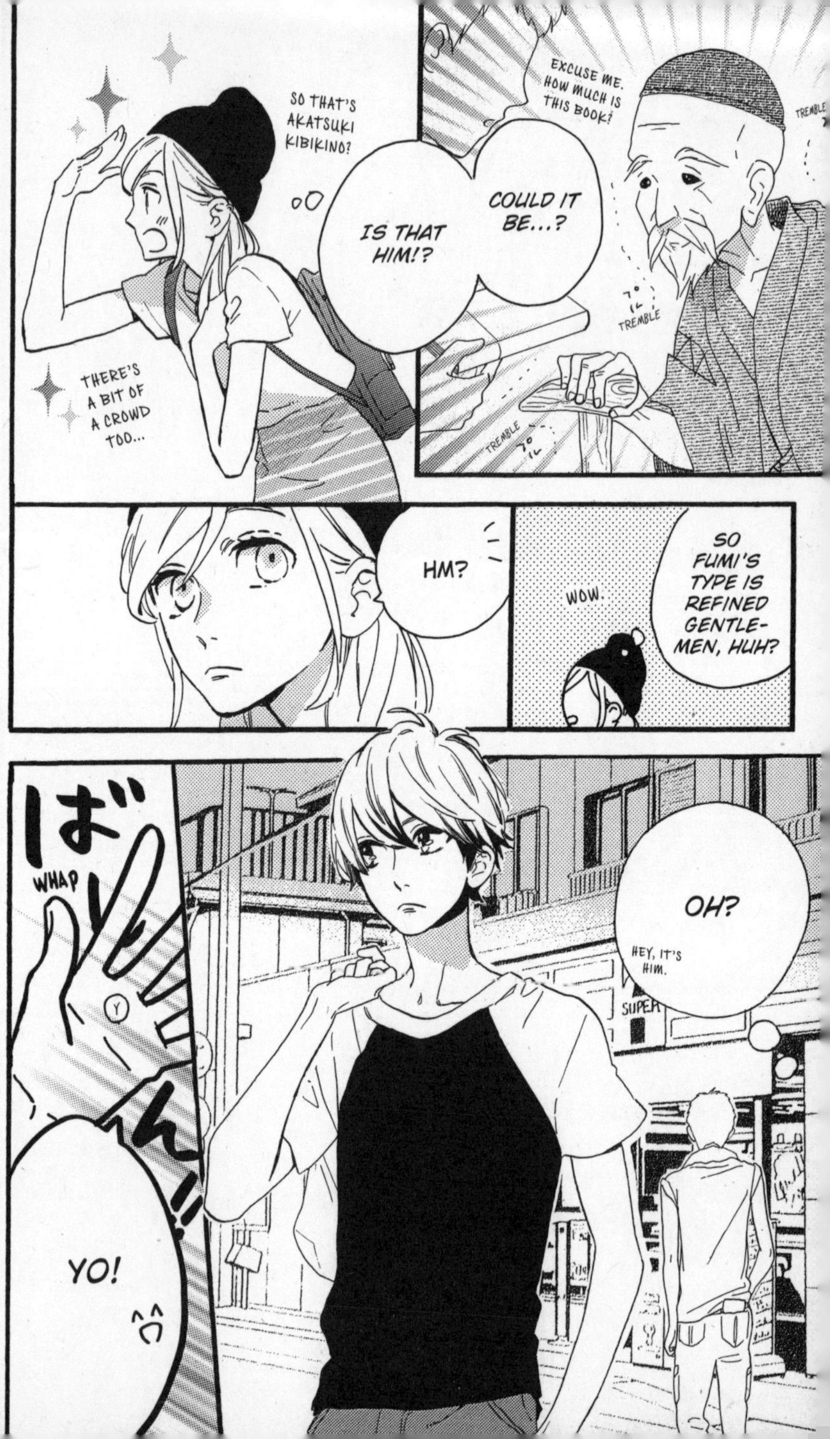
EXCUSE ME. HOW MUCH IS THIS BOOK?
TREMBLE
TREMBLE
TREMBLE
COULD IT BE...?
IS THAT HIM!?
SO THAT'S AKATSUKI KIBIKINO?
THERE'S A BIT OF A CROWD TOO...
SO FUMI'S TYPE IS REFINED GENTLE-MEN, HUH?
WOW.
HM?
OH?
HEY, IT'S HIM.
SUPER
ばん!!
WHAP
YO!

MOTOMIYA BOOKS IS OVER HERE.

MOTO-MIYA?

AH... OH RIGHT, THAT'S A THING, ISN'T IT?

HUH!?

NICE RUNNING INTO YOU. ARE YOU ALSO HEADED TO THE BOOK SIGNING?

WHAT'S YOUR DEAL!

THAT HURTS!

IRK

―3

HEY, DON'T GO SPLITTING HAIRS JUST 'COS I FOUND IT FIRST.

IT'S AT MIYAMOTO BOOKS AT 3:00.

DIDN'T SHE SAY IT WAS AT MIYAMOTO BOOKS?

WHY ARE YOU PATRONIZING ME!

...SO I'LL DO YOU A SOLID AND TAG ALONG WITH YOU, I GUESS.

...BUT FUMI'S NOT HERE...

WELL, I CAN'T SAY I LIKE YOU MUCH...

WHAT!?

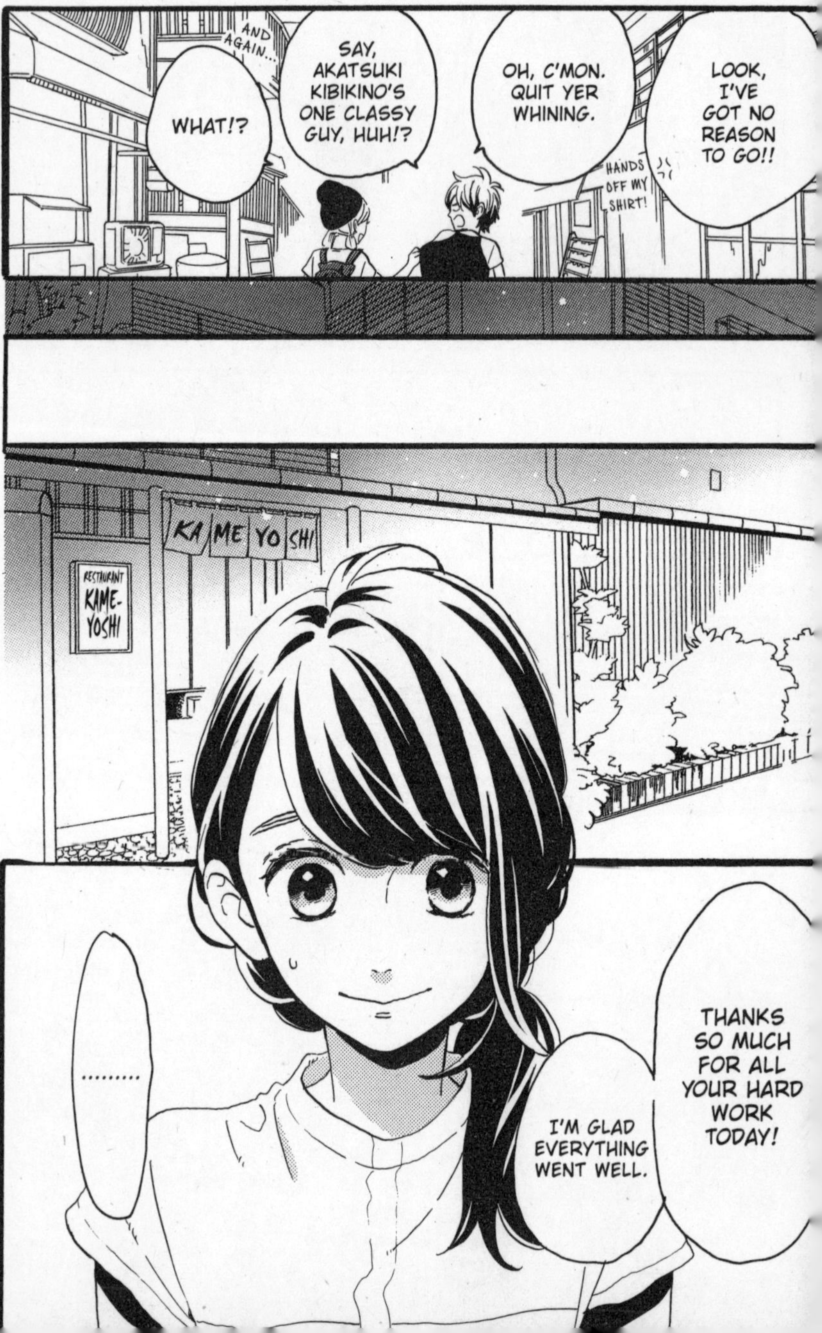
LOOK, I'VE GOT NO REASON TO GO!!
HANDS OFF MY SHIRT!
OH, C'MON. QUIT YER WHINING.
SAY, AKATSUKI KIBIKINO'S ONE CLASSY GUY, HUH!?
AND AGAIN...
WHAT!?
KA ME YO SHI
RESTAURANT KAME-YOSHI
THANKS SO MUCH FOR ALL YOUR HARD WORK TODAY!
I'M GLAD EVERYTHING WENT WELL.
....

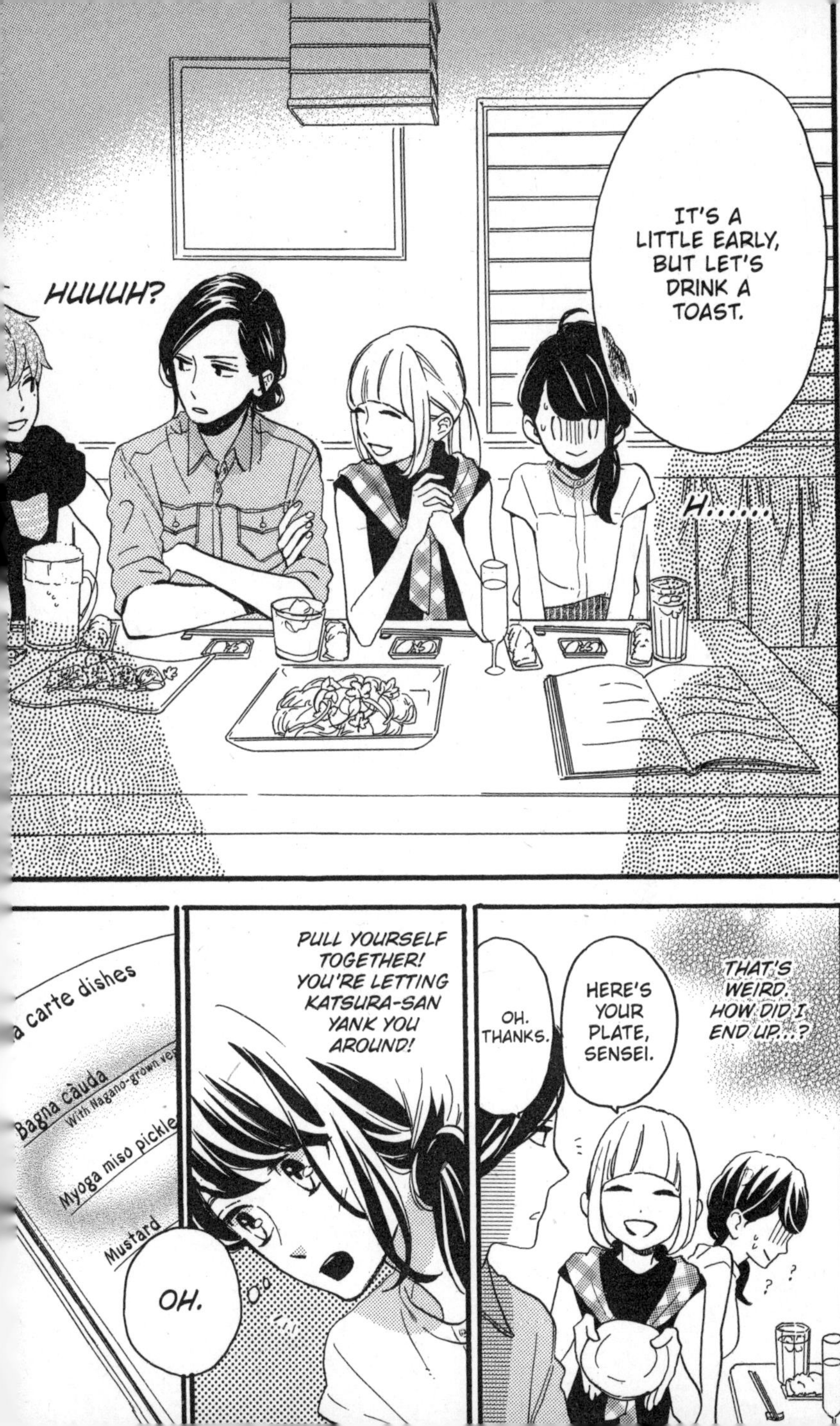
IT'S A LITTLE EARLY, BUT LET'S DRINK A TOAST.
H......
HUUUH?
THAT'S WEIRD. HOW DID I END UP...?
HERE'S YOUR PLATE, SENSEI.
OH. THANKS.
PULL YOURSELF TOGETHER! YOU'RE LETTING KATSURA-SAN YANK YOU AROUND!
a carte dishes
Bagna càuda
With Nagano-grown
Myoga miso pickle
Mustard
OH.

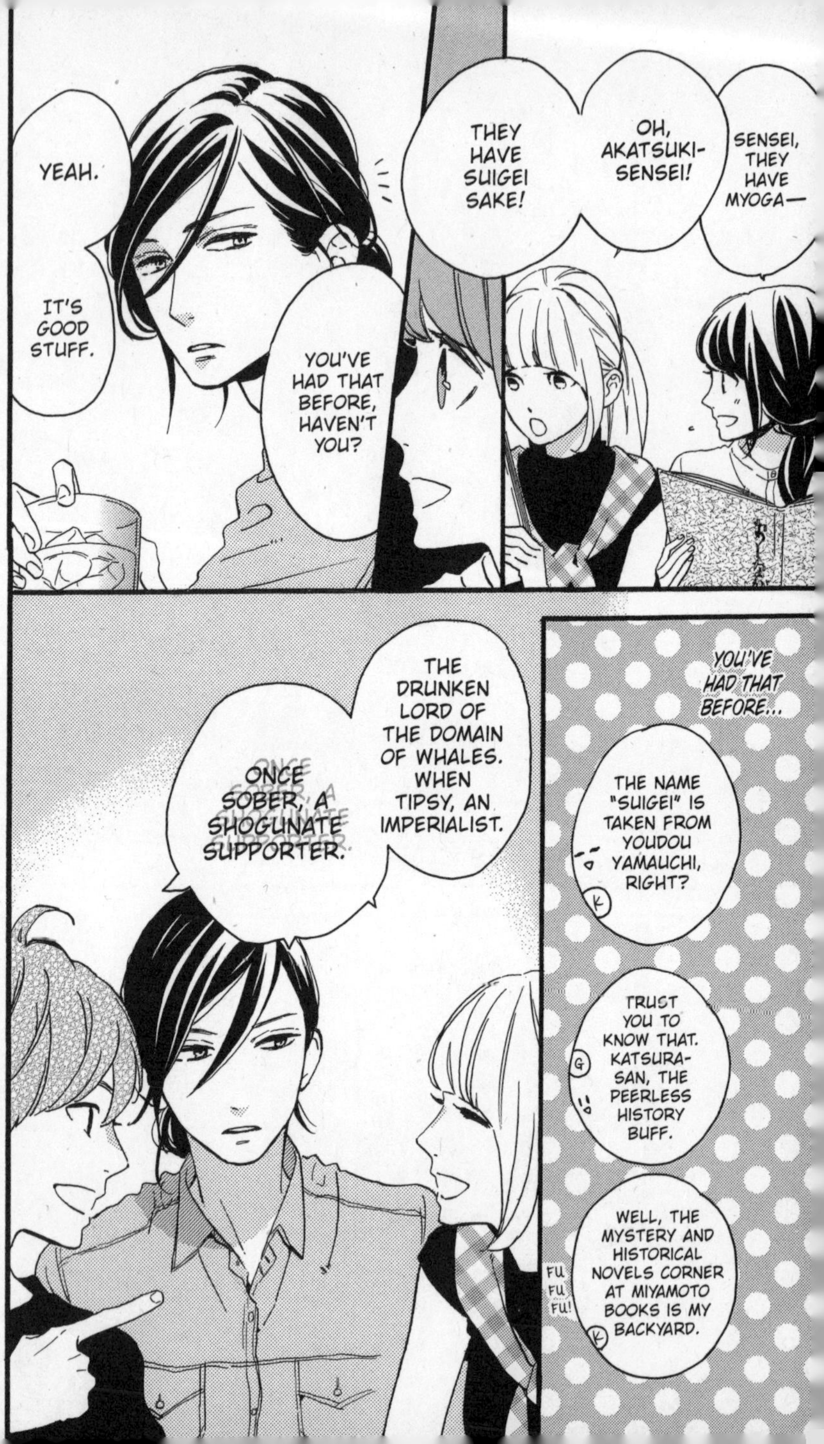
SENSEI, THEY HAVE MYOGA—
OH, AKATSUKI-SENSEI!
THEY HAVE SUIGEI SAKE!
YOU'VE HAD THAT BEFORE, HAVEN'T YOU?
YEAH.
IT'S GOOD STUFF.
YOU'VE HAD THAT BEFORE...
THE NAME "SUIGEI" IS TAKEN FROM YOUDOU YAMAUCHI, RIGHT?
TRUST YOU TO KNOW THAT. KATSURA-SAN, THE PEERLESS HISTORY BUFF.
FU FU FU!
WELL, THE MYSTERY AND HISTORICAL NOVELS CORNER AT MIYAMOTO BOOKS IS MY BACKYARD.
THE DRUNKEN LORD OF THE DOMAIN OF WHALES. WHEN TIPSY, AN IMPERIALIST.
ONCE SOBER, A SHOGUNATE SUPPORTER.

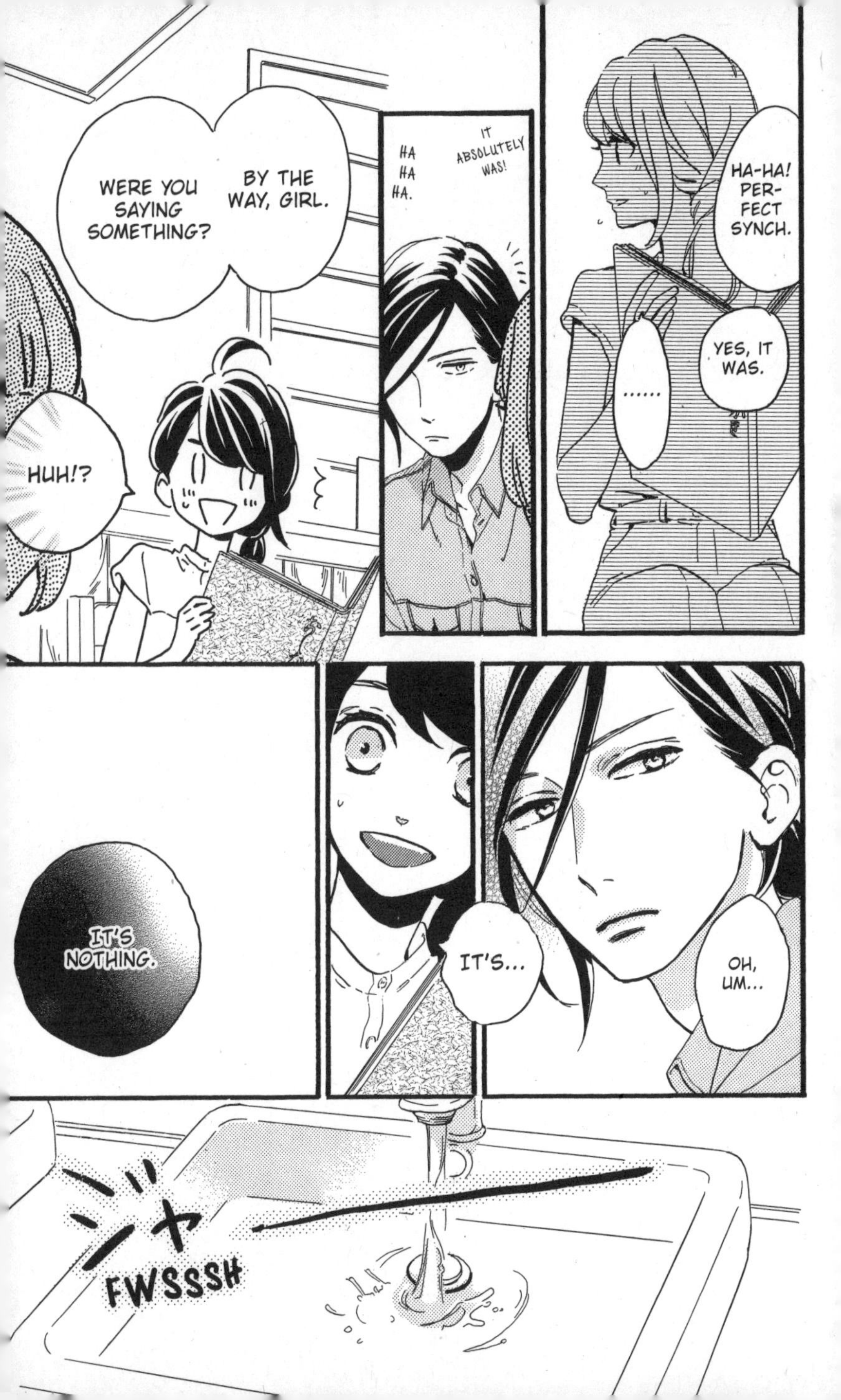
HA-HA! PERFECT SYNCH.
YES, IT WAS.
......
IT ABSOLUTELY WAS!
HA HA HA.
BY THE WAY, GIRL.
WERE YOU SAYING SOMETHING?
HUH!?
OH, UM...
IT'S...
IT'S NOTHING.
FWSSSH

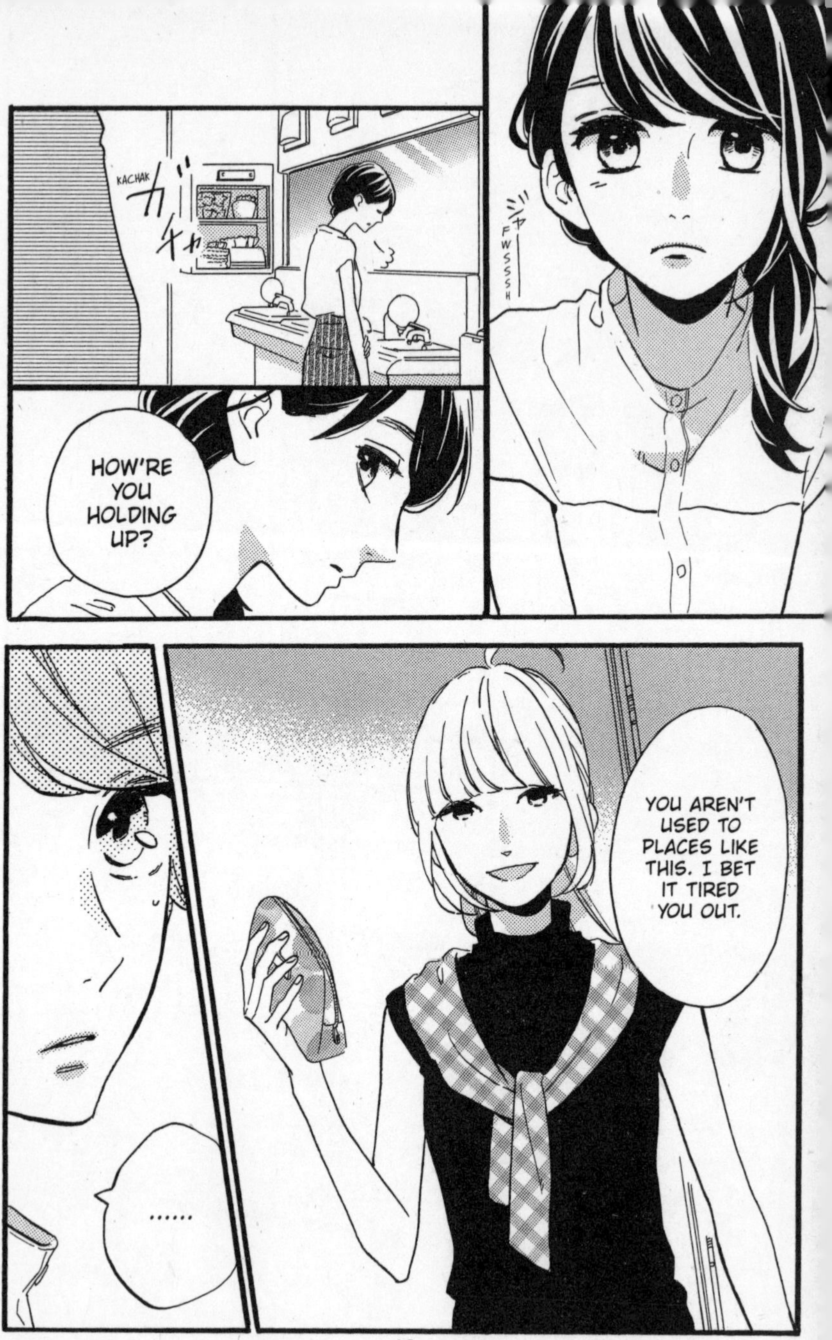
ジャ
FWSSSH
KACHAK
ガチャ
HOW'RE YOU HOLDING UP?
YOU AREN'T USED TO PLACES LIKE THIS. I BET IT TIRED YOU OUT.
......

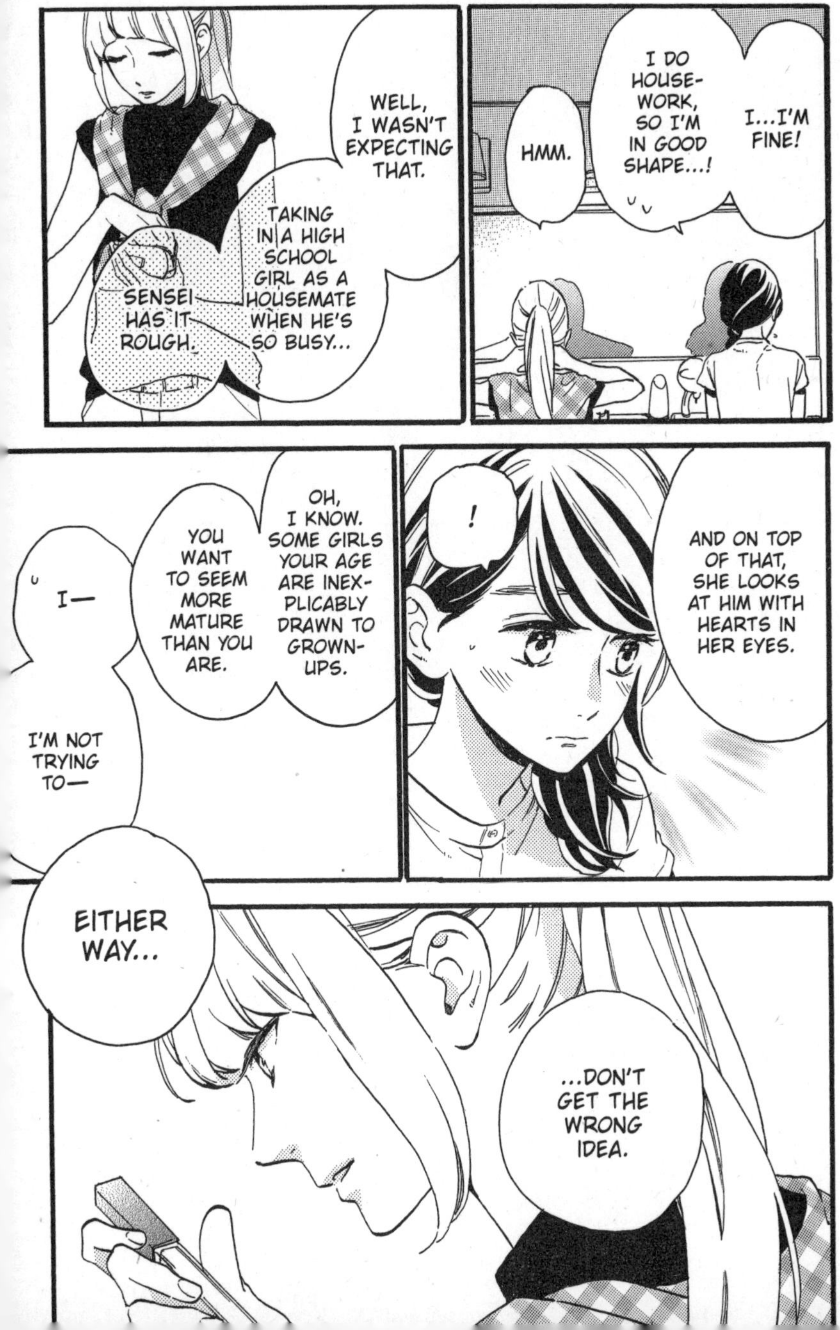
I...I'M FINE!
I DO HOUSE-WORK, SO I'M IN GOOD SHAPE...!
HMM.
WELL, I WASN'T EXPECTING THAT.
TAKING IN A HIGH SCHOOL GIRL AS A HOUSEMATE WHEN HE'S SO BUSY...
SENSEI HAS IT ROUGH.
AND ON TOP OF THAT, SHE LOOKS AT HIM WITH HEARTS IN HER EYES.
!
OH, I KNOW. SOME GIRLS YOUR AGE ARE INEXPLICABLY DRAWN TO GROWN-UPS.
YOU WANT TO SEEM MORE MATURE THAN YOU ARE.
I—
I'M NOT TRYING TO—
EITHER WAY...
...DON'T GET THE WRONG IDEA.

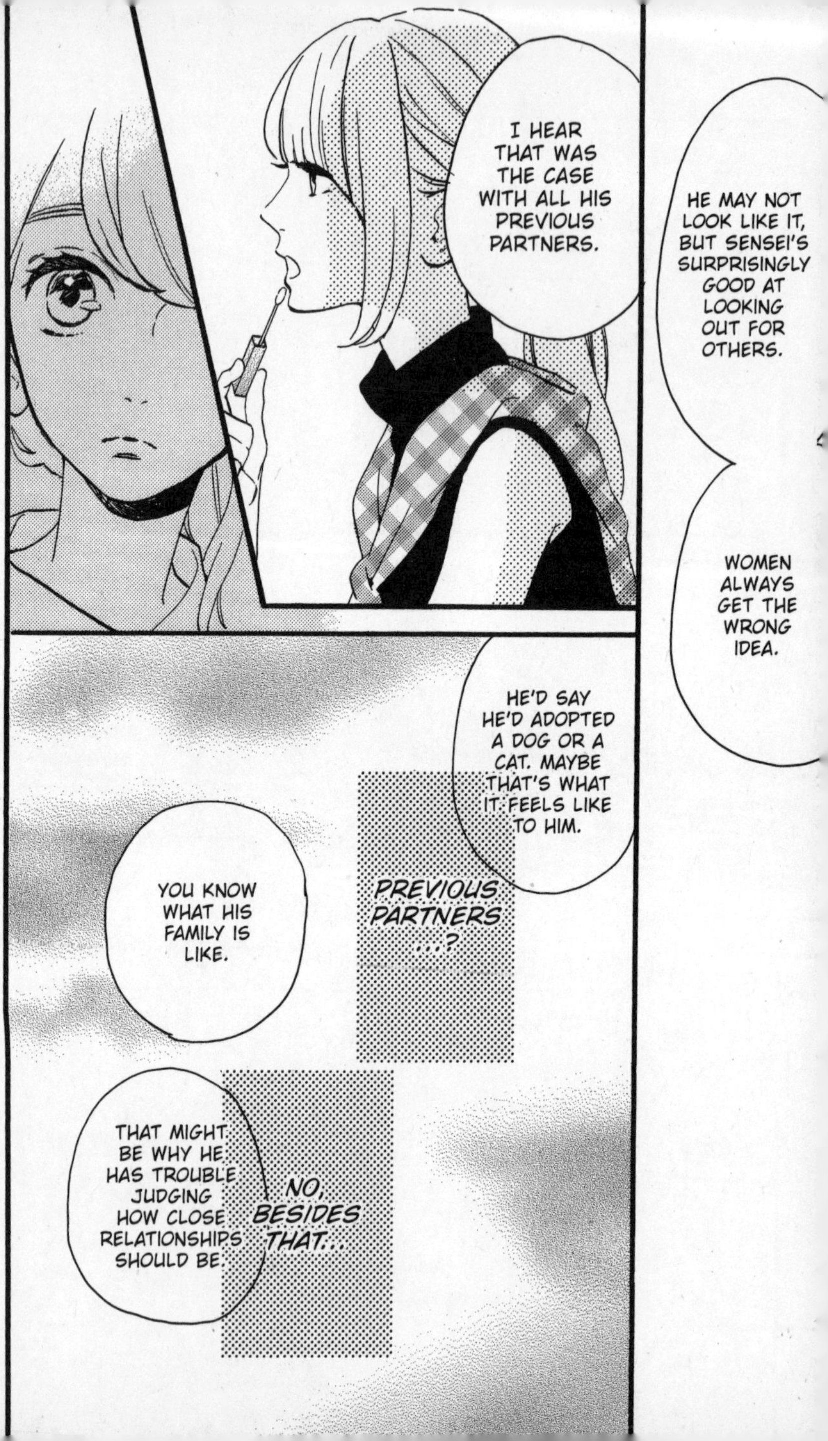
HE MAY NOT LOOK LIKE IT, BUT SENSEI'S SURPRISINGLY GOOD AT LOOKING OUT FOR OTHERS.
WOMEN ALWAYS GET THE WRONG IDEA.
I HEAR THAT WAS THE CASE WITH ALL HIS PREVIOUS PARTNERS.
HE'D SAY HE'D ADOPTED A DOG OR A CAT. MAYBE THAT'S WHAT IT FEELS LIKE TO HIM.
PREVIOUS PARTNERS...?
YOU KNOW WHAT HIS FAMILY IS LIKE.
THAT MIGHT BE WHY HE HAS TROUBLE JUDGING HOW CLOSE RELATIONSHIPS SHOULD BE.
NO, BESIDES THAT...

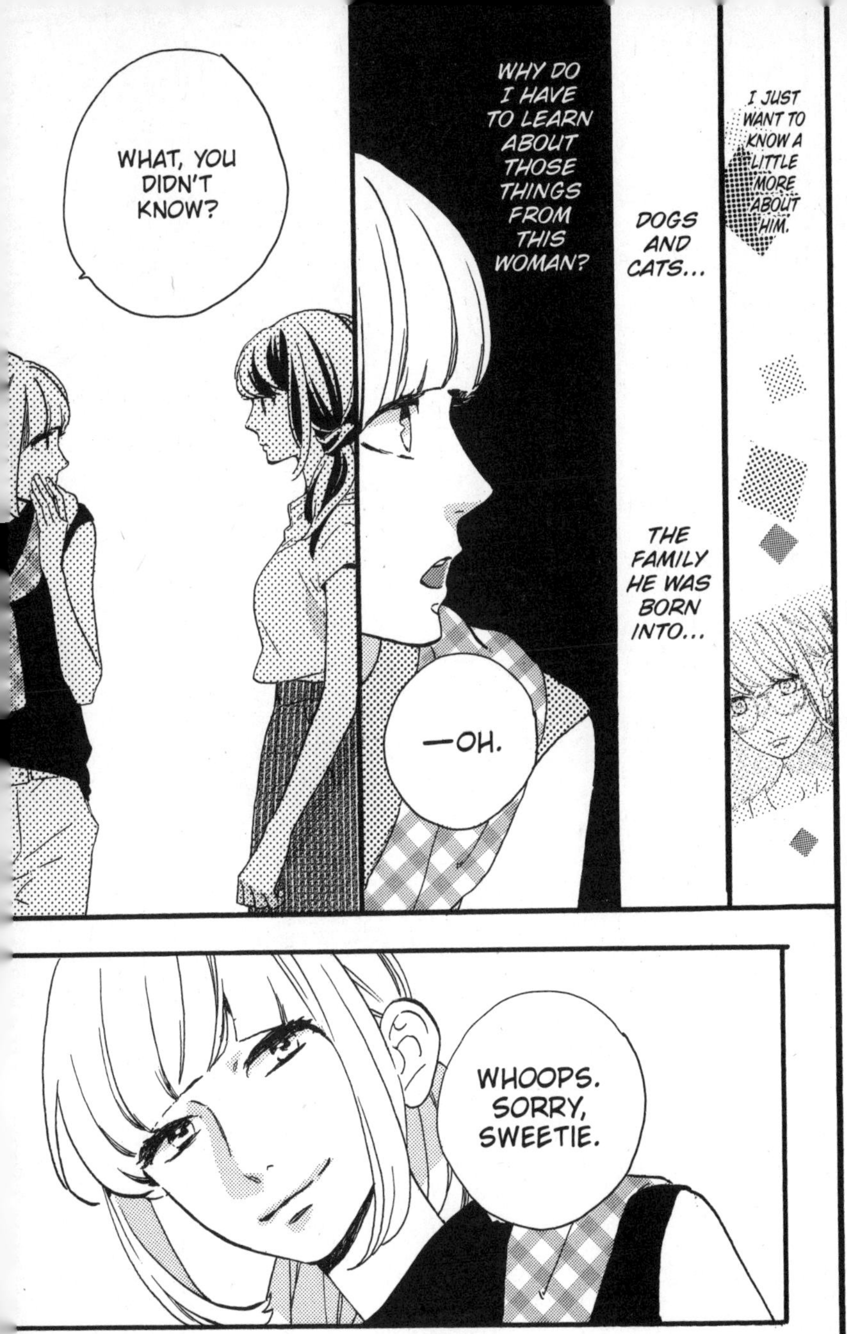
I JUST WANT TO KNOW A LITTLE MORE ABOUT HIM.
DOGS AND CATS...
THE FAMILY HE WAS BORN INTO...
WHY DO I HAVE TO LEARN ABOUT THOSE THINGS FROM THIS WOMAN?
—OH.
WHAT, YOU DIDN'T KNOW?
WHOOPS. SORRY, SWEETIE.

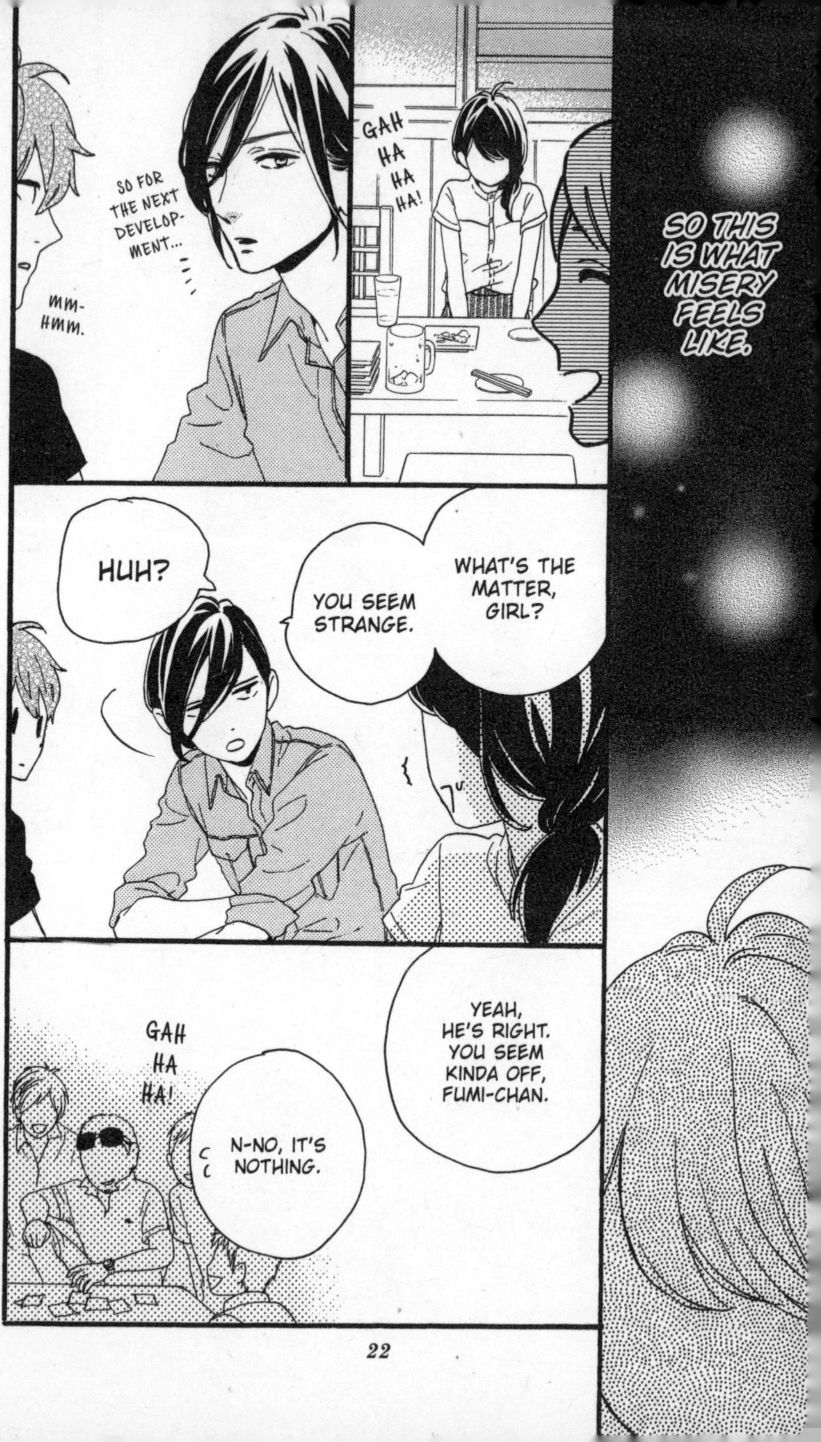
SO THIS IS WHAT MISERY FEELS LIKE.
GAH HA HA HA!
SO FOR THE NEXT DEVELOPMENT...
MM-HMM.
WHAT'S THE MATTER, GIRL?
YOU SEEM STRANGE.
HUH?
YEAH, HE'S RIGHT. YOU SEEM KINDA OFF, FUMI-CHAN.
N-NO, IT'S NOTHING.
GAH HA HA!

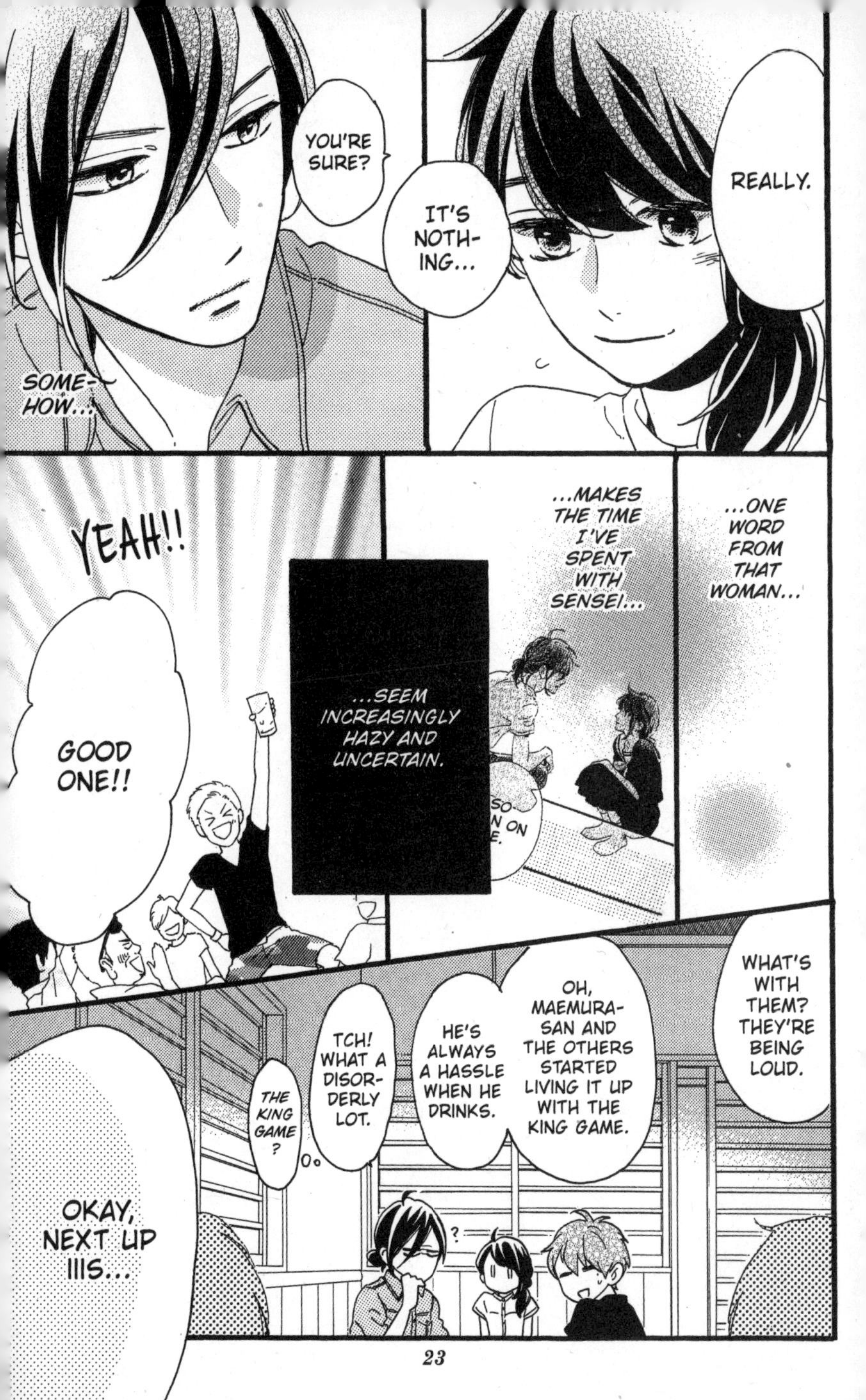
REALLY.
IT'S NOTHING...
YOU'RE SURE?
SOME-HOW...
...ONE WORD FROM THAT WOMAN...
...MAKES THE TIME I'VE SPENT WITH SENSEI...
...SEEM INCREASINGLY HAZY AND UNCERTAIN.
YEAH!!
GOOD ONE!!
WHAT'S WITH THEM? THEY'RE BEING LOUD.
OH, MAEMURA-SAN AND THE OTHERS STARTED LIVING IT UP WITH THE KING GAME.
HE'S ALWAYS A HASSLE WHEN HE DRINKS.
TCH! WHAT A DISORDERLY LOT.
THE KING GAME?
OKAY, NEXT UP IIIS...

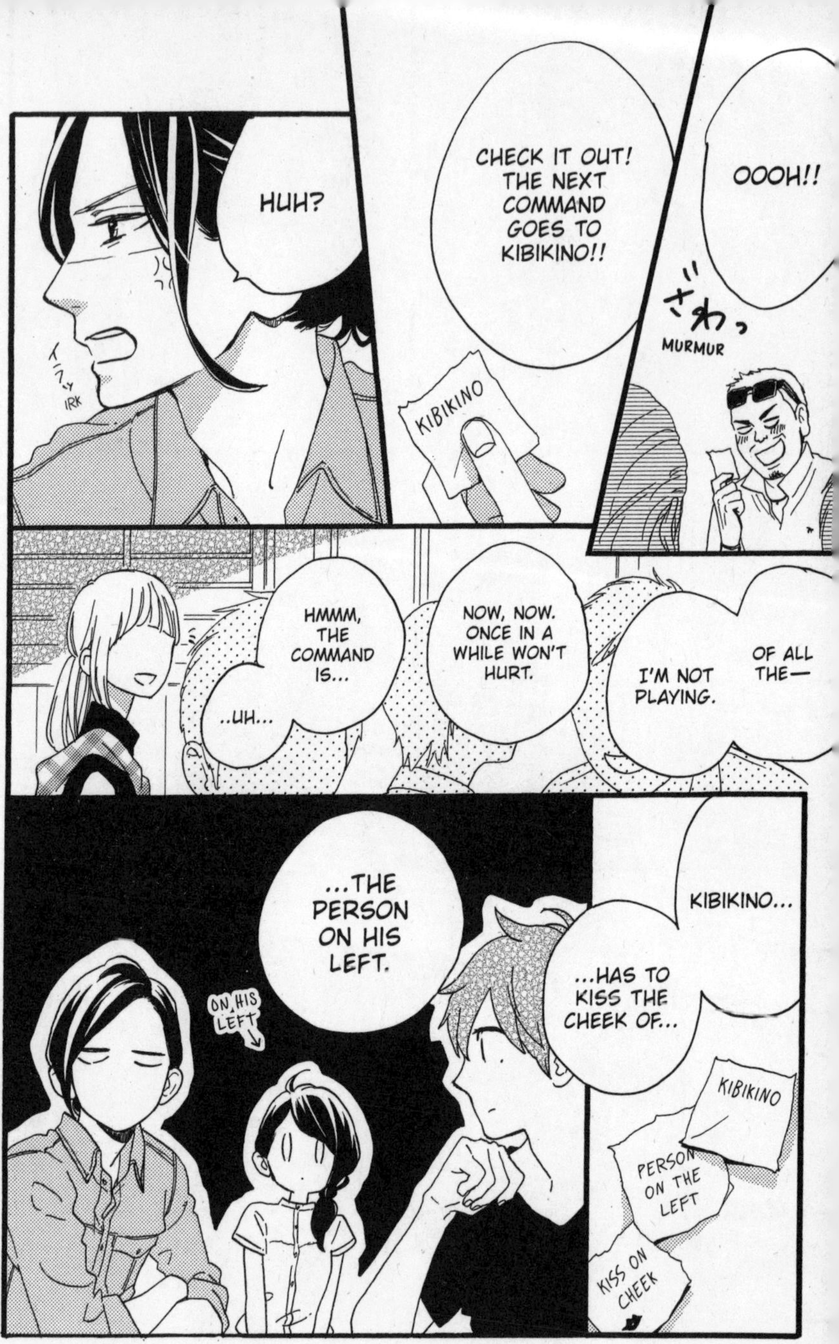
CHECK IT OUT! THE NEXT COMMAND GOES TO KIBIKINO!!
KIBIKINO
OOOH!!
ざわっ
MURMUR
HUH?
イラッ
IRK
OF ALL THE—
I'M NOT PLAYING.
NOW, NOW. ONCE IN A WHILE WON'T HURT.
HMMM, THE COMMAND IS...
...UH...
KIBIKINO...
...HAS TO KISS THE CHEEK OF...
KIBIKINO
PERSON ON THE LEFT
KISS ON CHEEK
...THE PERSON ON HIS LEFT.
ON HIS LEFT

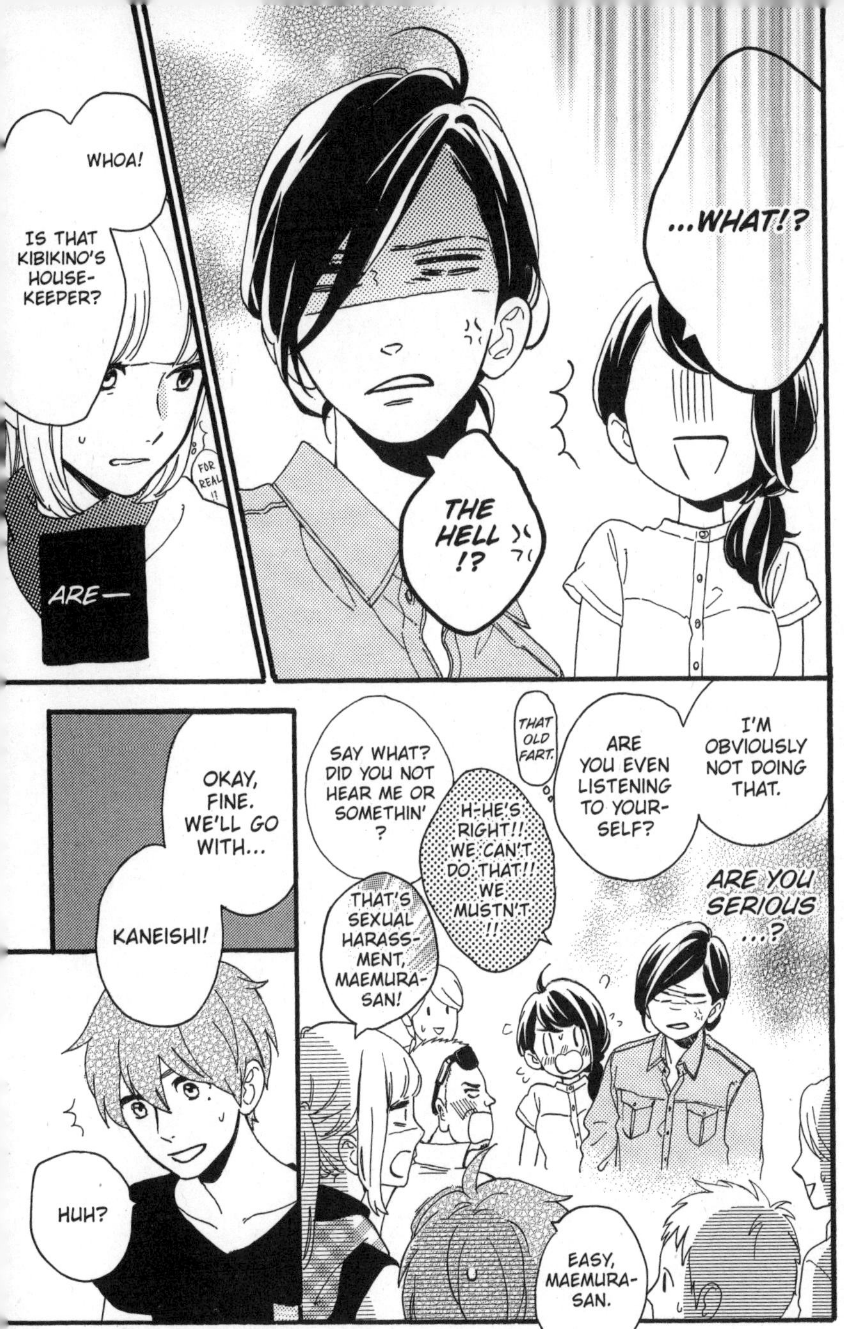
...WHAT!?
THE HELL!?
WHOA!
IS THAT KIBIKINO'S HOUSE-KEEPER?
FOR REAL!?
ARE—
I'M OBVIOUSLY NOT DOING THAT.
ARE YOU EVEN LISTENING TO YOURSELF?
THAT OLD FART.
ARE YOU SERIOUS...?
SAY WHAT? DID YOU NOT HEAR ME OR SOMETHIN'?
H-HE'S RIGHT!! WE CAN'T DO THAT!! WE MUSTN'T!!
THAT'S SEXUAL HARASSMENT, MAEMURA-SAN!
EASY, MAEMURA-SAN.
OKAY, FINE. WE'LL GO WITH...
KANEISHI!
HUH?

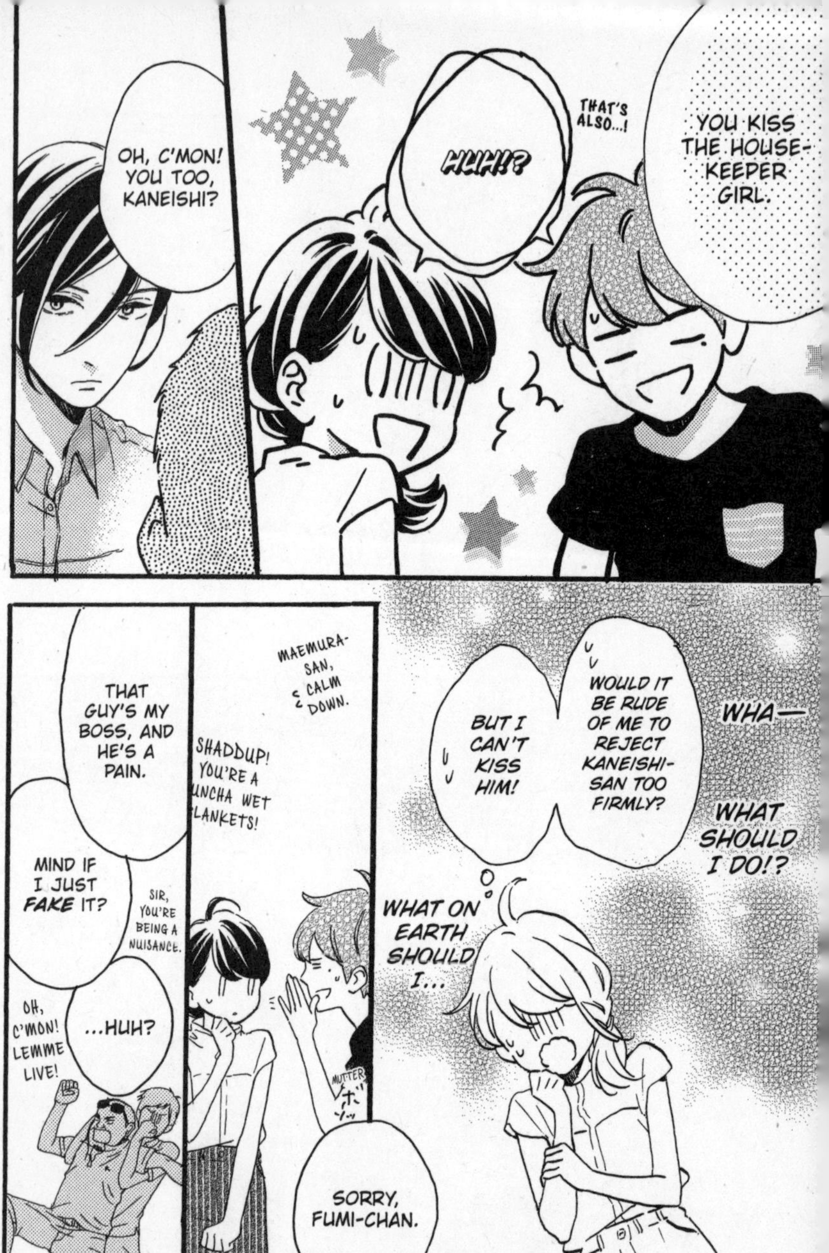
YOU KISS THE HOUSE-KEEPER GIRL.
THAT'S ALSO...!
HUH!?
OH, C'MON! YOU TOO, KANEISHI?
WHA—
WHAT SHOULD I DO!?
WOULD IT BE RUDE OF ME TO REJECT KANEISHI-SAN TOO FIRMLY?
BUT I CAN'T KISS HIM!
WHAT ON EARTH SHOULD I...
MAEMURA-SAN, CALM DOWN.
SHADDUP! YOU'RE A UNCHA WET LANKETS!
SIR, YOU'RE BEING A NUISANCE.
MUTTER
SORRY, FUMI-CHAN.
THAT GUY'S MY BOSS, AND HE'S A PAIN.
MIND IF I JUST *FAKE* IT?
...HUH?
OH, C'MON! LEMME LIVE!

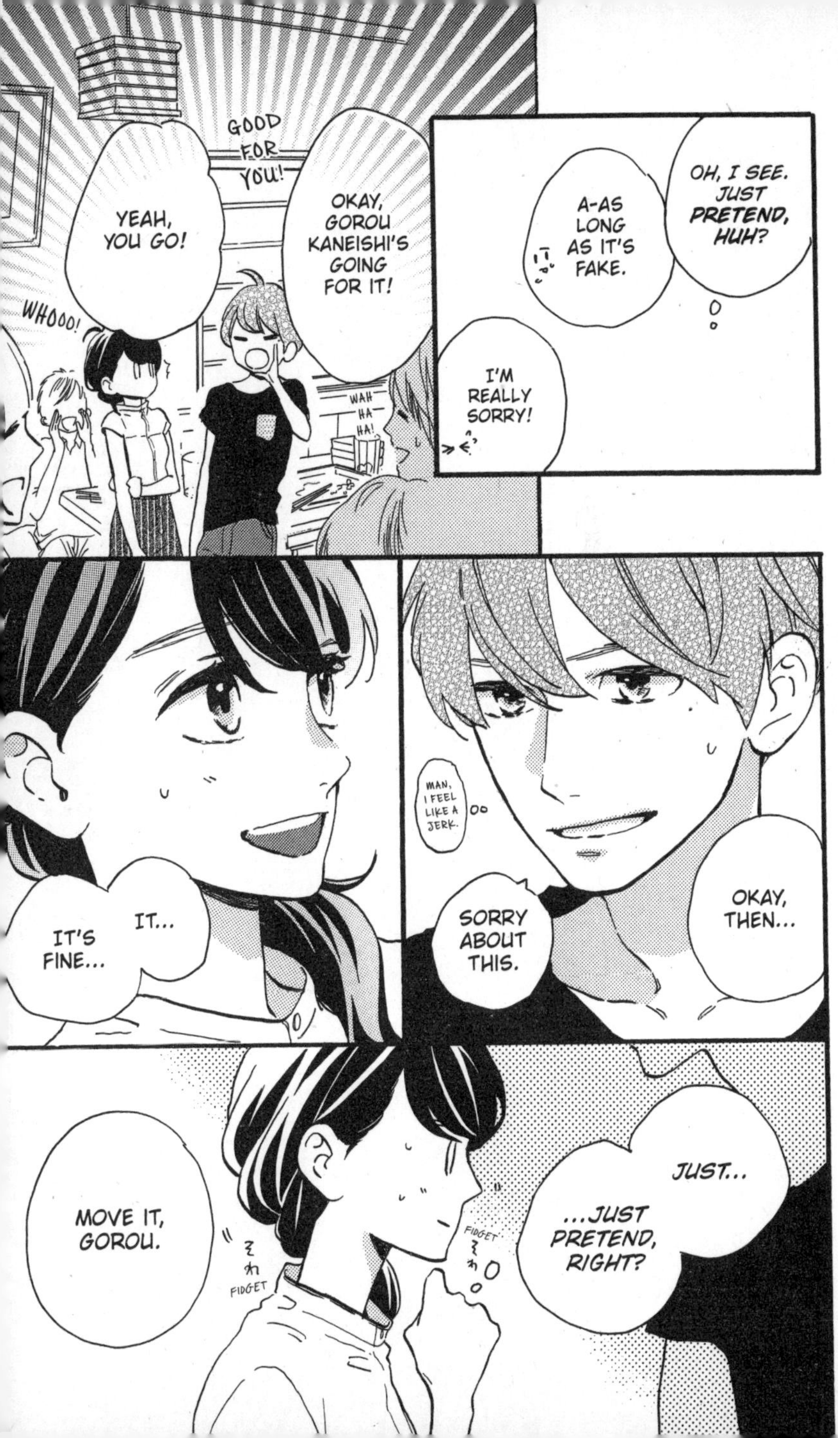
OH, I SEE. JUST PRETEND, HUH?
A-AS LONG AS IT'S FAKE.
I'M REALLY SORRY!
OKAY, GOROU KANEISHI'S GOING FOR IT!
GOOD FOR YOU!
YEAH, YOU GO!
WHOOO!
WAH HA HA!
OKAY, THEN...
SORRY ABOUT THIS.
MAN, I FEEL LIKE A JERK.
IT...
IT'S FINE...
JUST...
...JUST PRETEND, RIGHT?
FIDGET
FIDGET
MOVE IT, GOROU.

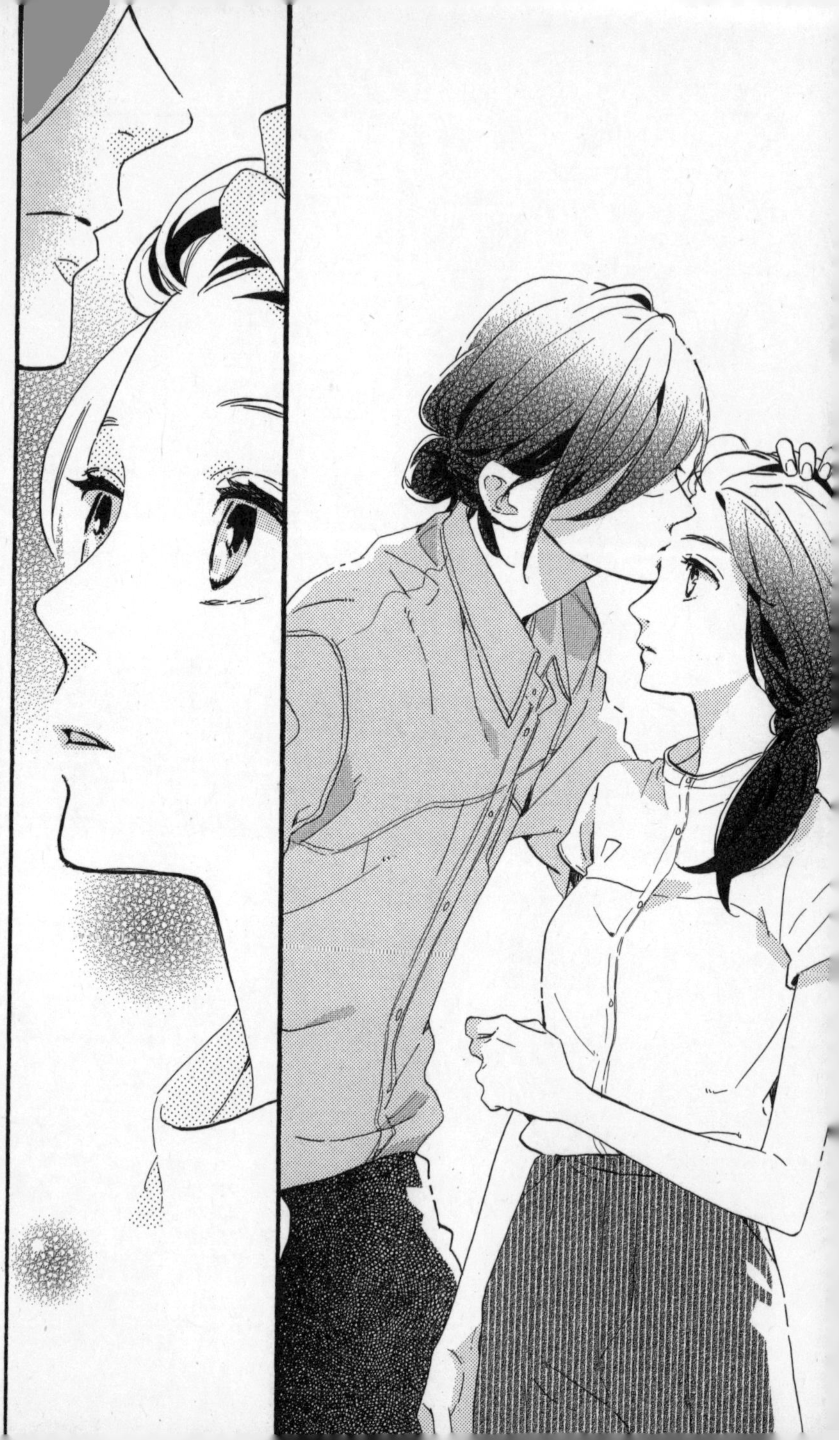

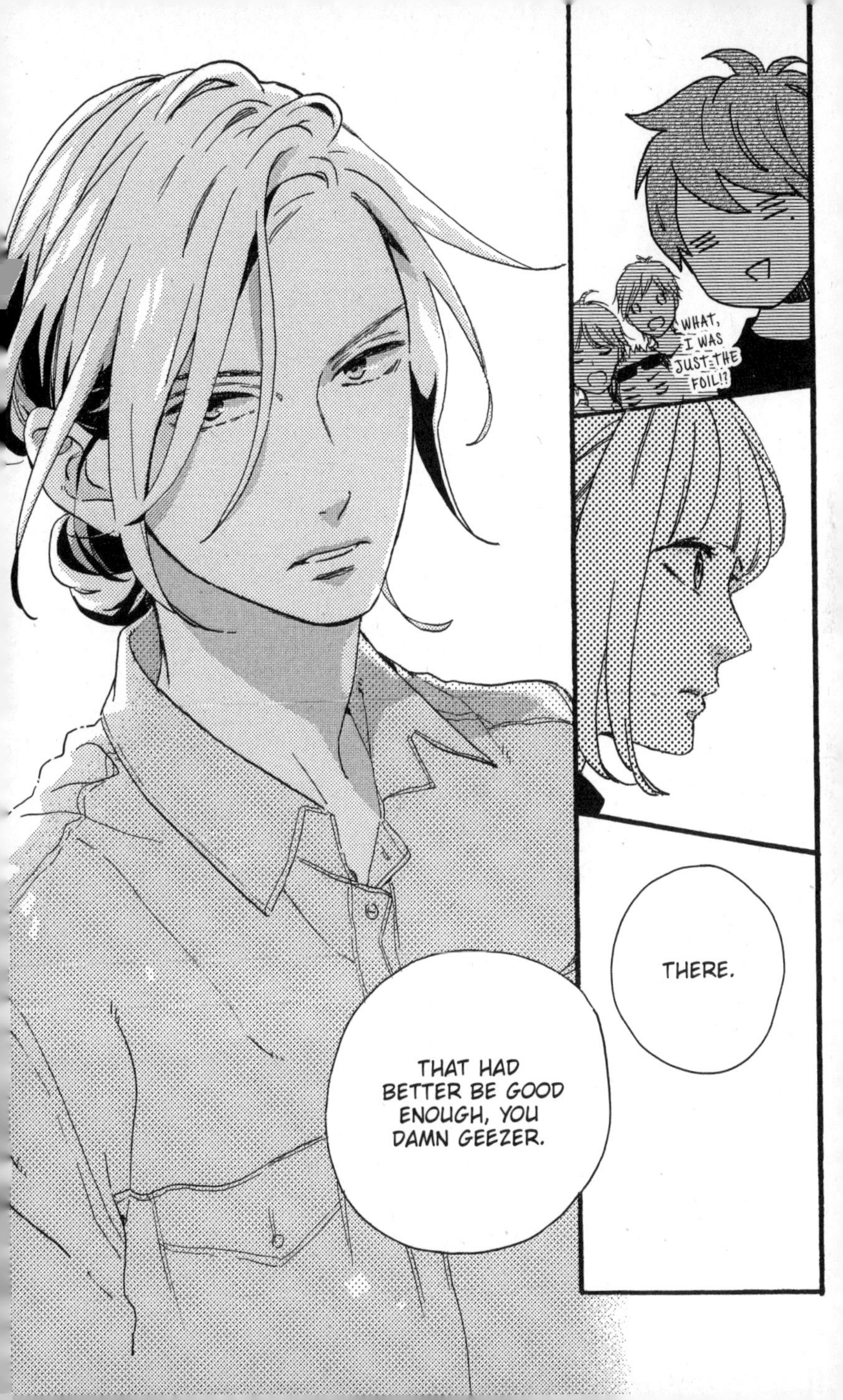
WHAT, I WAS JUST THE FOIL!?
THERE.
THAT HAD BETTER BE GOOD ENOUGH, YOU DAMN GEEZER.

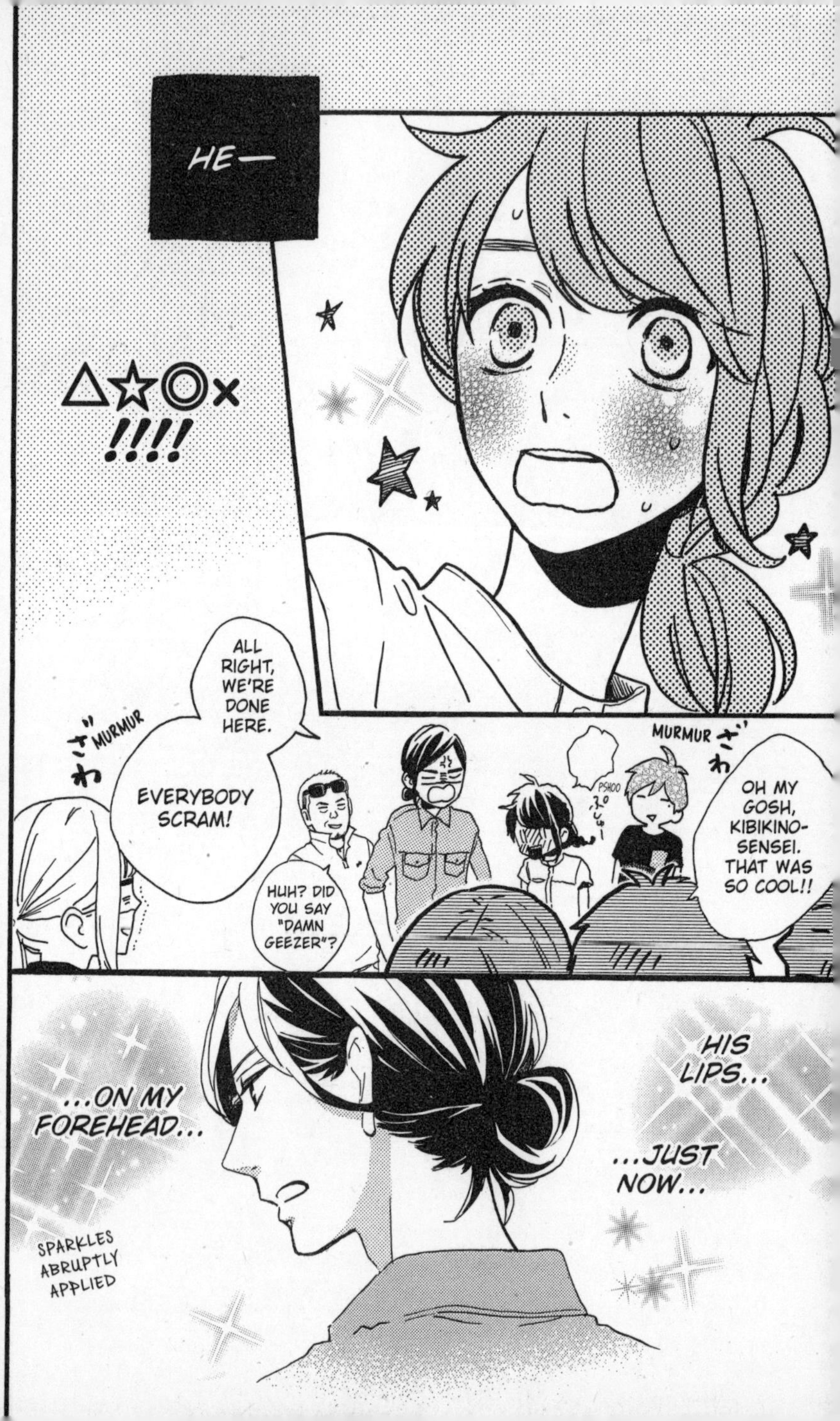
HE—
△☆◎x!!!!
MURMUR ざわ
OH MY GOSH, KIBIKINO-SENSEI. THAT WAS SO COOL!!
PSHOO
ALL RIGHT, WE'RE DONE HERE.
EVERYBODY SCRAM!
HUH? DID YOU SAY "DAMN GEEZER"?
ざわ MURMUR
HIS LIPS...
...JUST NOW...
...ON MY FOREHEAD...
SPARKLES ABRUPTLY APPLIED

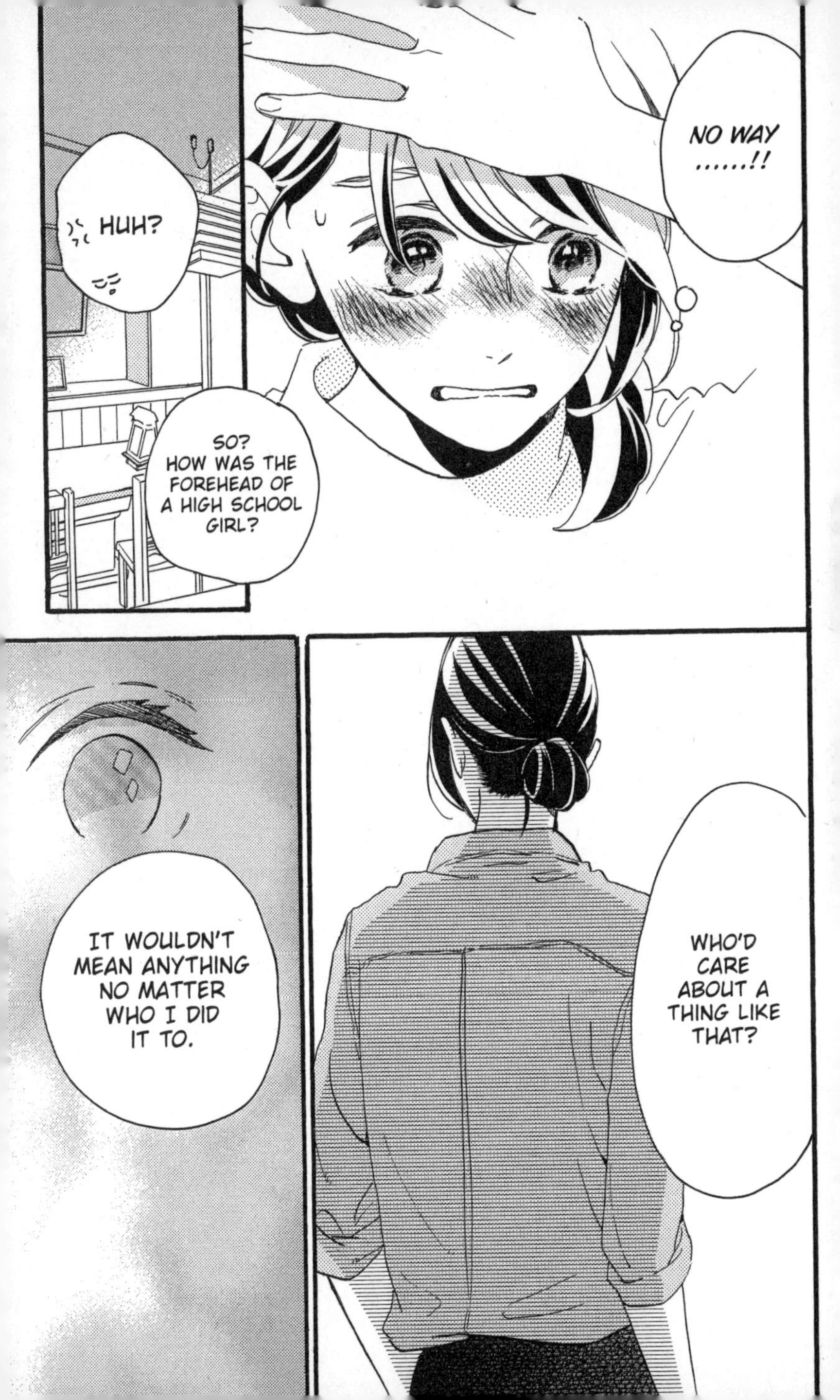
NO WAY ......!!
SO? HOW WAS THE FOREHEAD OF A HIGH SCHOOL GIRL?
HUH?
WHO'D CARE ABOUT A THING LIKE THAT?
IT WOULDN'T MEAN ANYTHING NO MATTER WHO I DID IT TO.

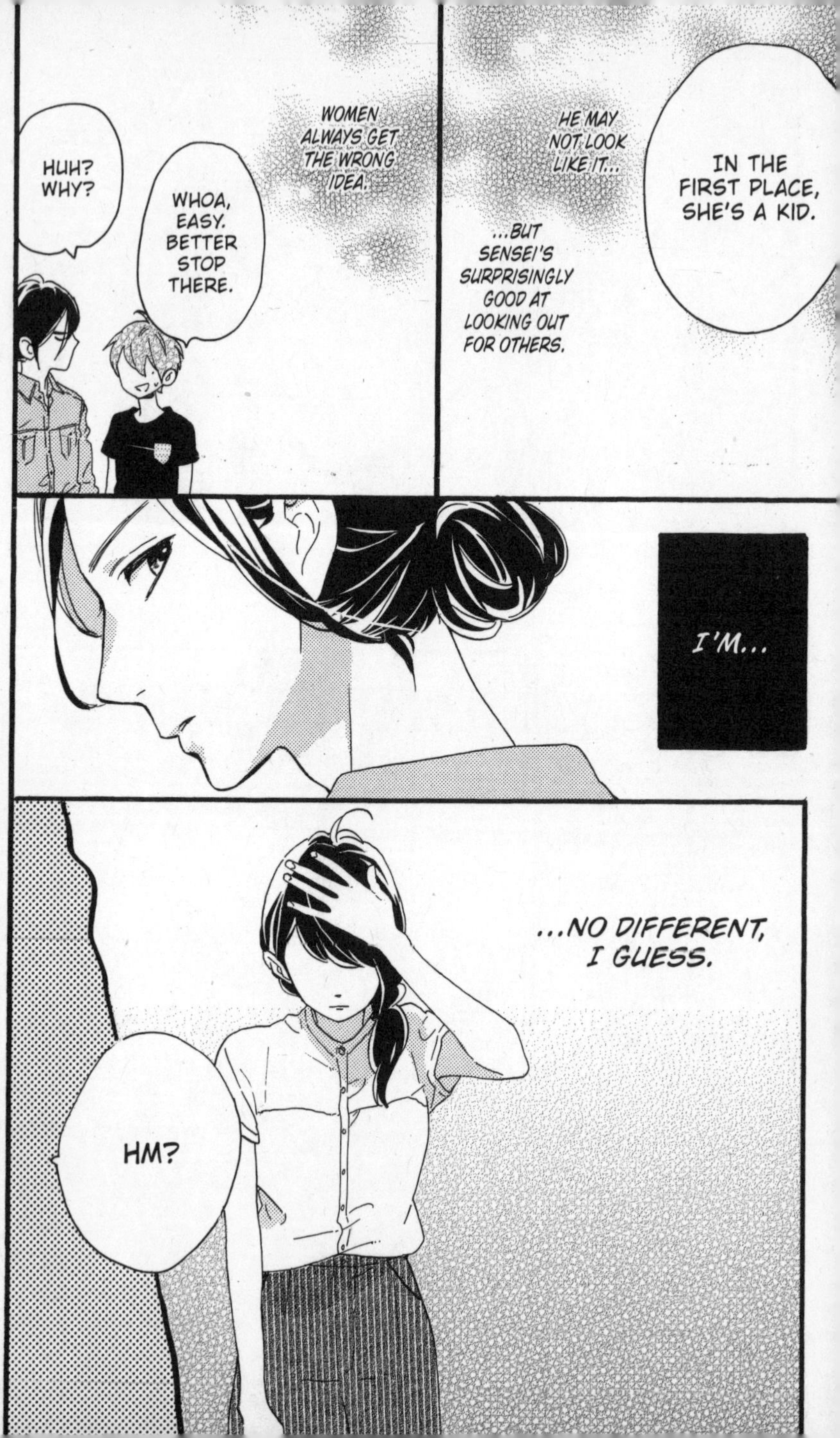
IN THE FIRST PLACE, SHE'S A KID.
HE MAY NOT LOOK LIKE IT...
...BUT SENSEI'S SURPRISINGLY GOOD AT LOOKING OUT FOR OTHERS.
WOMEN ALWAYS GET THE WRONG IDEA.
WHOA, EASY. BETTER STOP THERE.
HUH? WHY?
I'M...
...NO DIFFERENT, I GUESS.
HM?

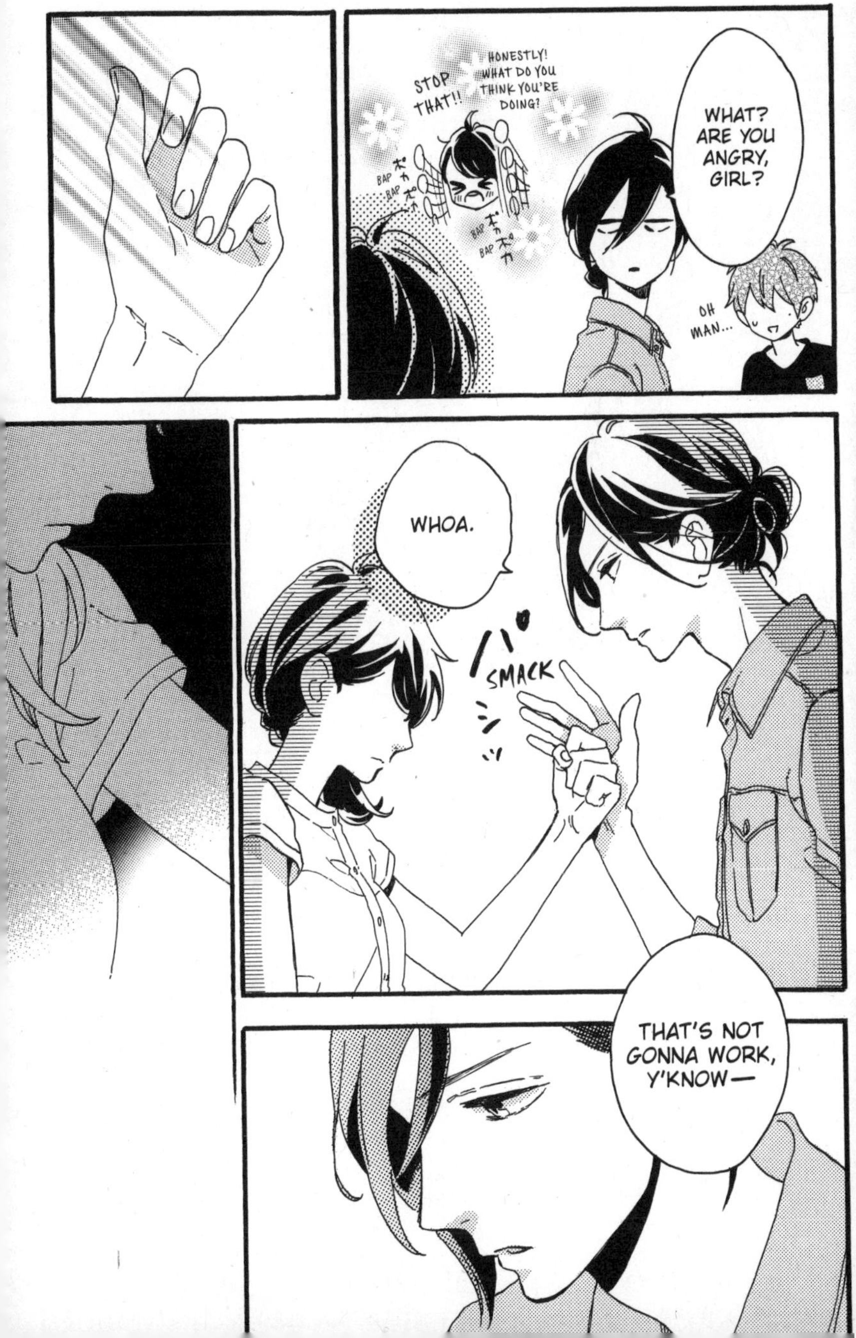
WHAT? ARE YOU ANGRY, GIRL?
HONESTLY! WHAT DO YOU THINK YOU'RE DOING?
STOP THAT!!
BAP BAP
BAP BAP
OH MAN...
WHOA.
SMACK
THAT'S NOT GONNA WORK, Y'KNOW—

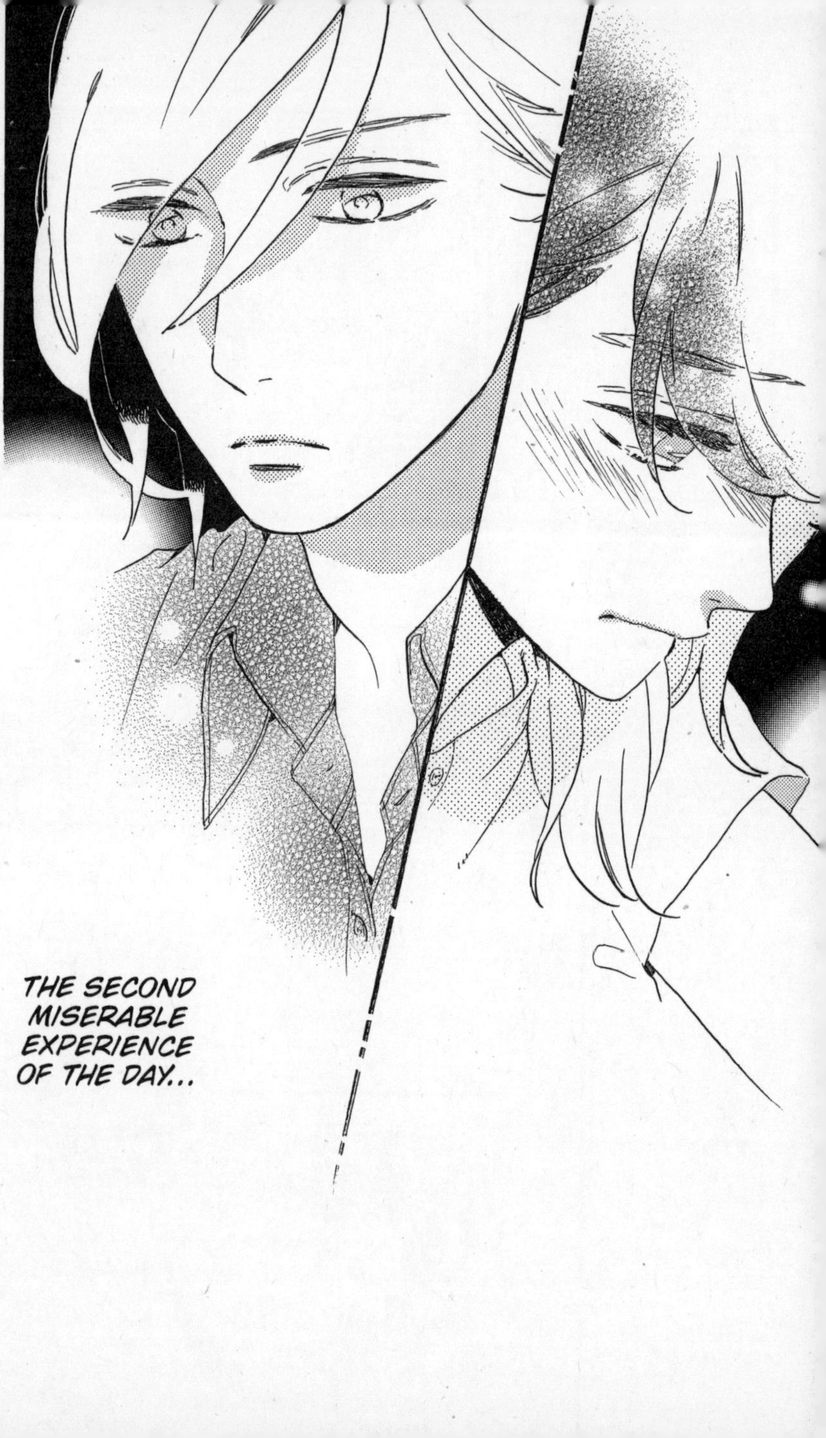
THE SECOND MISERABLE EXPERIENCE OF THE DAY...

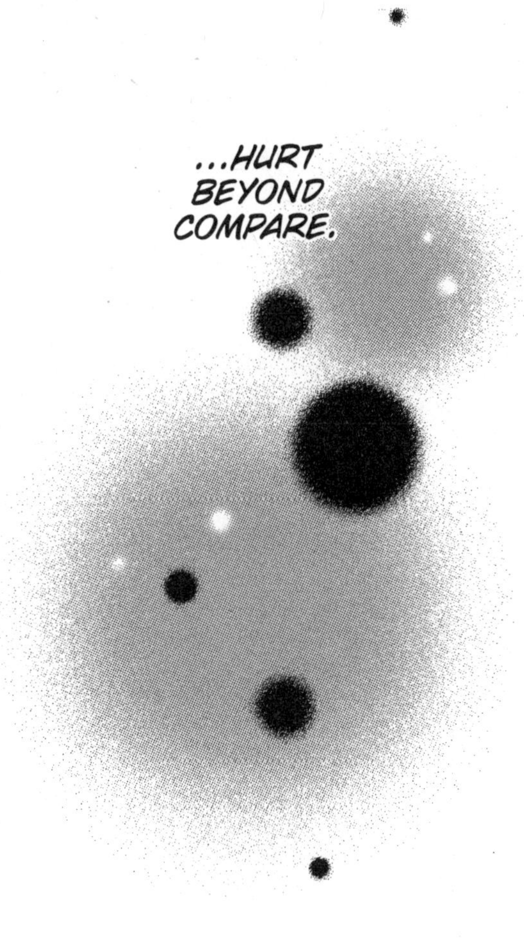
...HURT BEYOND COMPARE.

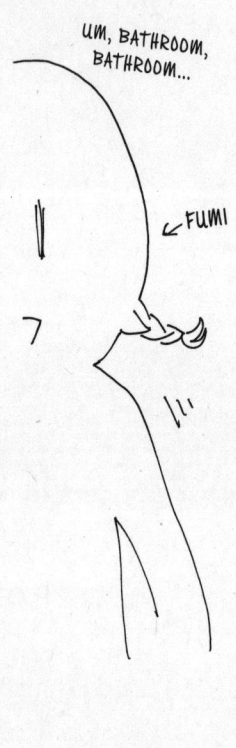

UM, BATHROOM,
BATHROOM...

← FUMI

KATSURA-SAN, WHO
WAITED FOR FUMI TO
MAKE A BATHROOM
TRIP AND HURRIEDLY
FOLLOWED HER SO SHE
COULD MAKE SARCASTIC
COMMENTS.

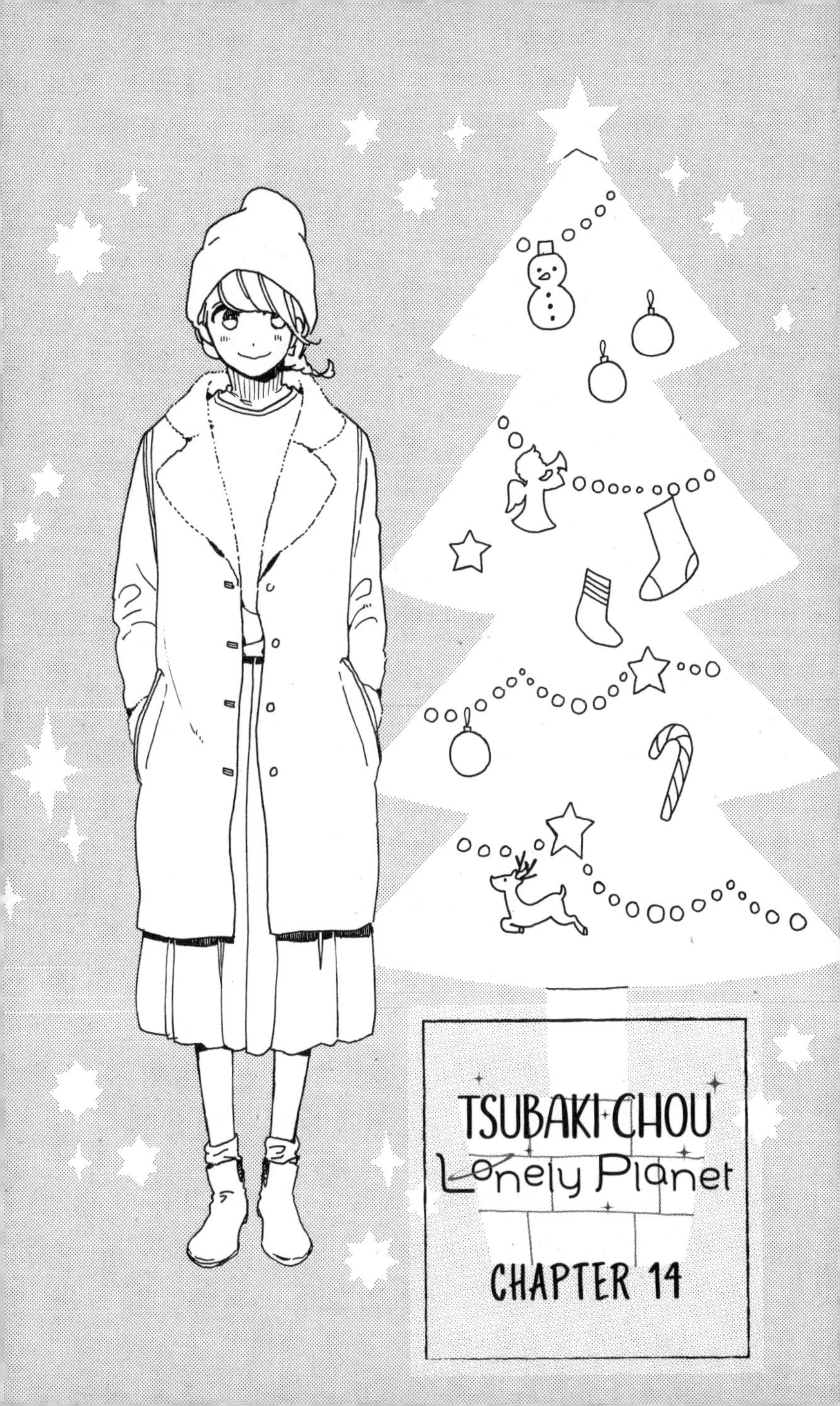
TSUBAKI-CHOU
Lonely Planet
CHAPTER 14

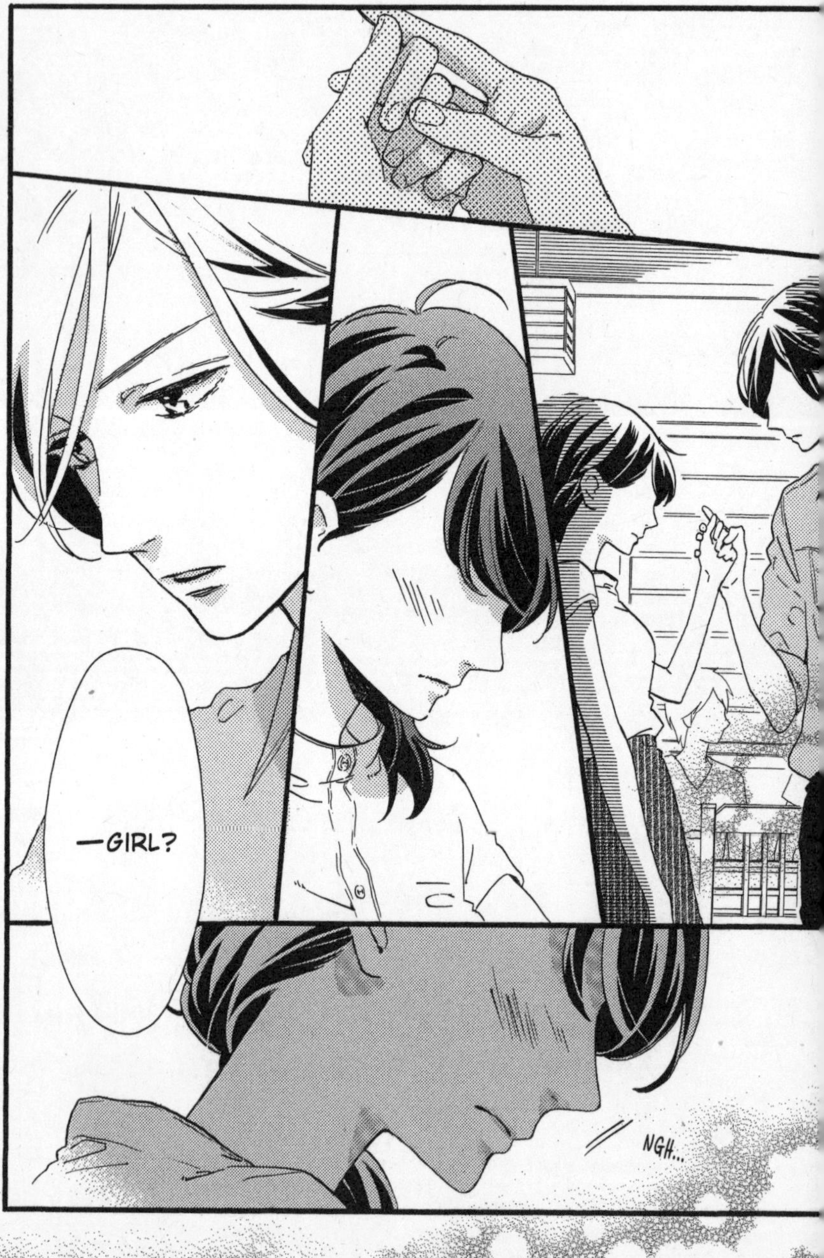
—GIRL?
NGH...

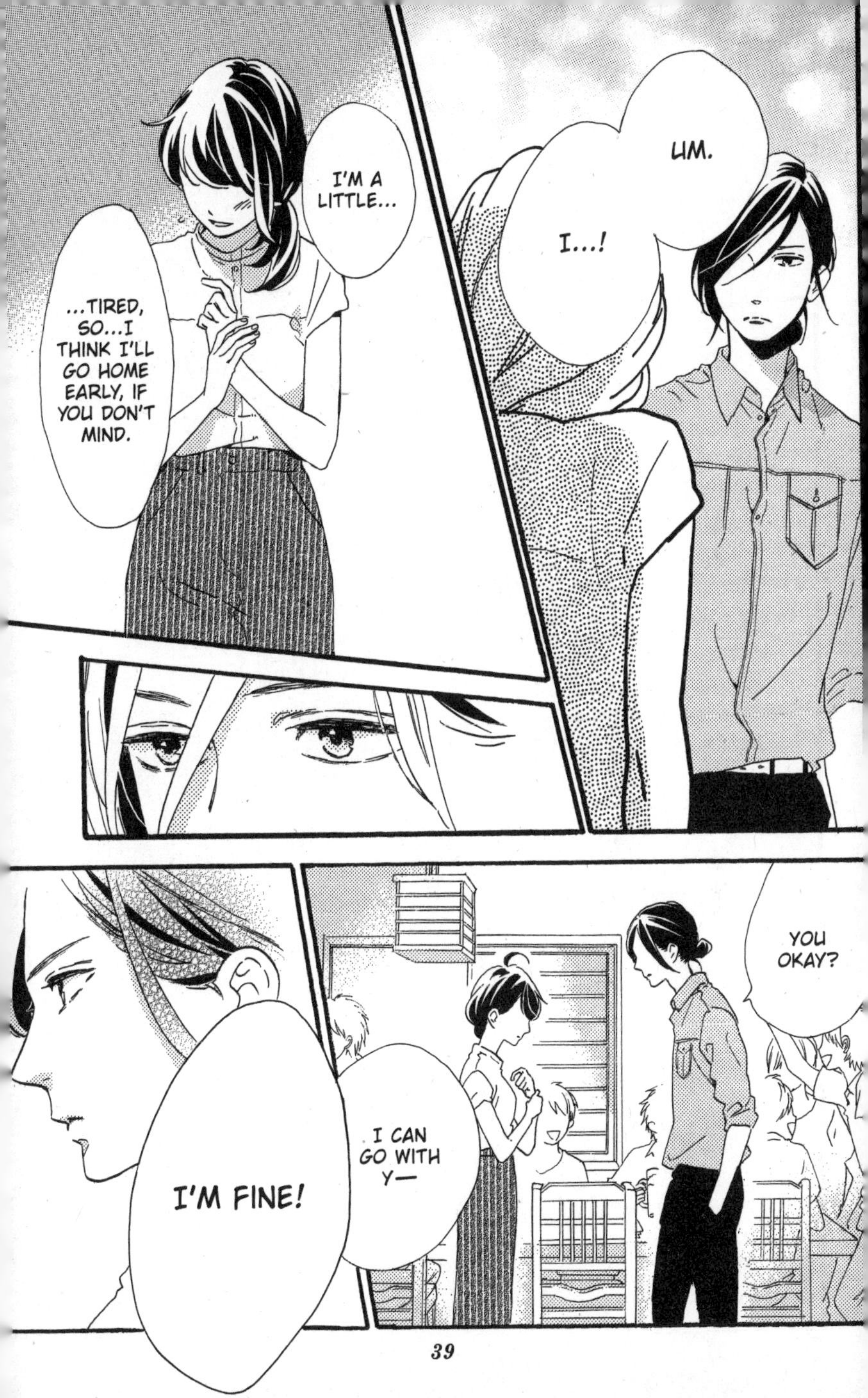
UM.
I...!
I'M A LITTLE...
...TIRED, SO...I THINK I'LL GO HOME EARLY, IF YOU DON'T MIND.
YOU OKAY?
I CAN GO WITH Y—
I'M FINE!

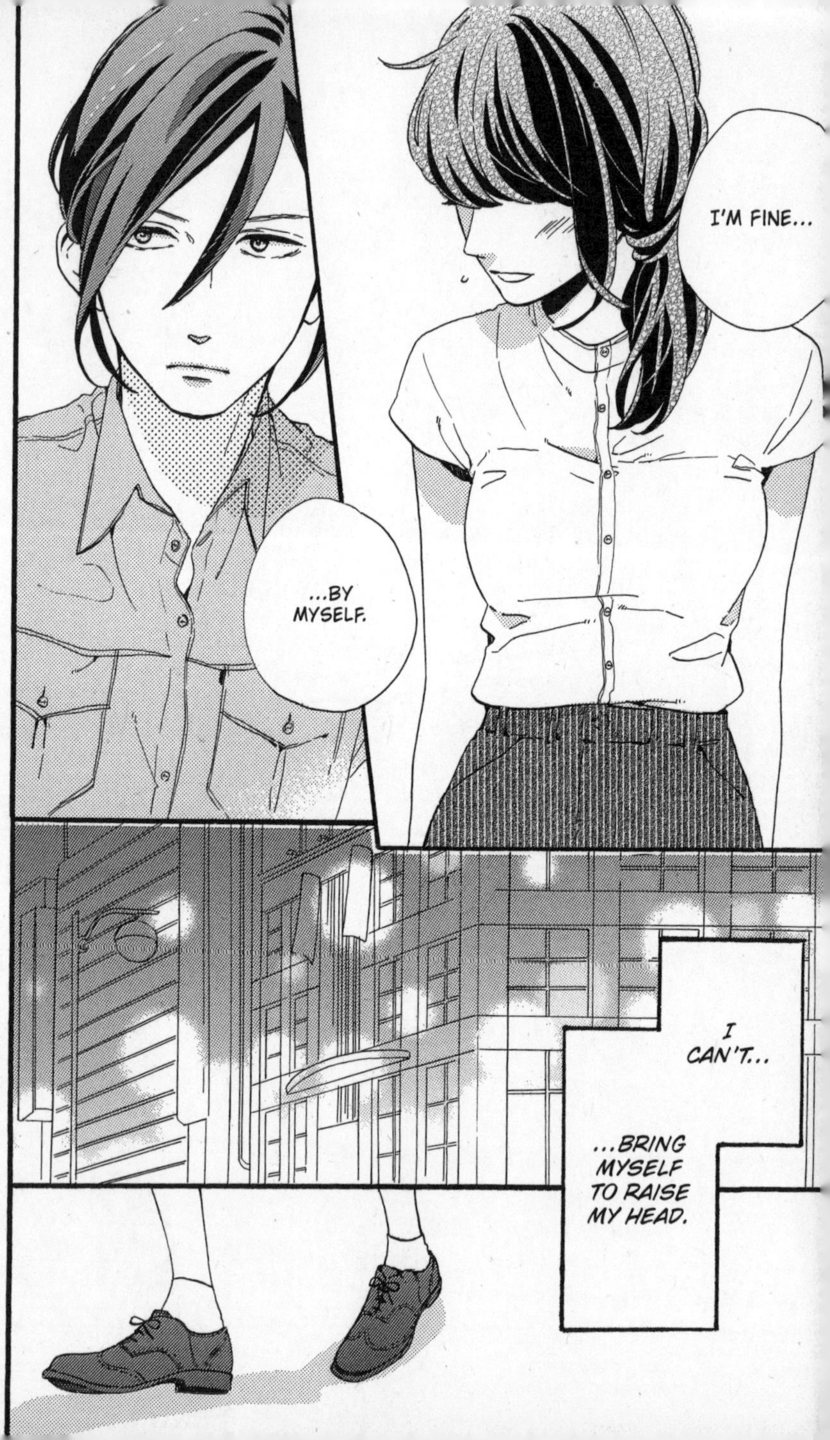
I'M FINE...
...BY MYSELF.
I CAN'T...
...BRING MYSELF TO RAISE MY HEAD.

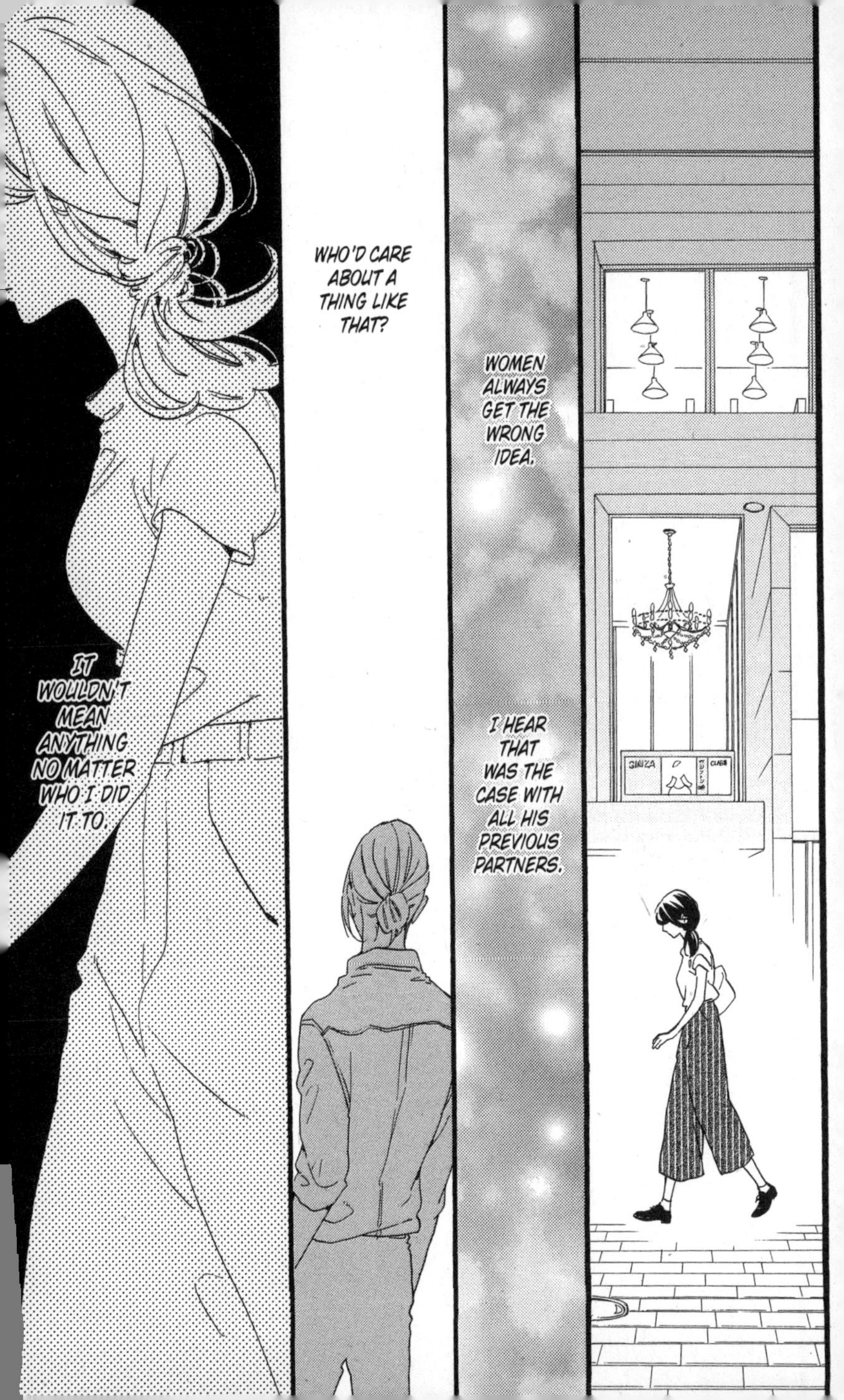

WOMEN ALWAYS GET THE WRONG IDEA.
I HEAR THAT WAS THE CASE WITH ALL HIS PREVIOUS PARTNERS.
WHO'D CARE ABOUT A THING LIKE THAT?
IT WOULDN'T MEAN ANYTHING NO MATTER WHO I DID IT TO.

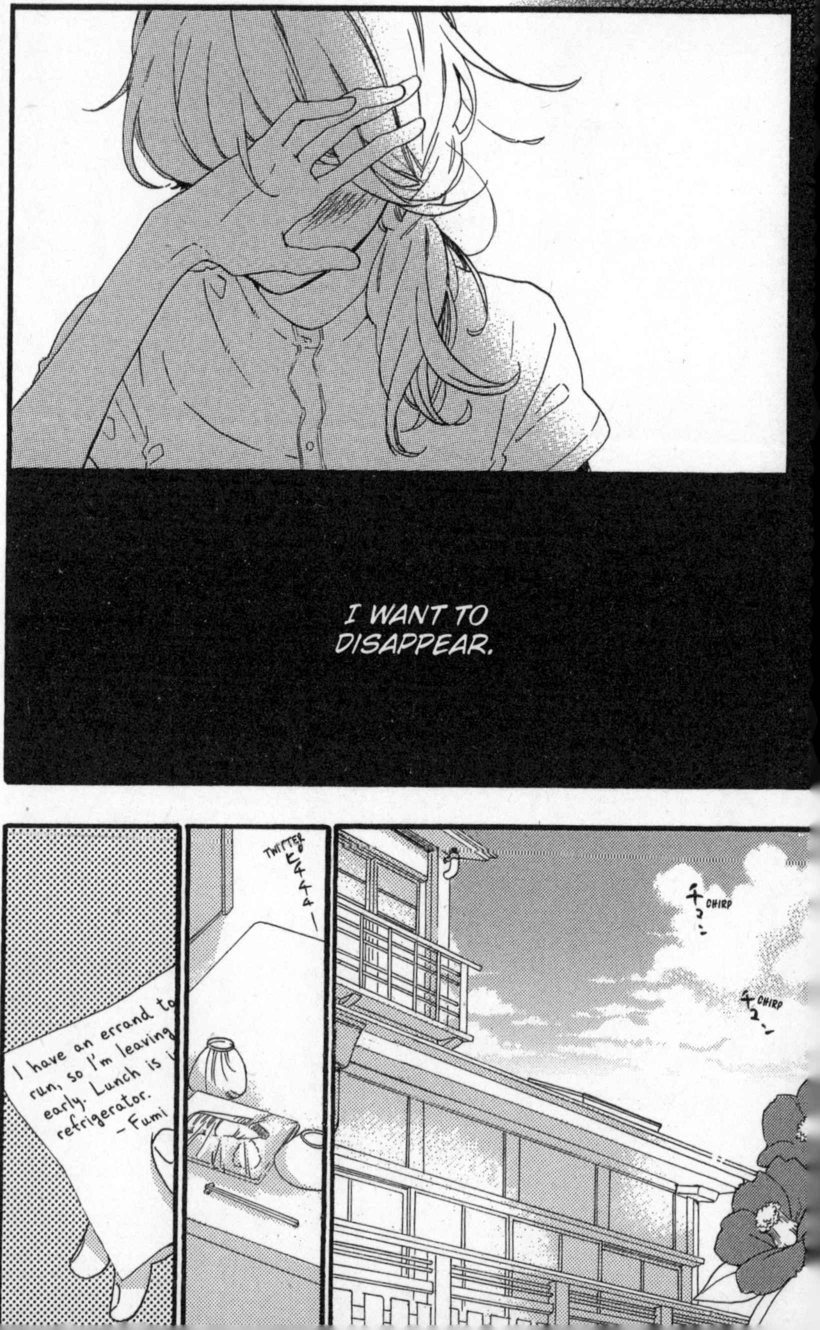
I WANT TO
DISAPPEAR.
CHIRP
CHIRP
TWITTER
I have an errand to
run, so I'm leaving
early. Lunch is i
refrigerator.
- Fumi

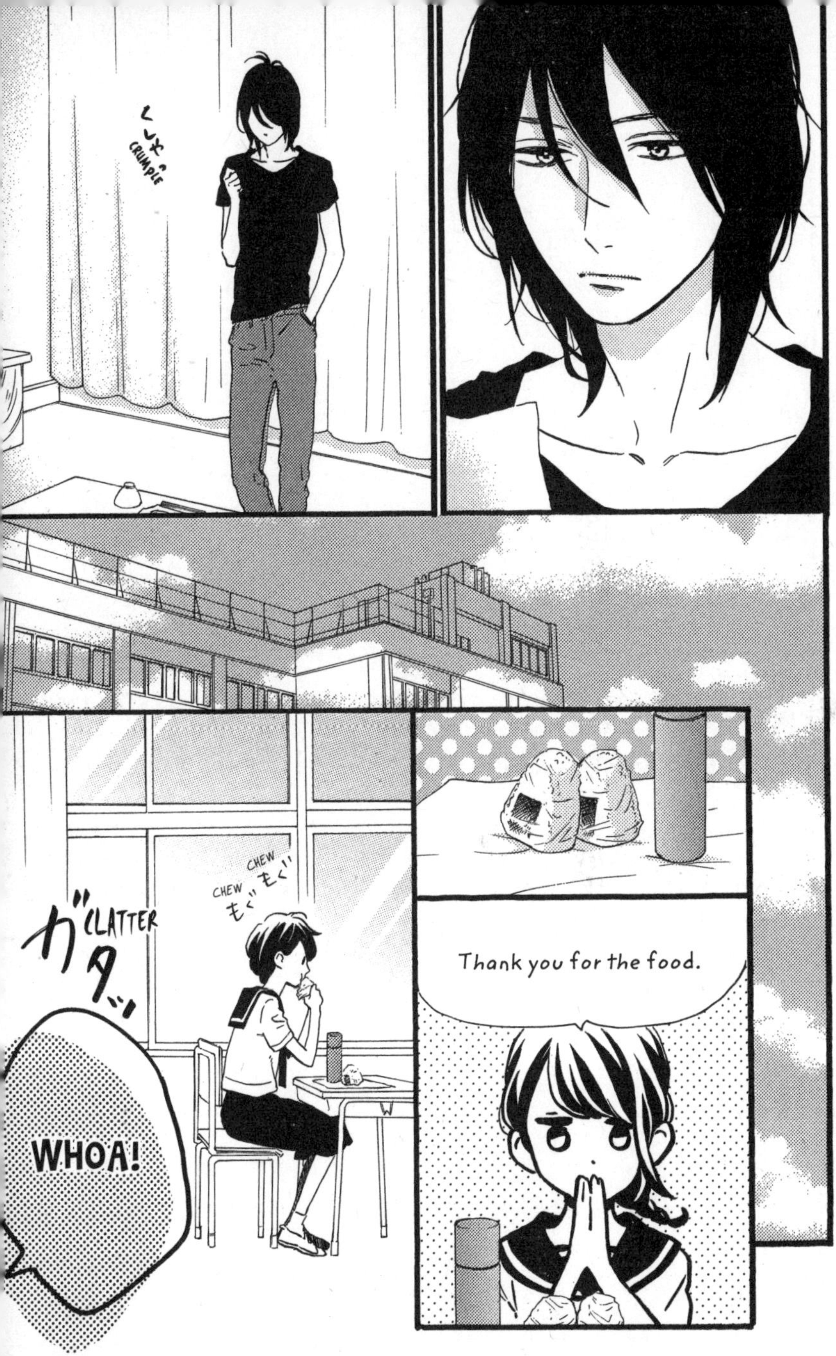
くしゃ
CRUMPLE
Thank you for the food.
CHEW
CHEW
もぐもぐ
ガタッ
CLATTER
WHOA!

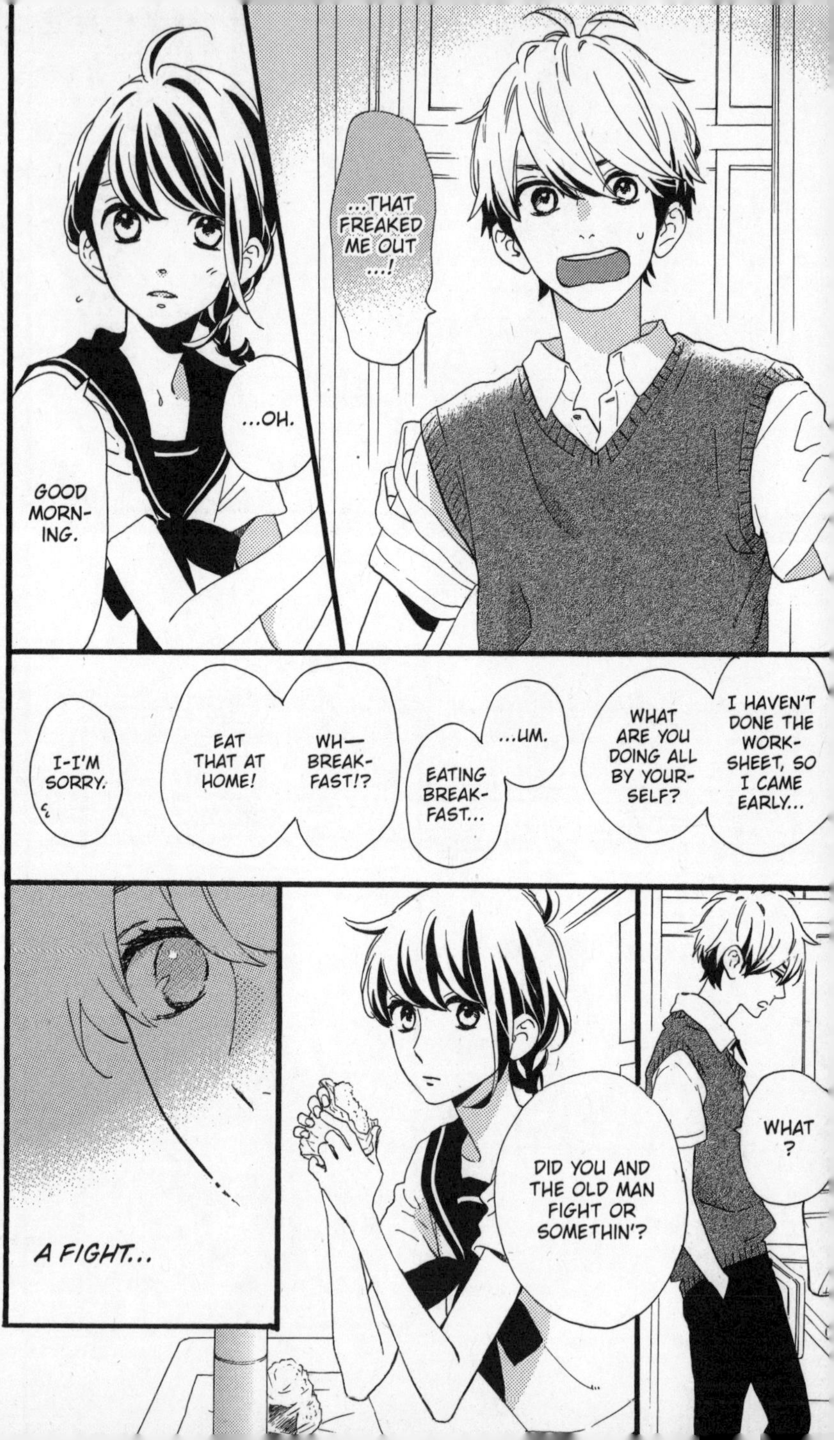
...THAT FREAKED ME OUT ...!
...OH.
GOOD MORN-ING.
I HAVEN'T DONE THE WORK-SHEET, SO I CAME EARLY...
WHAT ARE YOU DOING ALL BY YOUR-SELF?
...UM.
EATING BREAK-FAST...
WH— BREAK-FAST!?
EAT THAT AT HOME!
I-I'M SORRY.
WHAT?
DID YOU AND THE OLD MAN FIGHT OR SOMETHIN'?
A FIGHT...

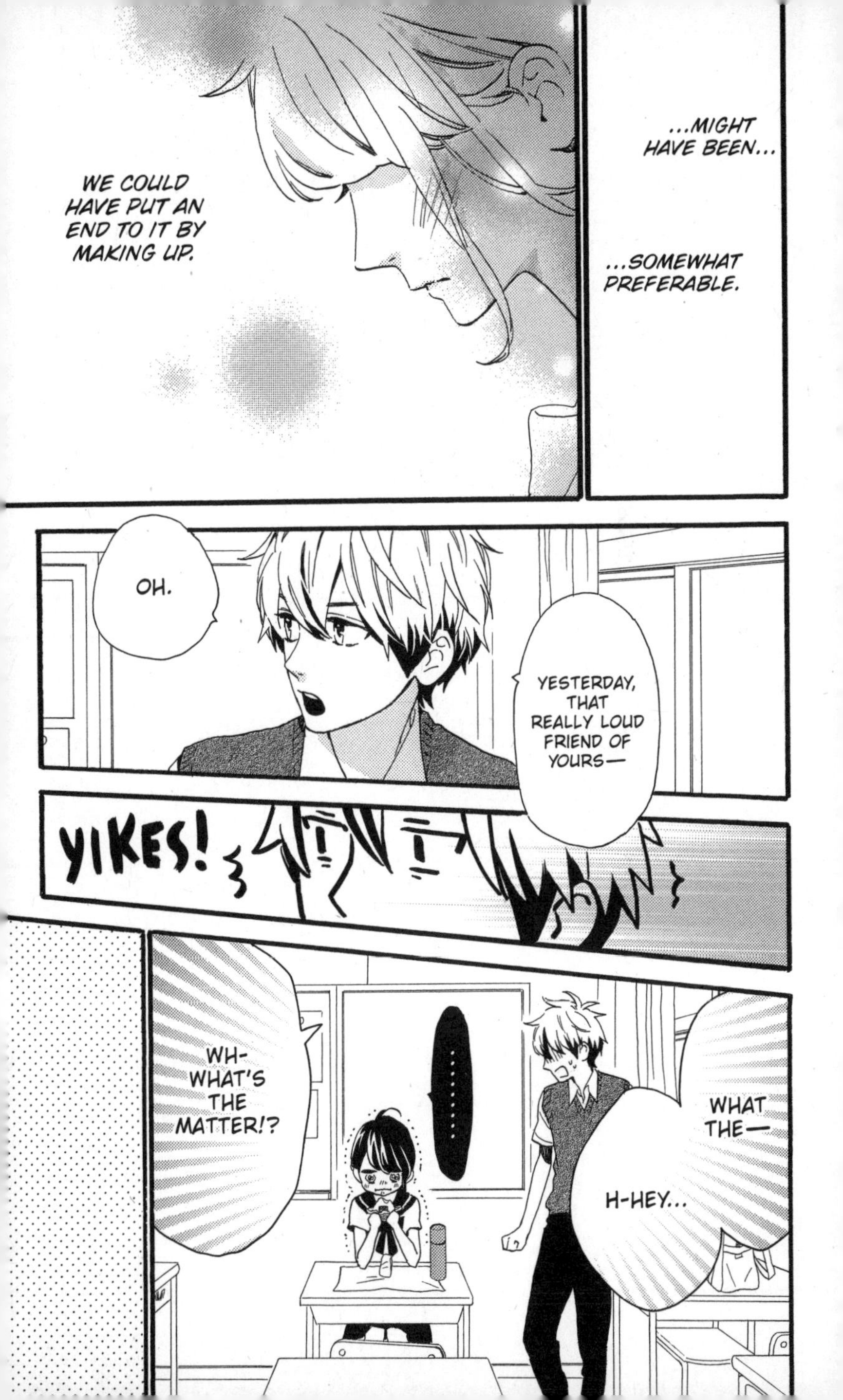
...MIGHT HAVE BEEN...
...SOMEWHAT PREFERABLE.
WE COULD HAVE PUT AN END TO IT BY MAKING UP.
OH.
YESTERDAY, THAT REALLY LOUD FRIEND OF YOURS—
YIKES!
WHAT THE—
H-HEY...
......
WH-WHAT'S THE MATTER!?

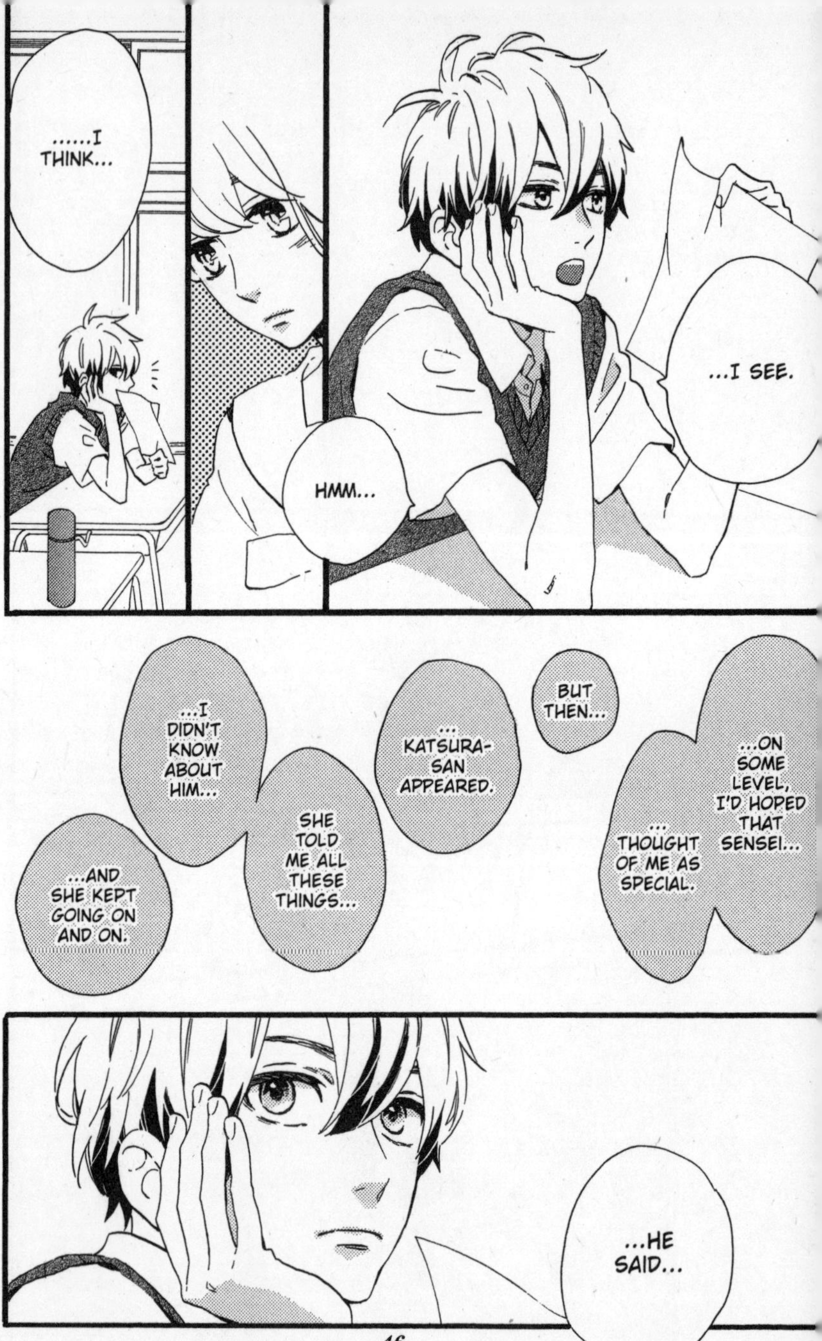
...I SEE.
HMM...
......I THINK...
...ON SOME LEVEL, I'D HOPED THAT SENSEI...
...THOUGHT OF ME AS SPECIAL.
BUT THEN...
...KATSURA-SAN APPEARED.
...I DIDN'T KNOW ABOUT HIM...
SHE TOLD ME ALL THESE THINGS...
...AND SHE KEPT GOING ON AND ON.
...HE SAID...

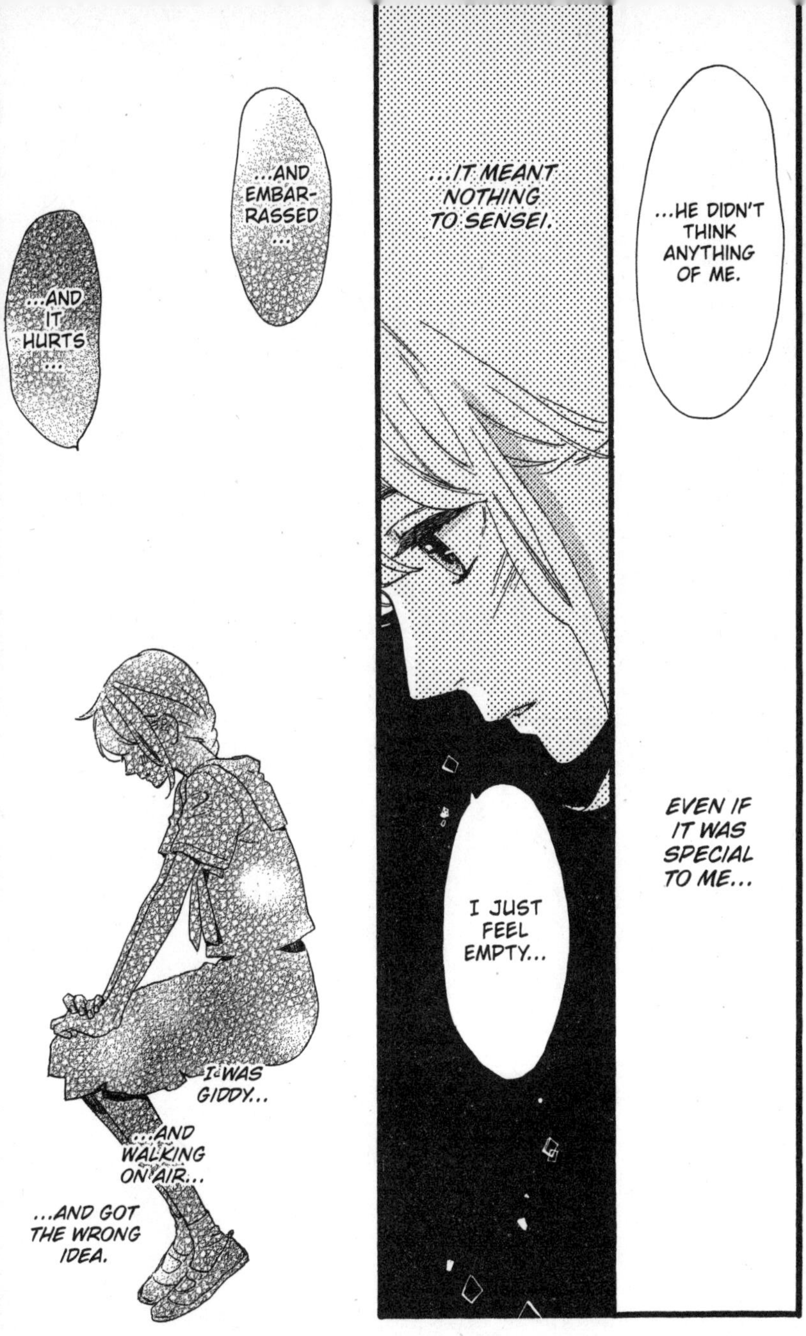
...HE DIDN'T THINK ANYTHING OF ME.
EVEN IF IT WAS SPECIAL TO ME...
...IT MEANT NOTHING TO SENSEI.
I JUST FEEL EMPTY...
...AND EMBARRASSED...
...AND IT HURTS...
I WAS GIDDY...
...AND WALKING ON AIR...
...AND GOT THE WRONG IDEA.

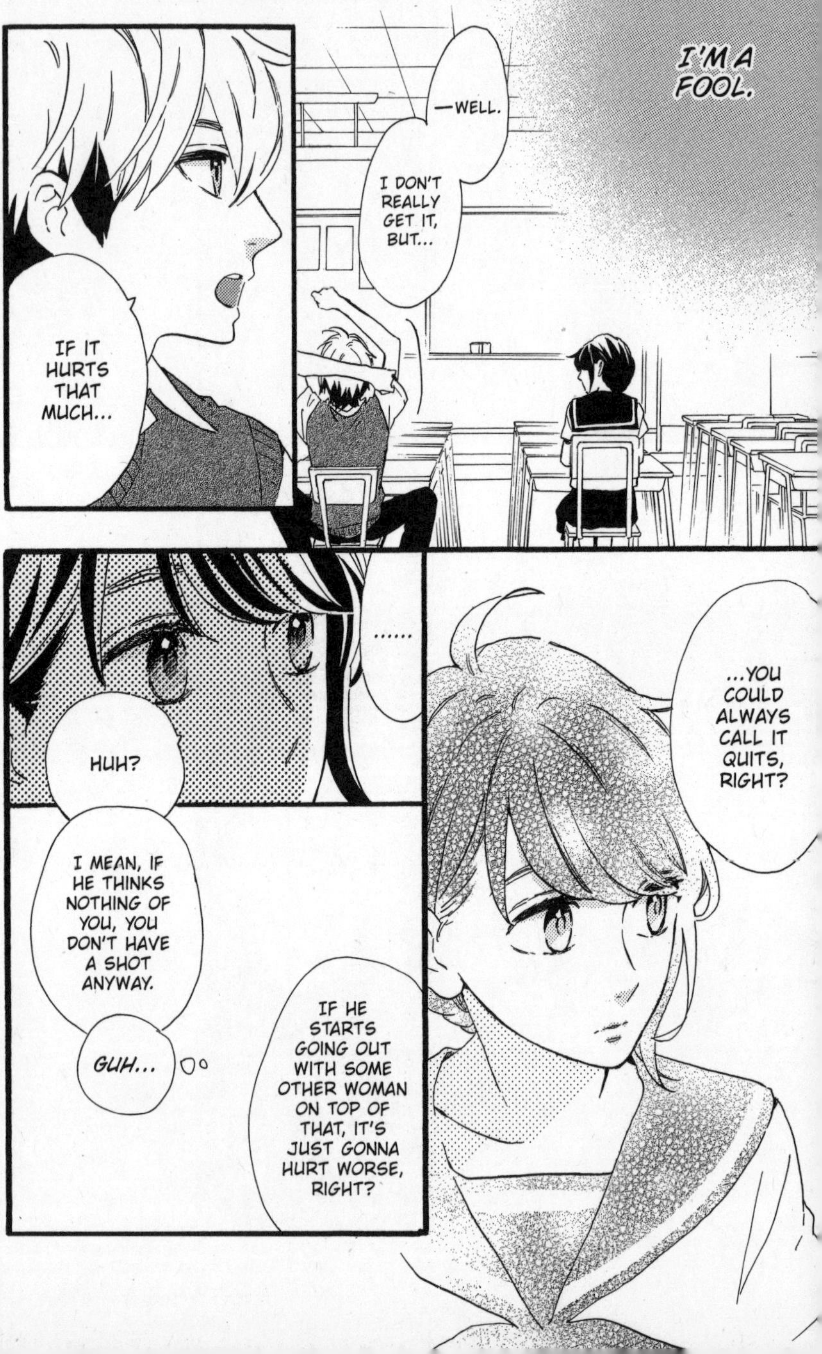
I'M A FOOL.
—WELL.
I DON'T REALLY GET IT, BUT...
IF IT HURTS THAT MUCH...
...YOU COULD ALWAYS CALL IT QUITS, RIGHT?
......
HUH?
I MEAN, IF HE THINKS NOTHING OF YOU, YOU DON'T HAVE A SHOT ANYWAY.
GUH...
IF HE STARTS GOING OUT WITH SOME OTHER WOMAN ON TOP OF THAT, IT'S JUST GONNA HURT WORSE, RIGHT?

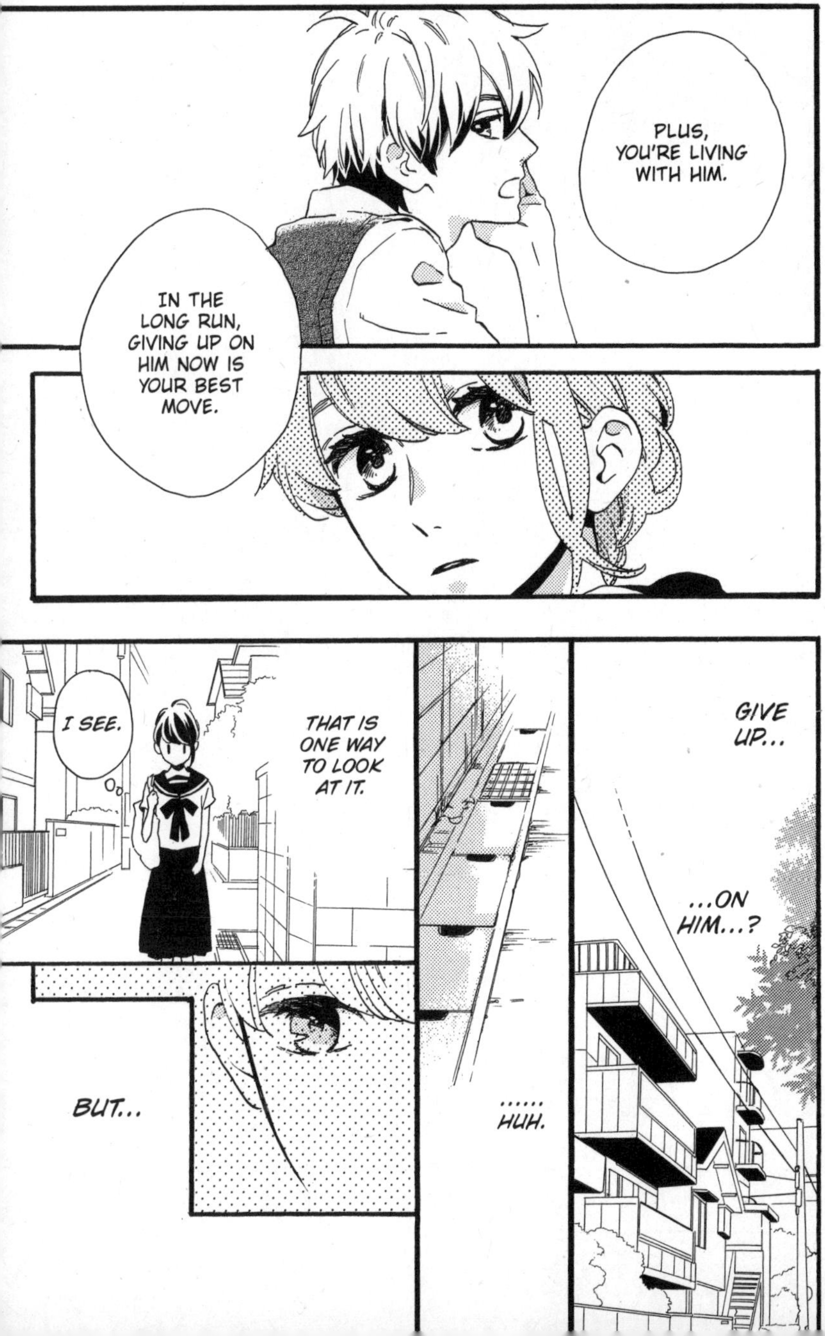
PLUS, YOU'RE LIVING WITH HIM.
IN THE LONG RUN, GIVING UP ON HIM NOW IS YOUR BEST MOVE.
GIVE UP...
...ON HIM...?
...... HUH.
I SEE.
THAT IS ONE WAY TO LOOK AT IT.
BUT...

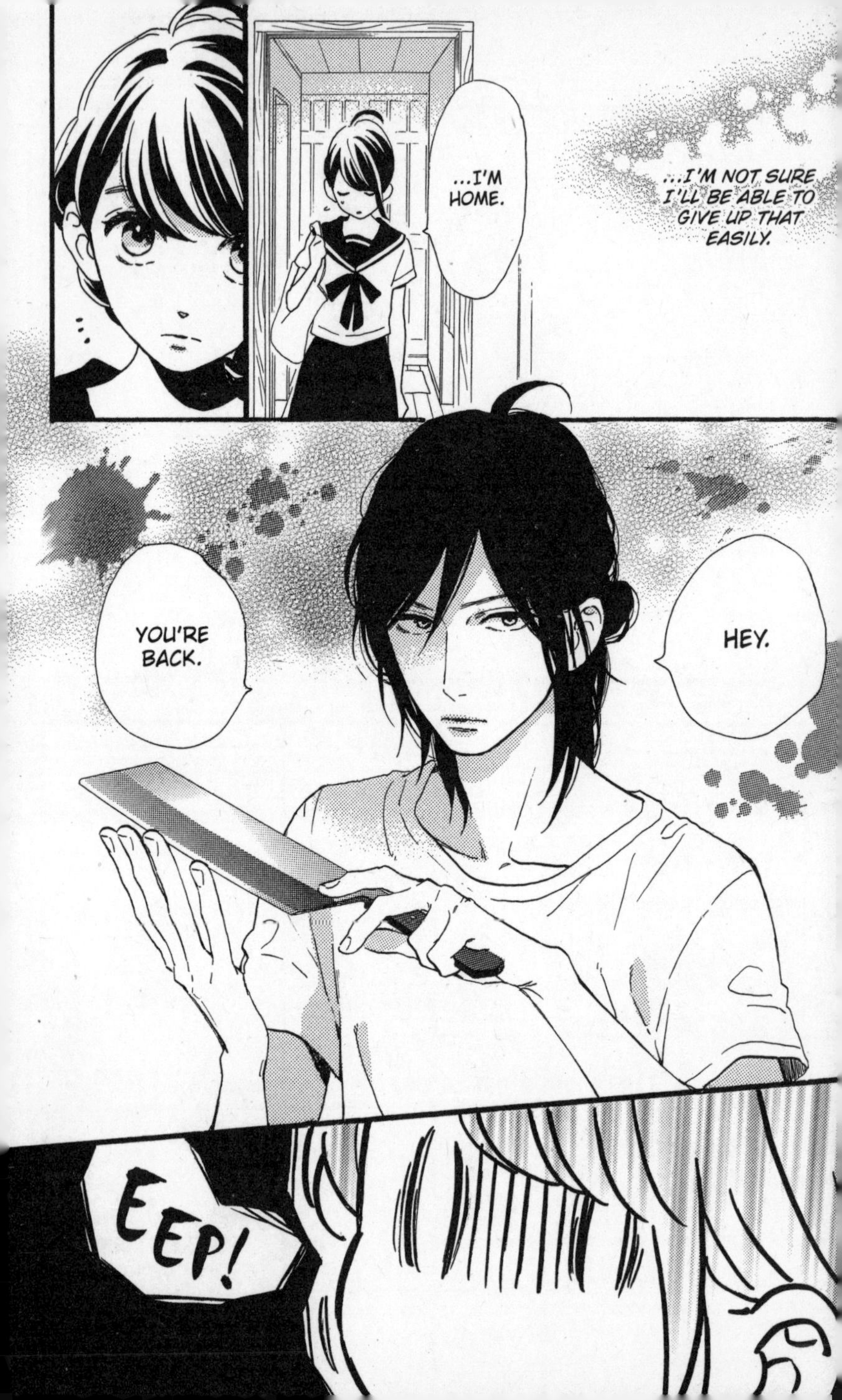
...I'M NOT SURE I'LL BE ABLE TO GIVE UP THAT EASILY.
...I'M HOME.
HEY.
YOU'RE BACK.
EEP!

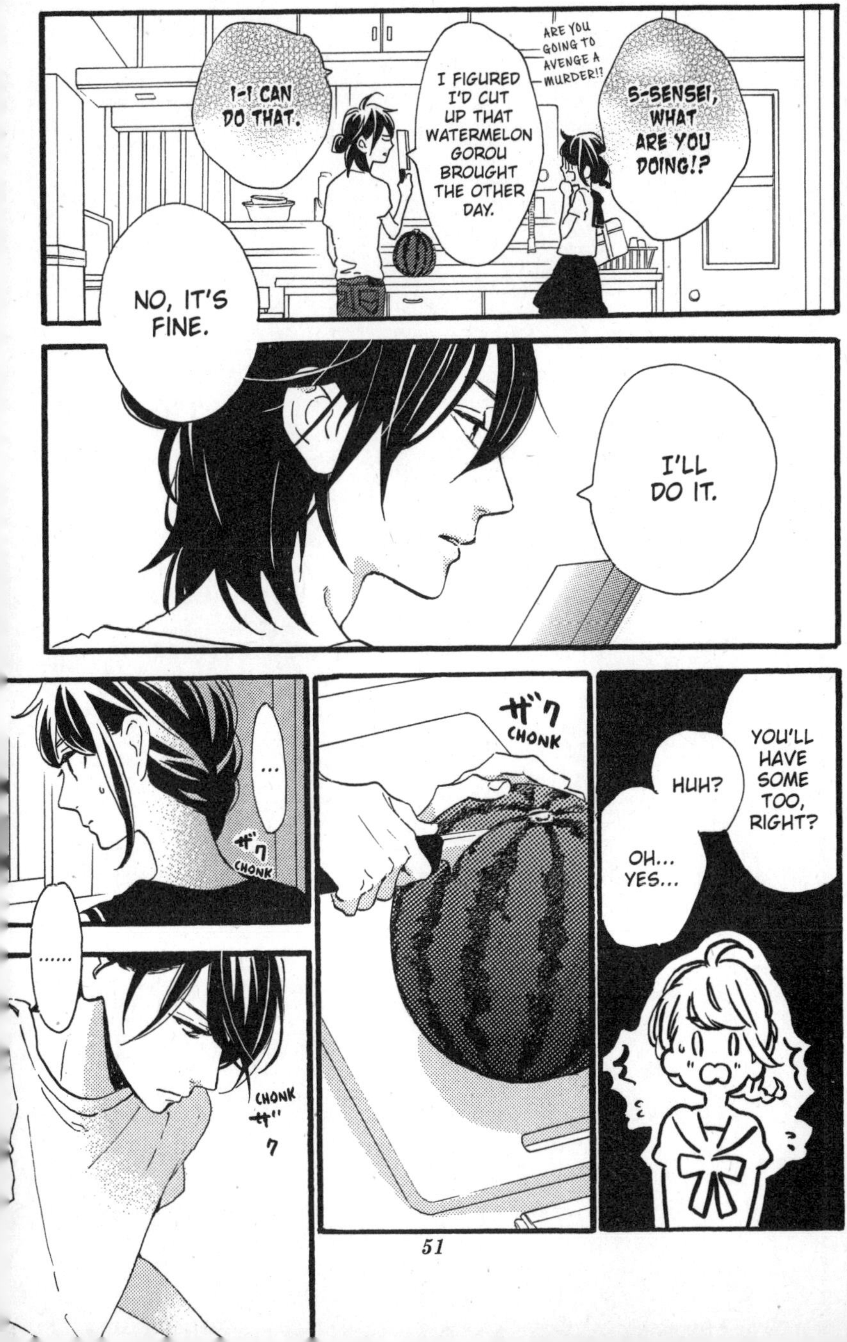
S-SENSEI, WHAT ARE YOU DOING!?
ARE YOU GOING TO AVENGE A MURDER!?
I FIGURED I'D CUT UP THAT WATERMELON GOROU BROUGHT THE OTHER DAY.
I-I CAN DO THAT.
NO, IT'S FINE.
I'LL DO IT.
YOU'LL HAVE SOME TOO, RIGHT?
HUH?
OH... YES...
ザク
CHONK
...
ザク
CHONK
......
CHONK
ザク

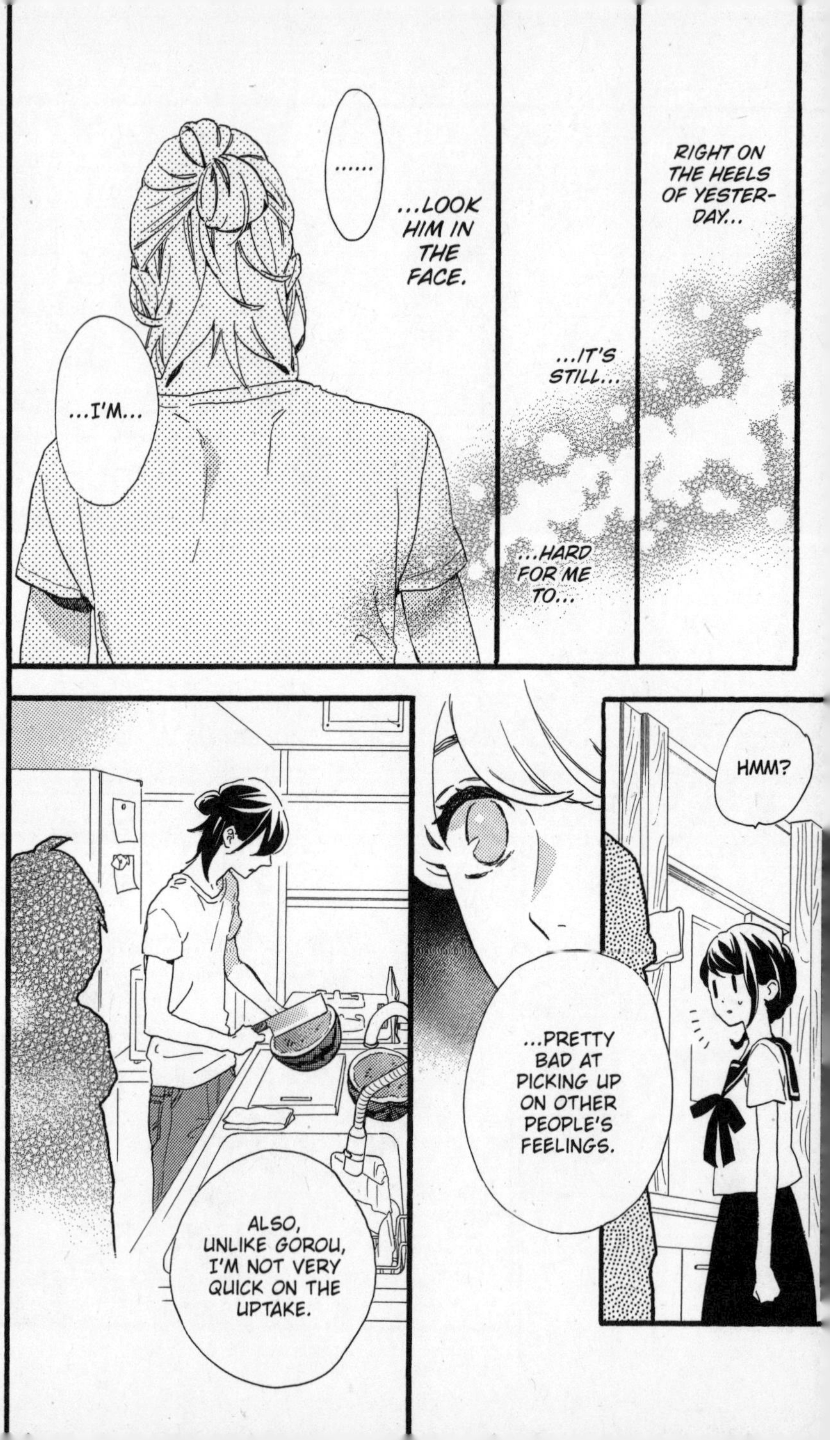
RIGHT ON THE HEELS OF YESTER-DAY...
...IT'S STILL...
...HARD FOR ME TO...
......
...LOOK HIM IN THE FACE.
...I'M...
HMM?
...PRETTY BAD AT PICKING UP ON OTHER PEOPLE'S FEELINGS.
ALSO, UNLIKE GOROU, I'M NOT VERY QUICK ON THE UPTAKE.

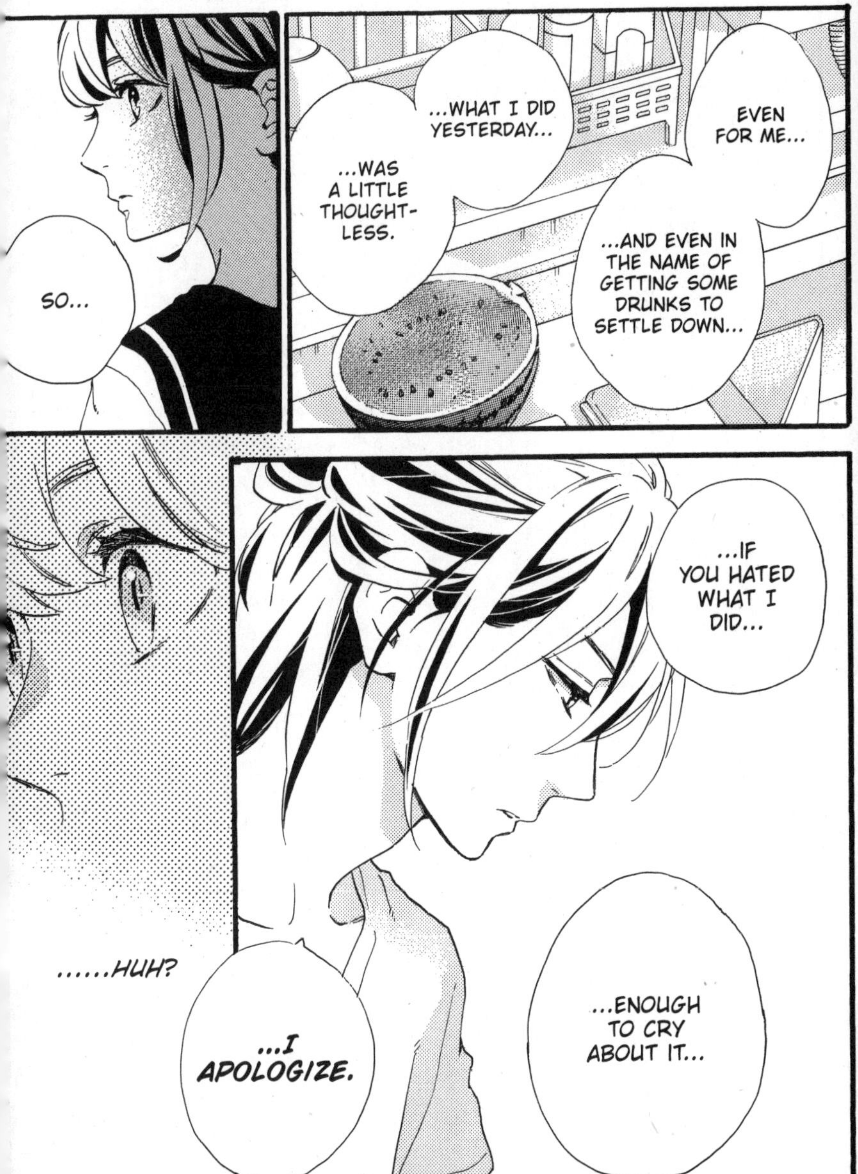
EVEN FOR ME...
...AND EVEN IN THE NAME OF GETTING SOME DRUNKS TO SETTLE DOWN...
...WHAT I DID YESTERDAY...
...WAS A LITTLE THOUGHTLESS.
SO...
...IF YOU HATED WHAT I DID...
...ENOUGH TO CRY ABOUT IT...
...I APOLOGIZE.
......HUH?

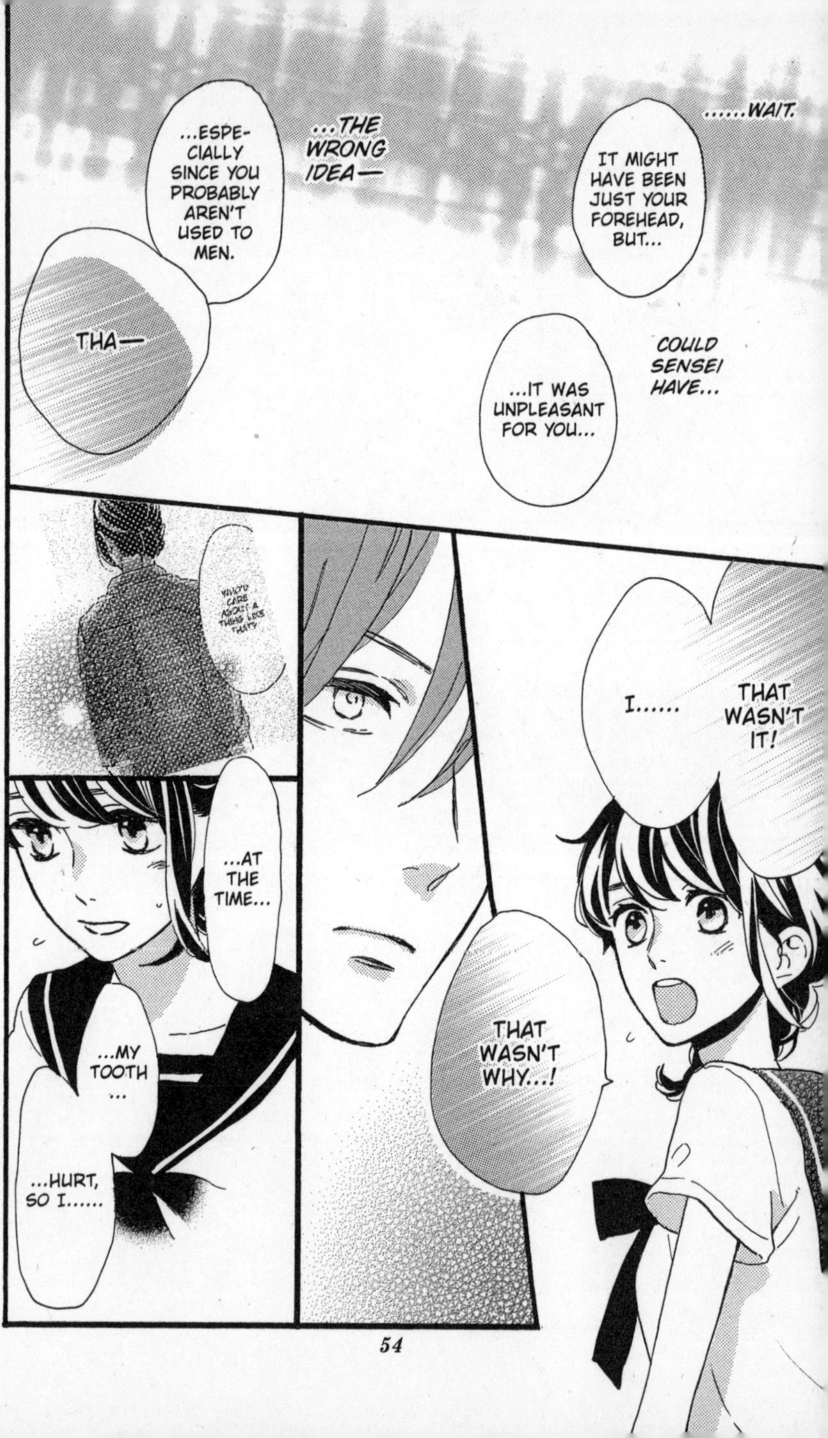
......WAIT.
IT MIGHT HAVE BEEN JUST YOUR FOREHEAD, BUT...
COULD SENSEI HAVE...
...IT WAS UNPLEASANT FOR YOU...
...THE WRONG IDEA—
...ESPE-CIALLY SINCE YOU PROBABLY AREN'T USED TO MEN.
THA—
THAT WASN'T IT!
I......
THAT WASN'T WHY...!
WHO'D CARE ABOUT A THING LIKE THAT?
...AT THE TIME...
...MY TOOTH ...
...HURT, SO I......

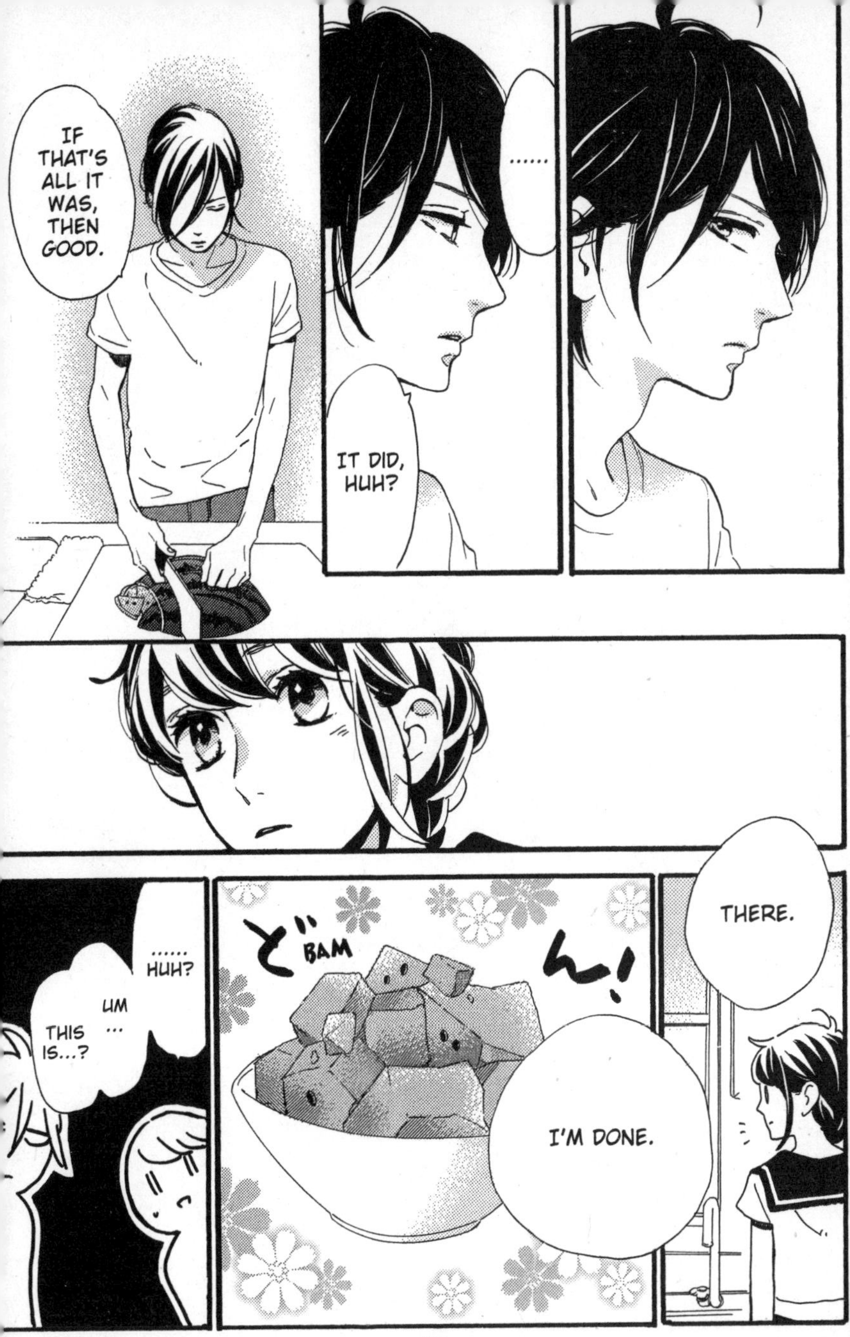
......
IT DID, HUH?
IF THAT'S ALL IT WAS, THEN GOOD.
THERE.
ど BAM
ん!
I'M DONE.
......HUH?
UM...
THIS IS...?

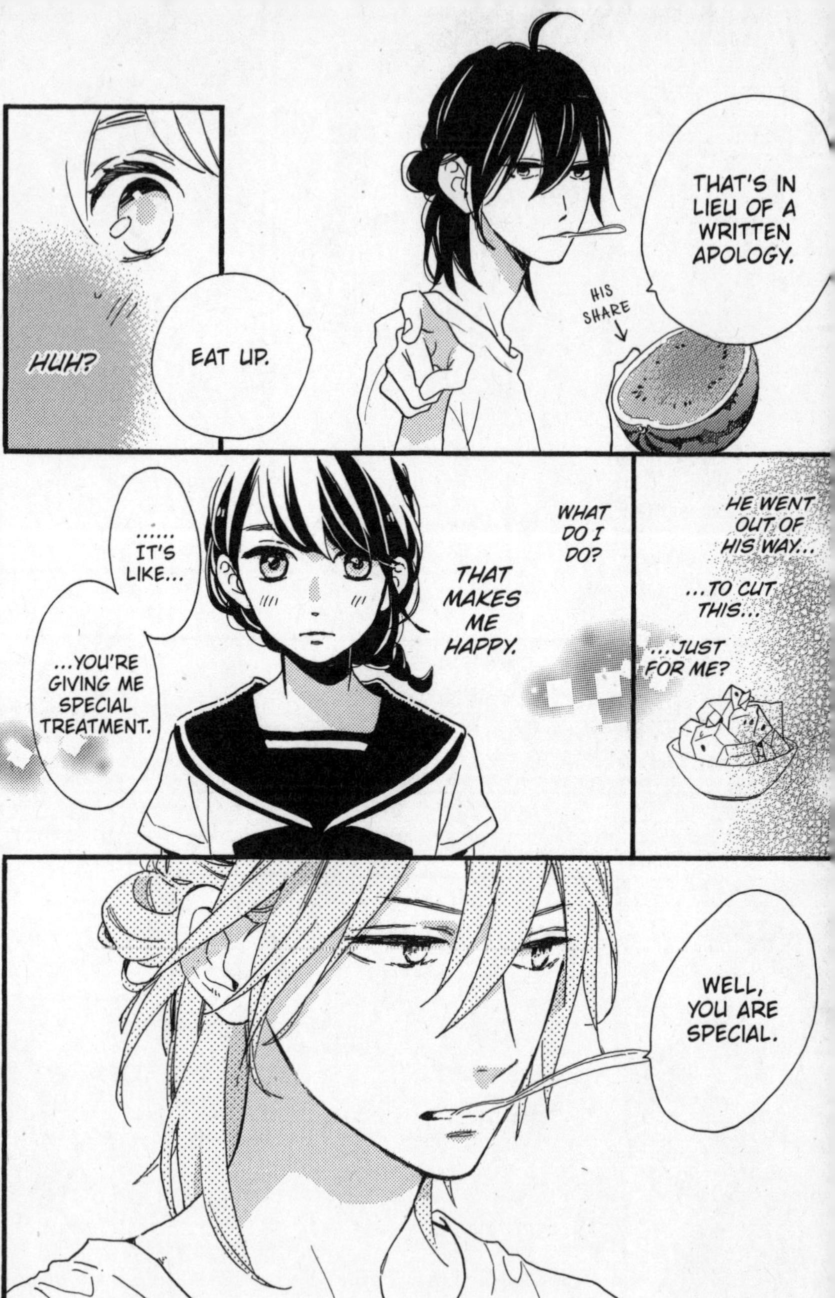
THAT'S IN LIEU OF A WRITTEN APOLOGY.
HIS SHARE
EAT UP.
HUH?
HE WENT OUT OF HIS WAY...
...TO CUT THIS...
...JUST FOR ME?
WHAT DO I DO?
THAT MAKES ME HAPPY.
......IT'S LIKE...
...YOU'RE GIVING ME SPECIAL TREATMENT.
WELL, YOU ARE SPECIAL.

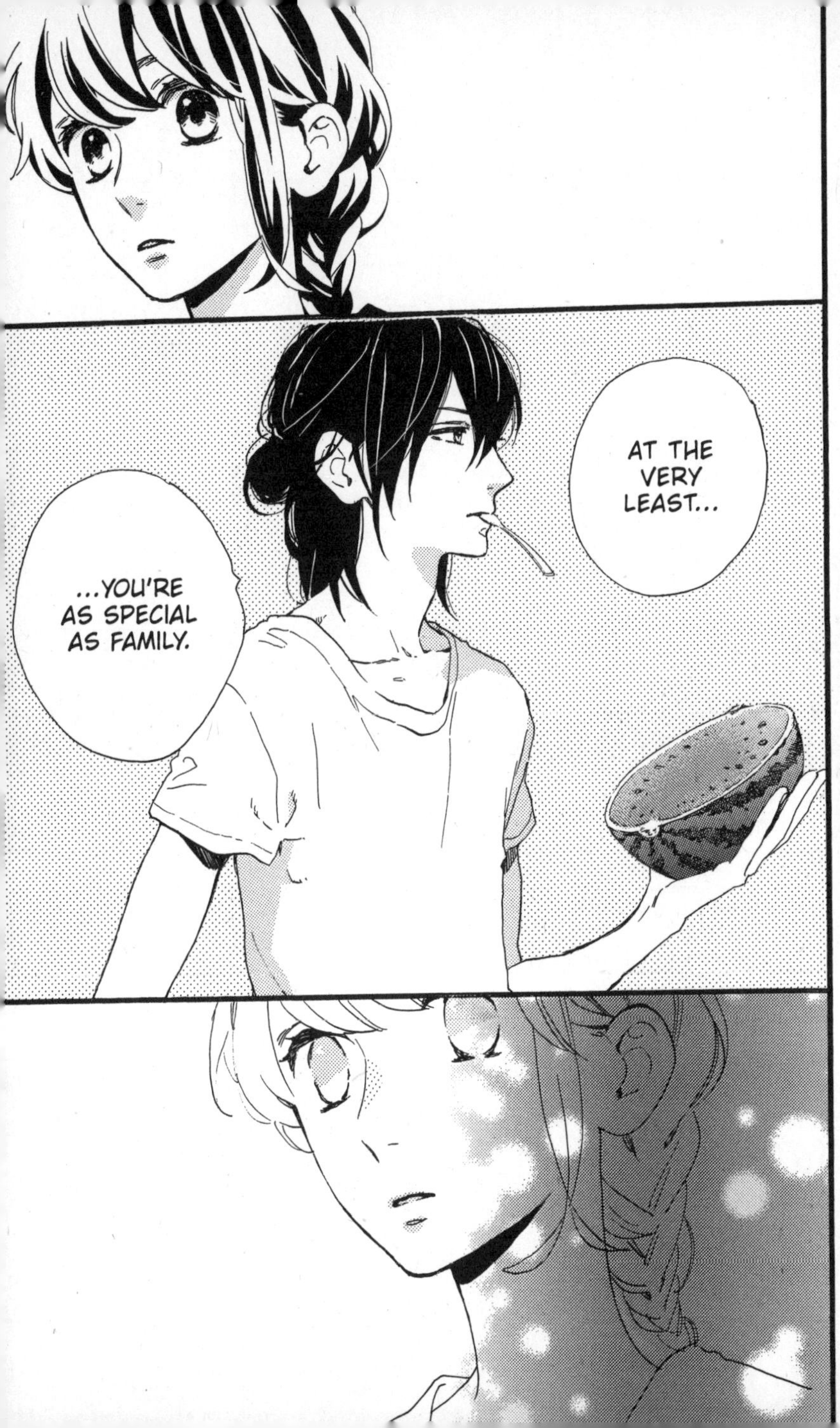
AT THE VERY LEAST...
...YOU'RE AS SPECIAL AS FAMILY.

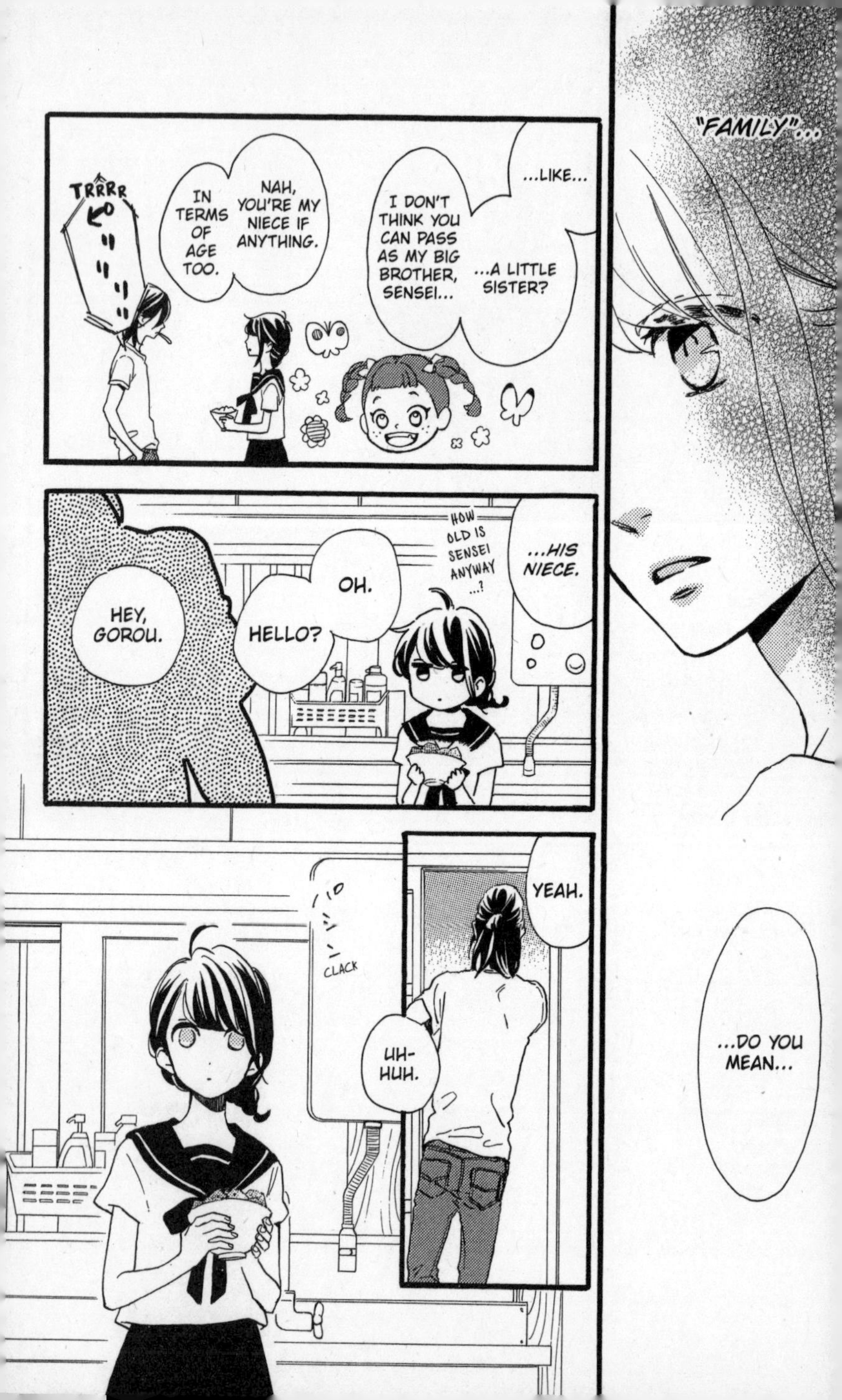
"FAMILY"...
...DO YOU MEAN...
...LIKE...
...A LITTLE SISTER?
I DON'T THINK YOU CAN PASS AS MY BIG BROTHER, SENSEI...
NAH, YOU'RE MY NIECE IF ANYTHING.
IN TERMS OF AGE TOO.
TRRRR
...HIS NIECE.
HOW OLD IS SENSEI ANYWAY...?
OH.
HELLO?
HEY, GOROU.
YEAH.
CLACK
UH-HUH.

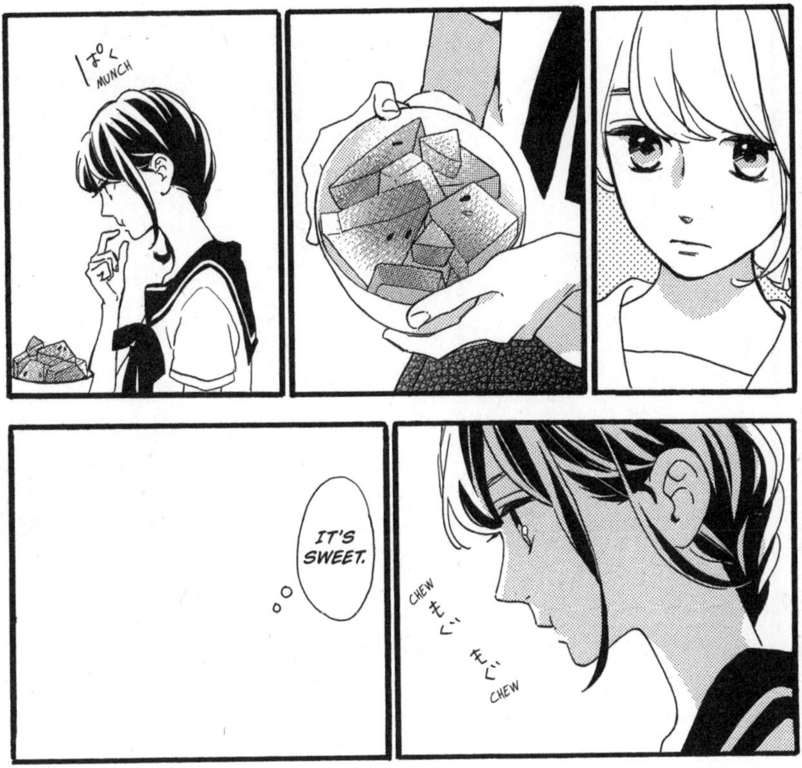
ぽく
MUNCH
もぐ CHEW
もぐ CHEW
IT'S SWEET.

I SEE.

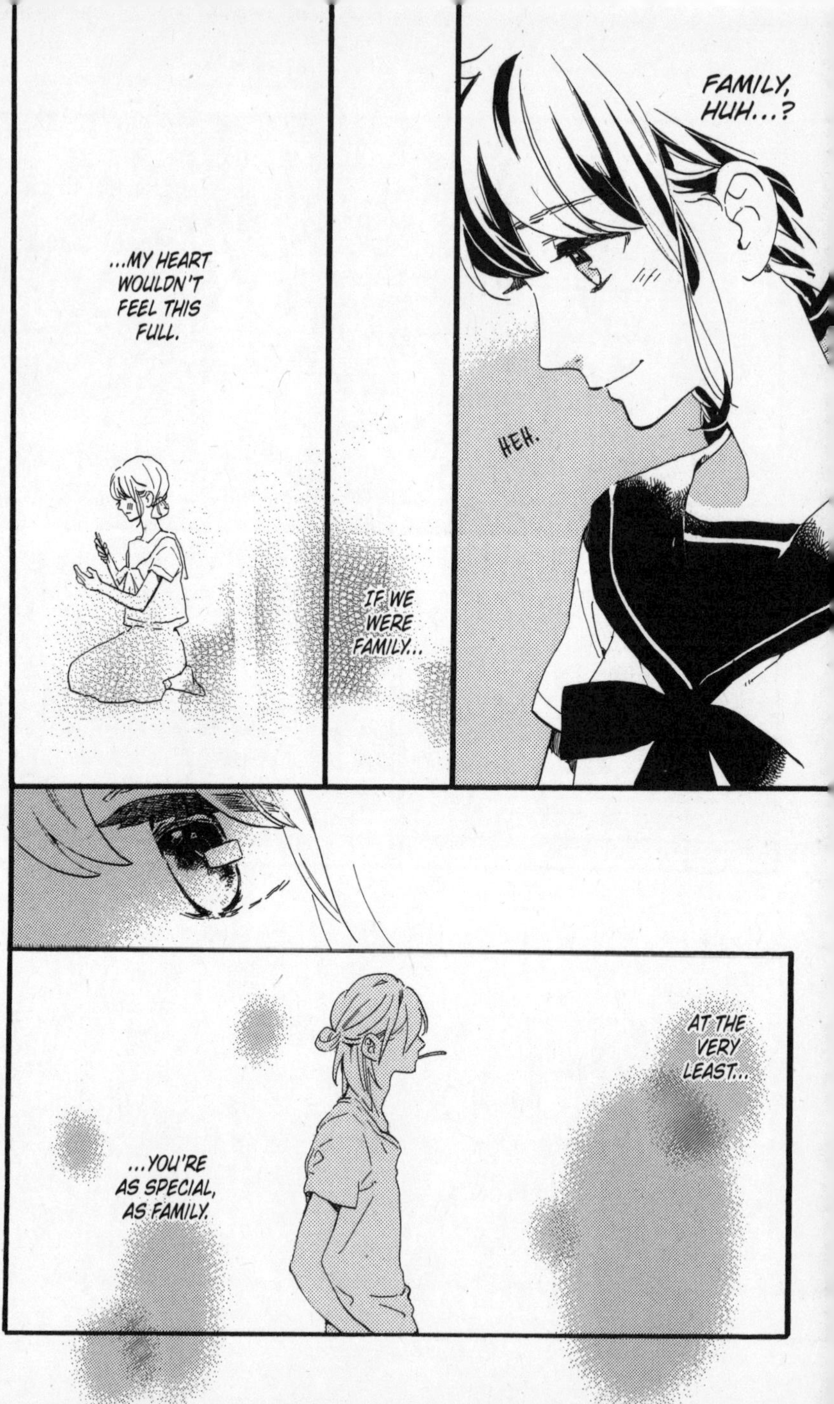
FAMILY, HUH...?
HEH.
IF WE WERE FAMILY...
...MY HEART WOULDN'T FEEL THIS FULL.
AT THE VERY LEAST...
...YOU'RE AS SPECIAL, AS FAMILY.

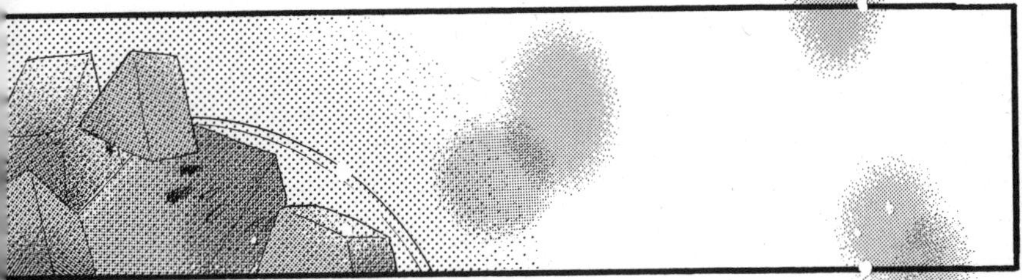

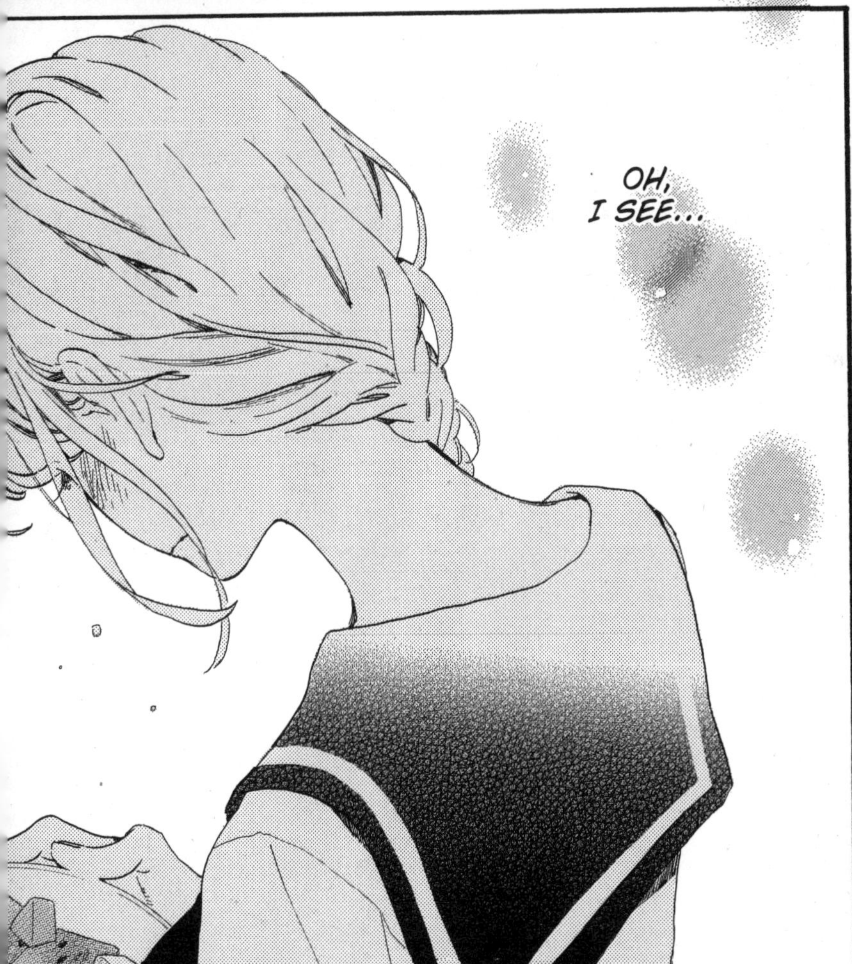
OH, I SEE...

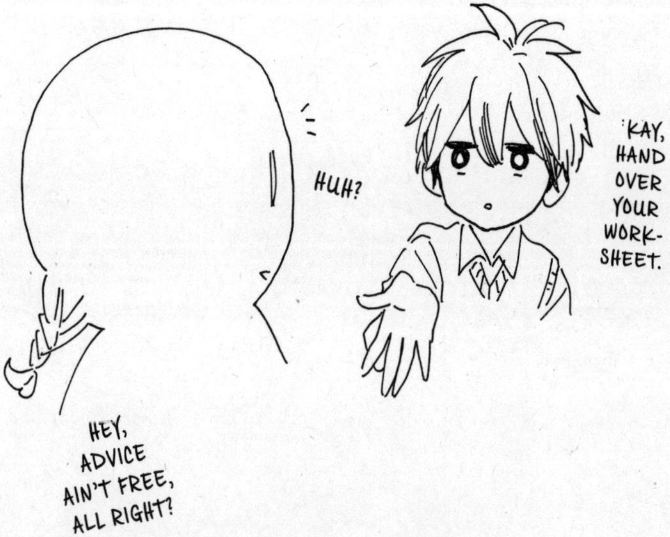
'KAY, HAND OVER YOUR WORK-SHEET.
HUH?
HEY, ADVICE AIN'T FREE, ALL RIGHT?

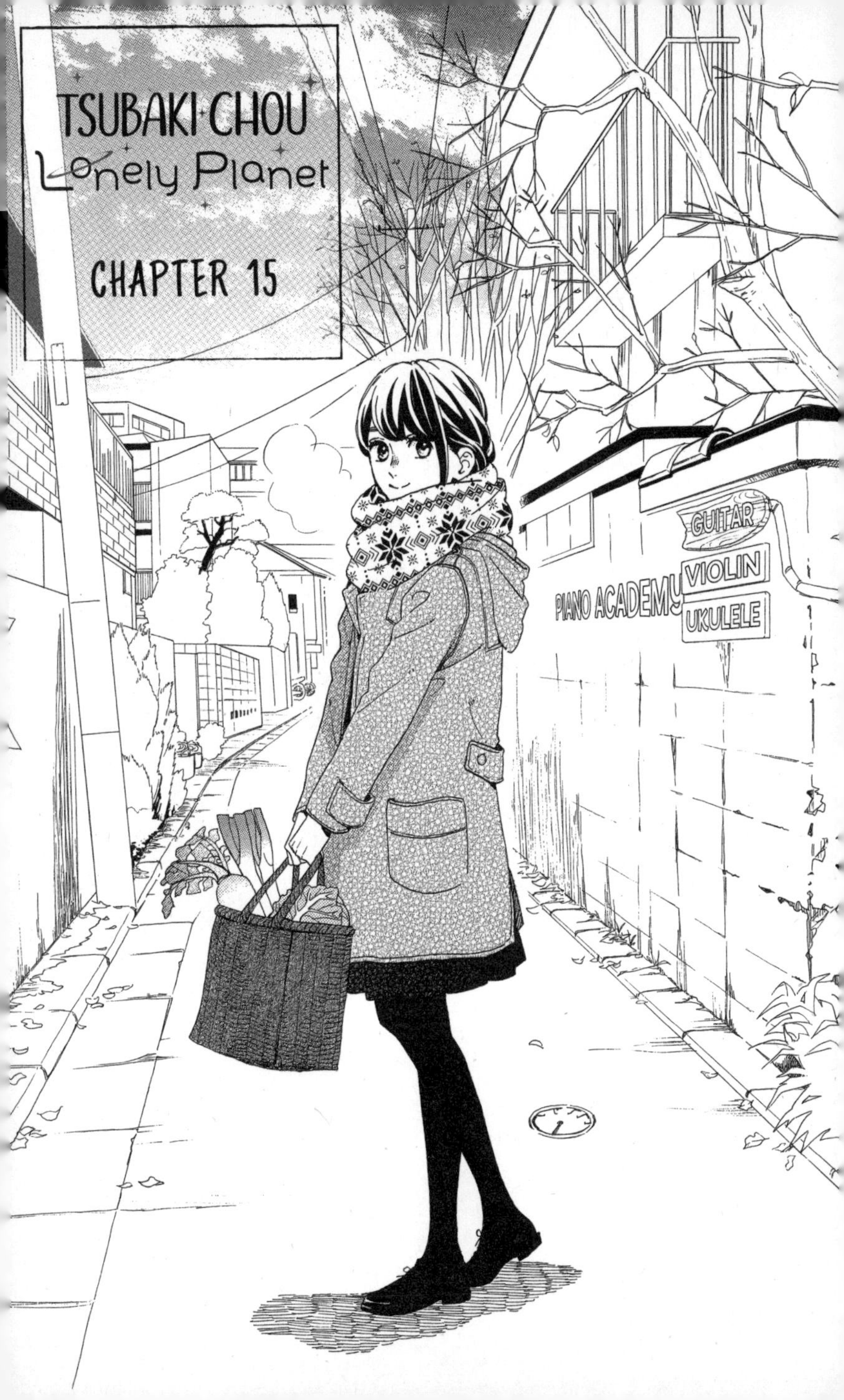
TSUBAKI-CHOU
Lonely Planet
CHAPTER 15
GUITAR
VIOLIN
PIANO ACADEMY
UKULELE

GIVING UP ON HIM NOW IS YOUR BEST MOVE.

AT THE VERY LEAST, YOU'RE AS SPECIAL AS FAMILY.

YEAH.

THAT'S RIGHT.

I SHOULD GIVE UP ON HIM ALREADY.

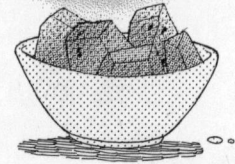

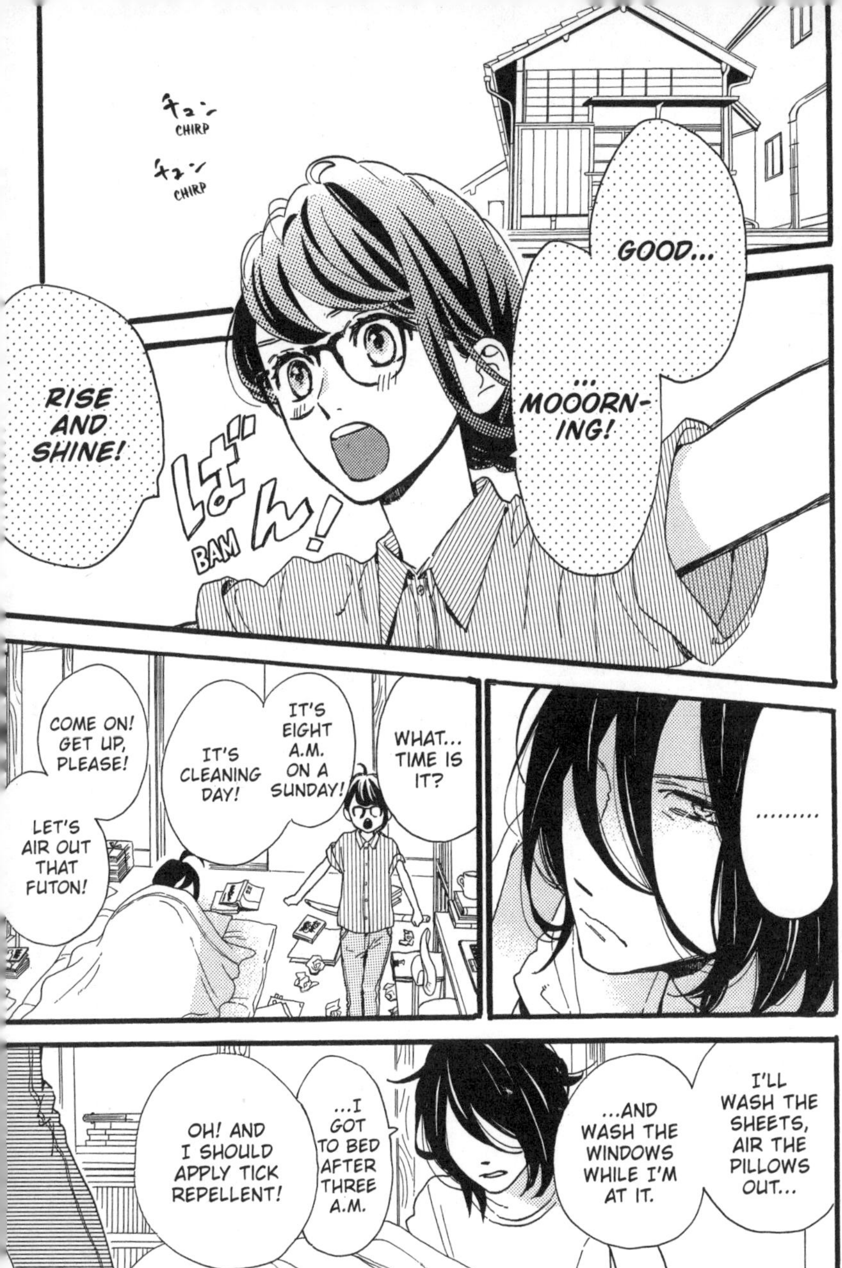
チュン
CHIRP
チュン
CHIRP
GOOD... ...MOOORNING!
RISE AND SHINE!
ばん
BAM
....
WHAT... TIME IS IT?
IT'S EIGHT A.M. ON A SUNDAY!
IT'S CLEANING DAY!
COME ON! GET UP, PLEASE!
LET'S AIR OUT THAT FUTON!
I'LL WASH THE SHEETS, AIR THE PILLOWS OUT...
...AND WASH THE WINDOWS WHILE I'M AT IT.
...I GOT TO BED AFTER THREE A.M.
OH! AND I SHOULD APPLY TICK REPELLENT!

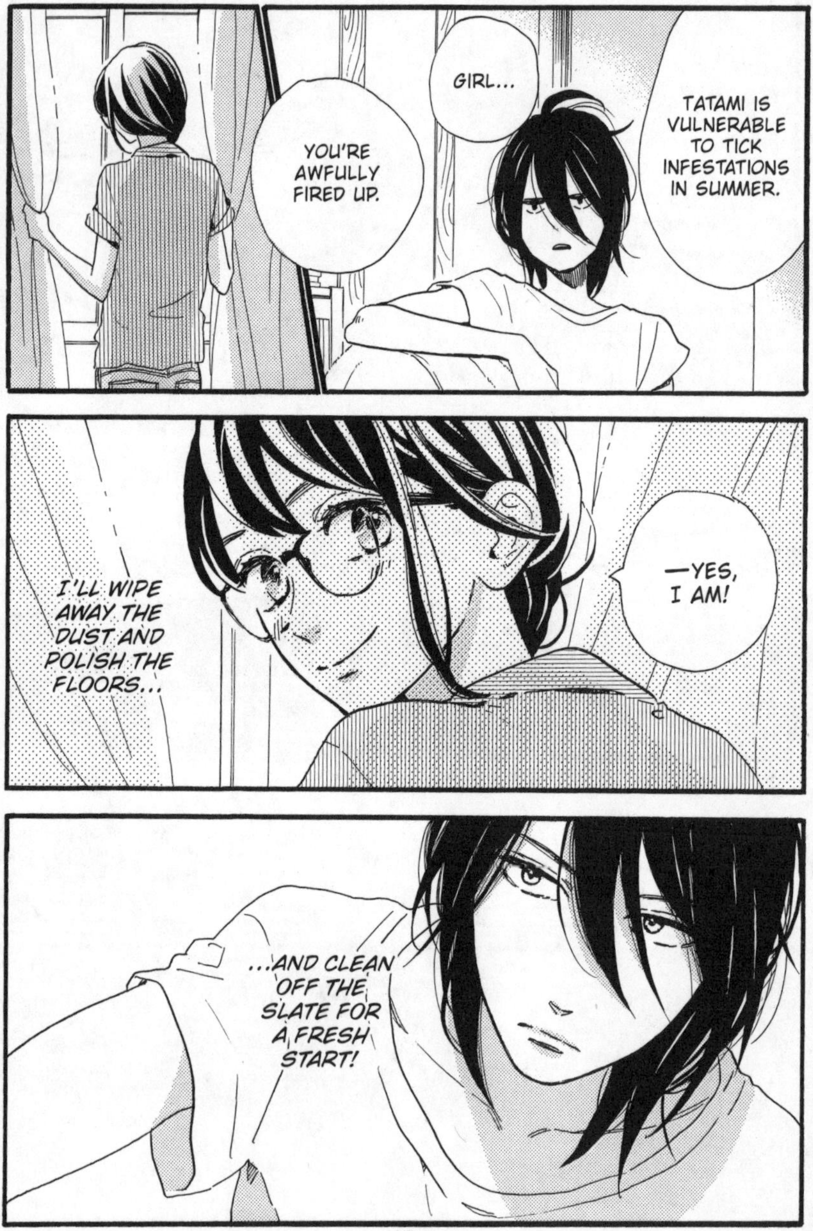
TATAMI IS VULNERABLE TO TICK INFESTATIONS IN SUMMER.
GIRL...
YOU'RE AWFULLY FIRED UP.
—YES, I AM!
I'LL WIPE AWAY THE DUST AND POLISH THE FLOORS...
...AND CLEAN OFF THE SLATE FOR A FRESH START!

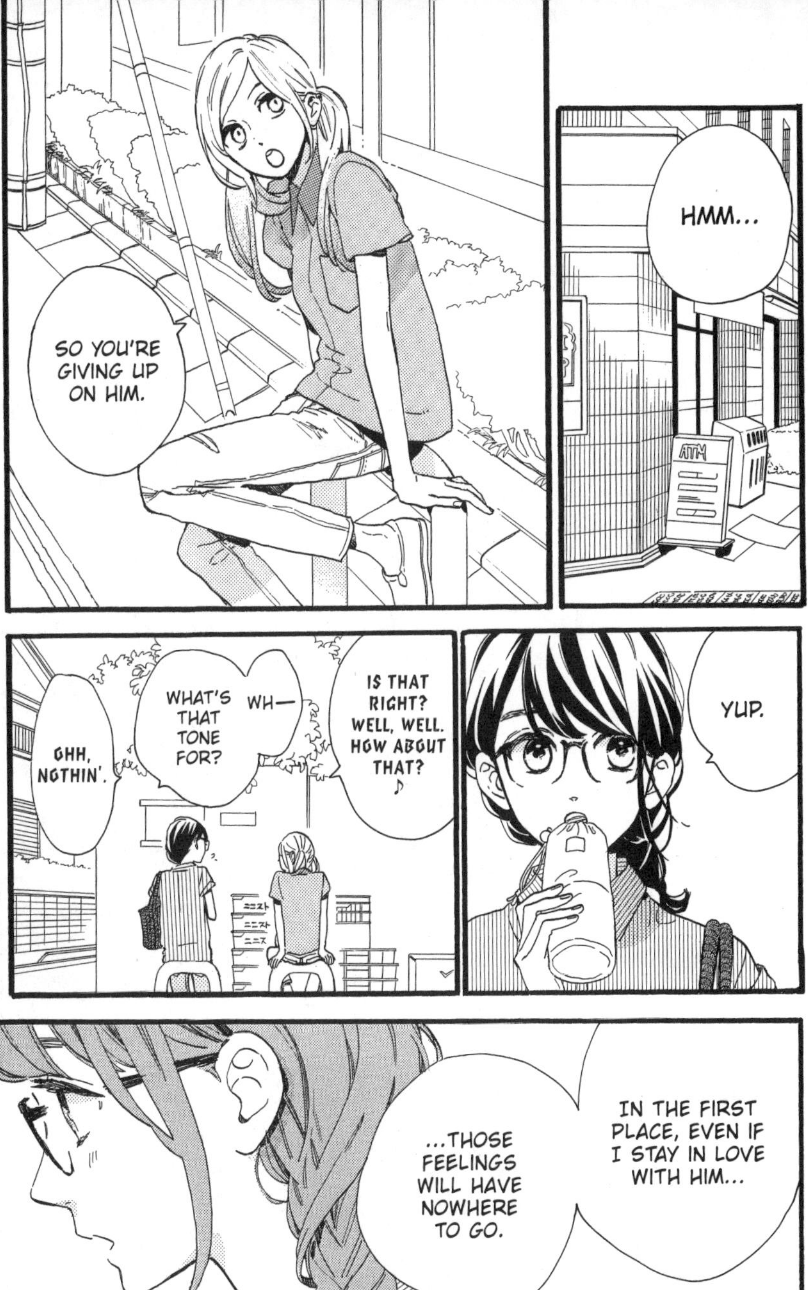
HMM...
SO YOU'RE GIVING UP ON HIM.
ATM
YUP.
IS THAT RIGHT? WELL, WELL. HOW ABOUT THAT? ♪
WH—
WHAT'S THAT TONE FOR?
OHH, NOTHIN'.
IN THE FIRST PLACE, EVEN IF I STAY IN LOVE WITH HIM...
...THOSE FEELINGS WILL HAVE NOWHERE TO GO.

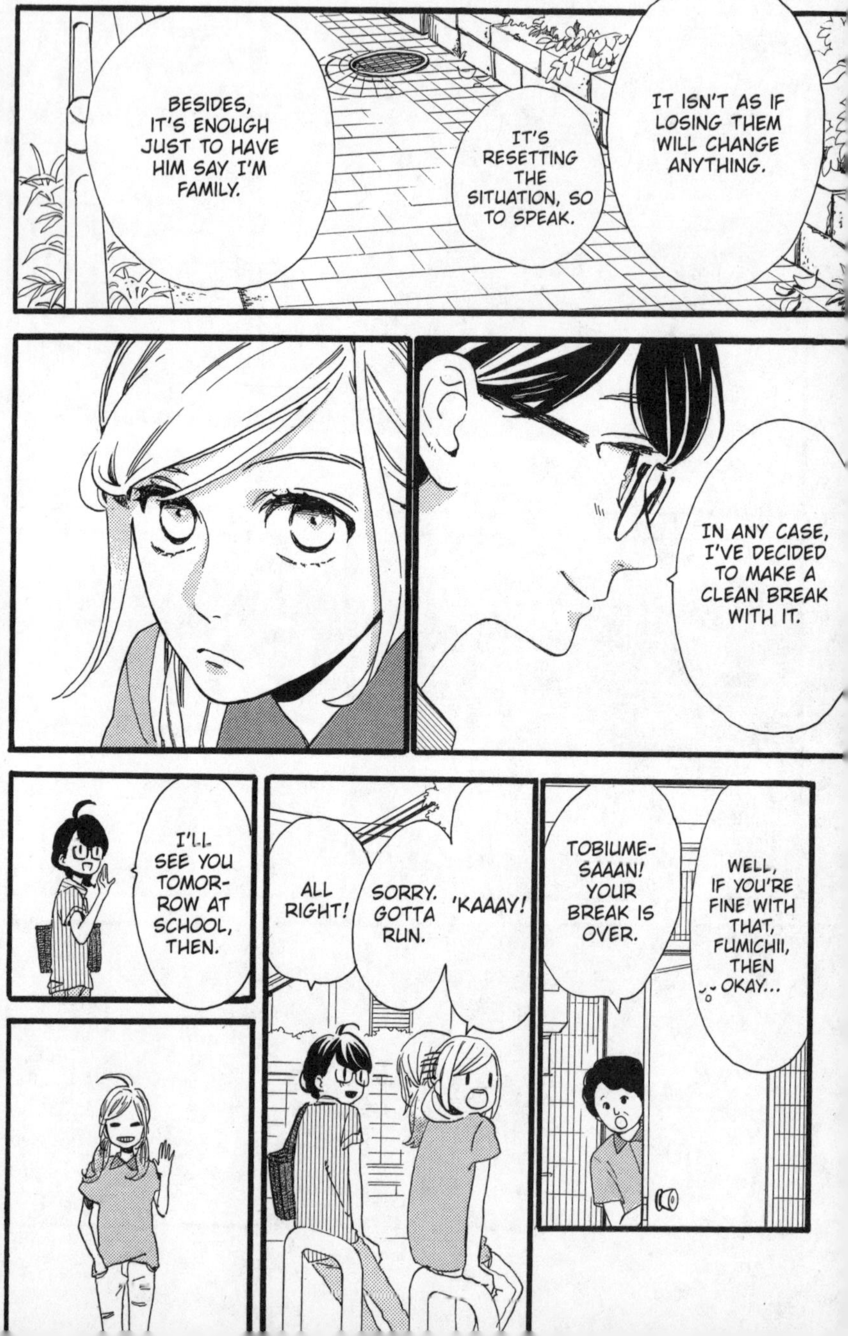
IT ISN'T AS IF LOSING THEM WILL CHANGE ANYTHING.
IT'S RESETTING THE SITUATION, SO TO SPEAK.
BESIDES, IT'S ENOUGH JUST TO HAVE HIM SAY I'M FAMILY.
IN ANY CASE, I'VE DECIDED TO MAKE A CLEAN BREAK WITH IT.
WELL, IF YOU'RE FINE WITH THAT, FUMICHII, THEN OKAY...
TOBIUME-SAAAN! YOUR BREAK IS OVER.
'KAAAY!
SORRY. GOTTA RUN.
ALL RIGHT!
I'LL SEE YOU TOMOR-ROW AT SCHOOL, THEN.

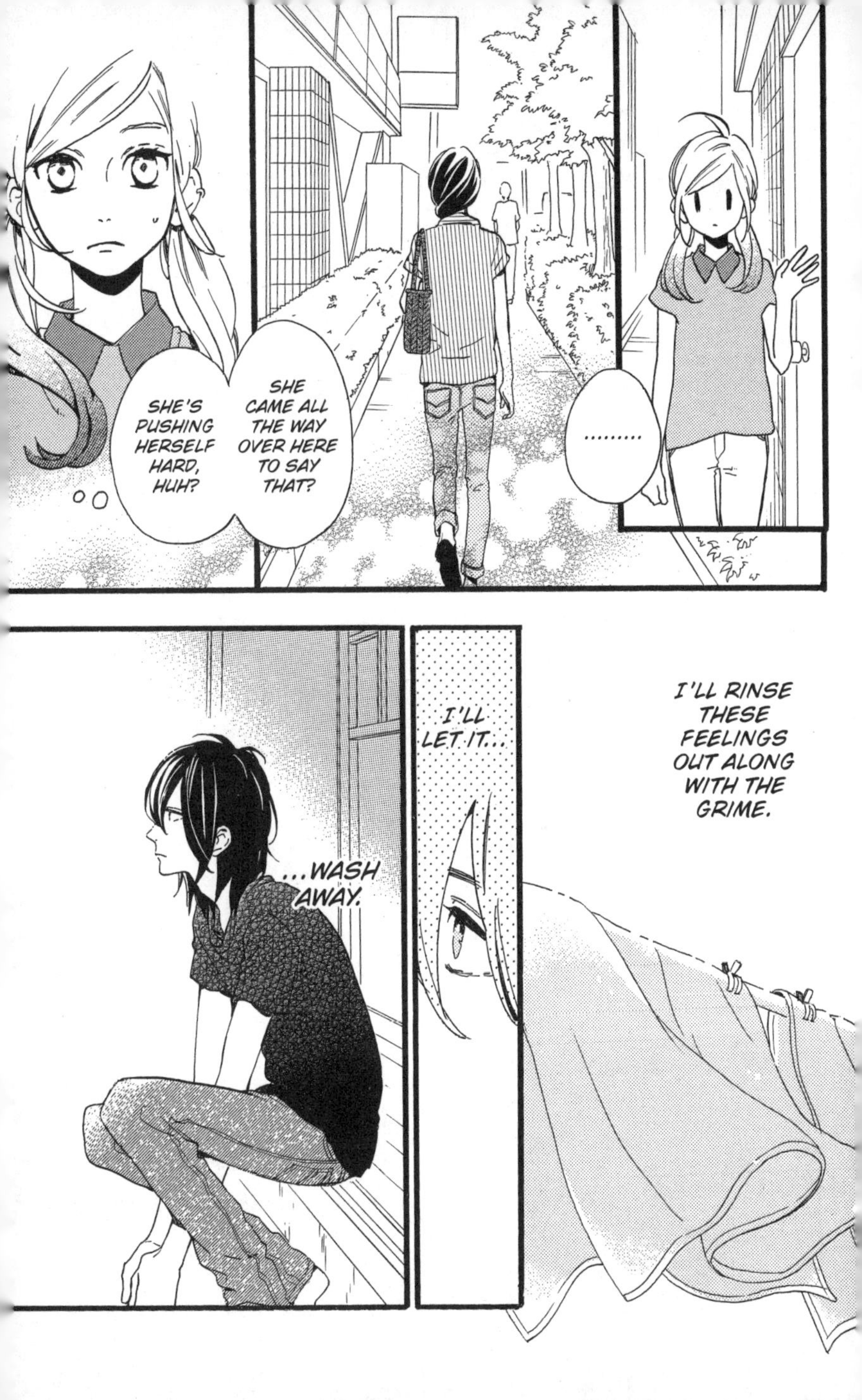
....
SHE CAME ALL THE WAY OVER HERE TO SAY THAT?
SHE'S PUSHING HERSELF HARD, HUH?
I'LL RINSE THESE FEELINGS OUT ALONG WITH THE GRIME.
I'LL LET IT...
...WASH AWAY.

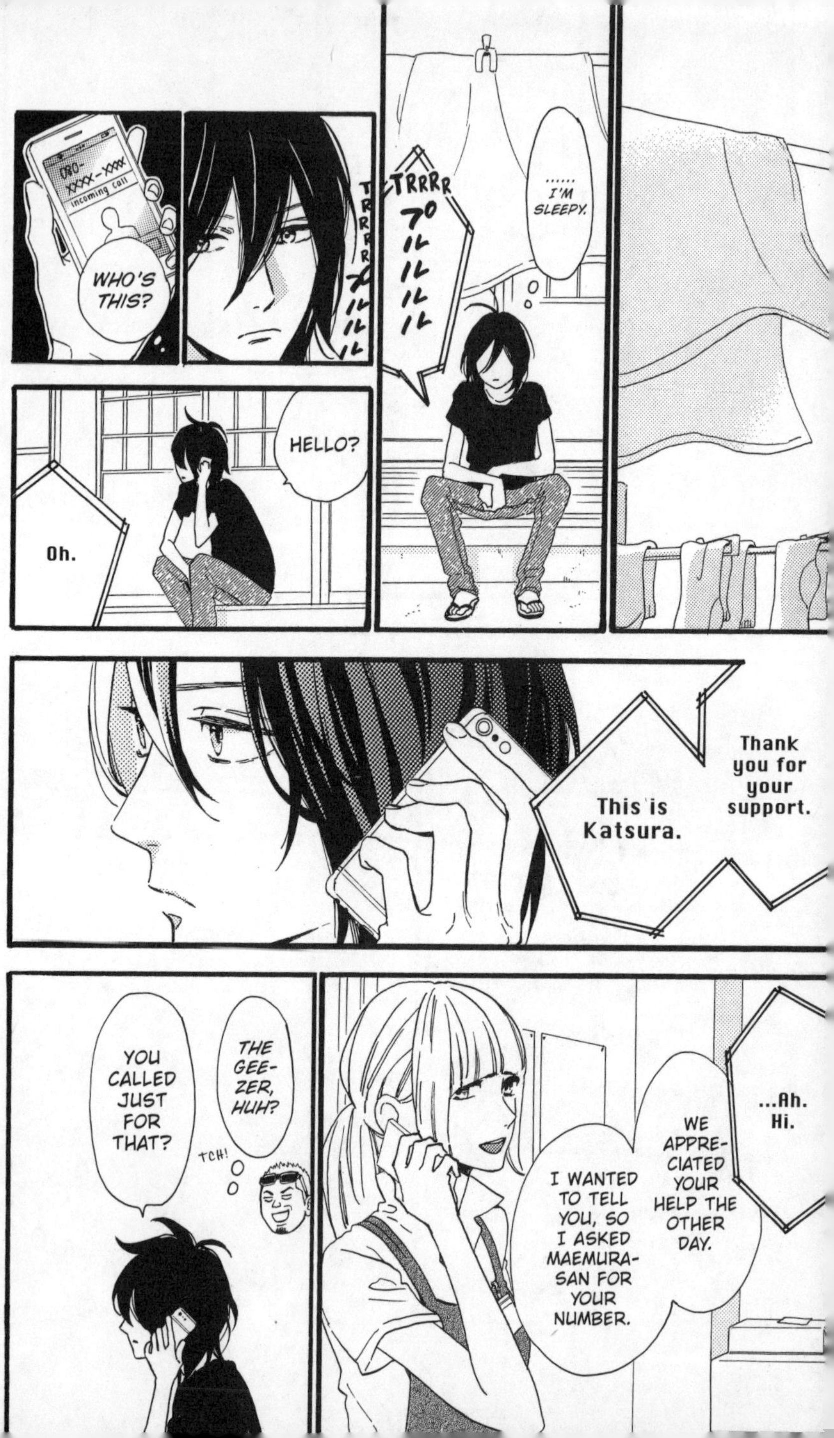

......
I'M SLEEPY.
TRRRR
プルルル
TRRRR
プルルル
080-
XXXX-XXXX
Incoming call
WHO'S THIS?
HELLO?
Oh.
Thank you for your support.
This is Katsura.
...Ah. Hi.
WE APPRECIATED YOUR HELP THE OTHER DAY.
I WANTED TO TELL YOU, SO I ASKED MAEMURA-SAN FOR YOUR NUMBER.
THE GEE-ZER, HUH?
TCH!
YOU CALLED JUST FOR THAT?

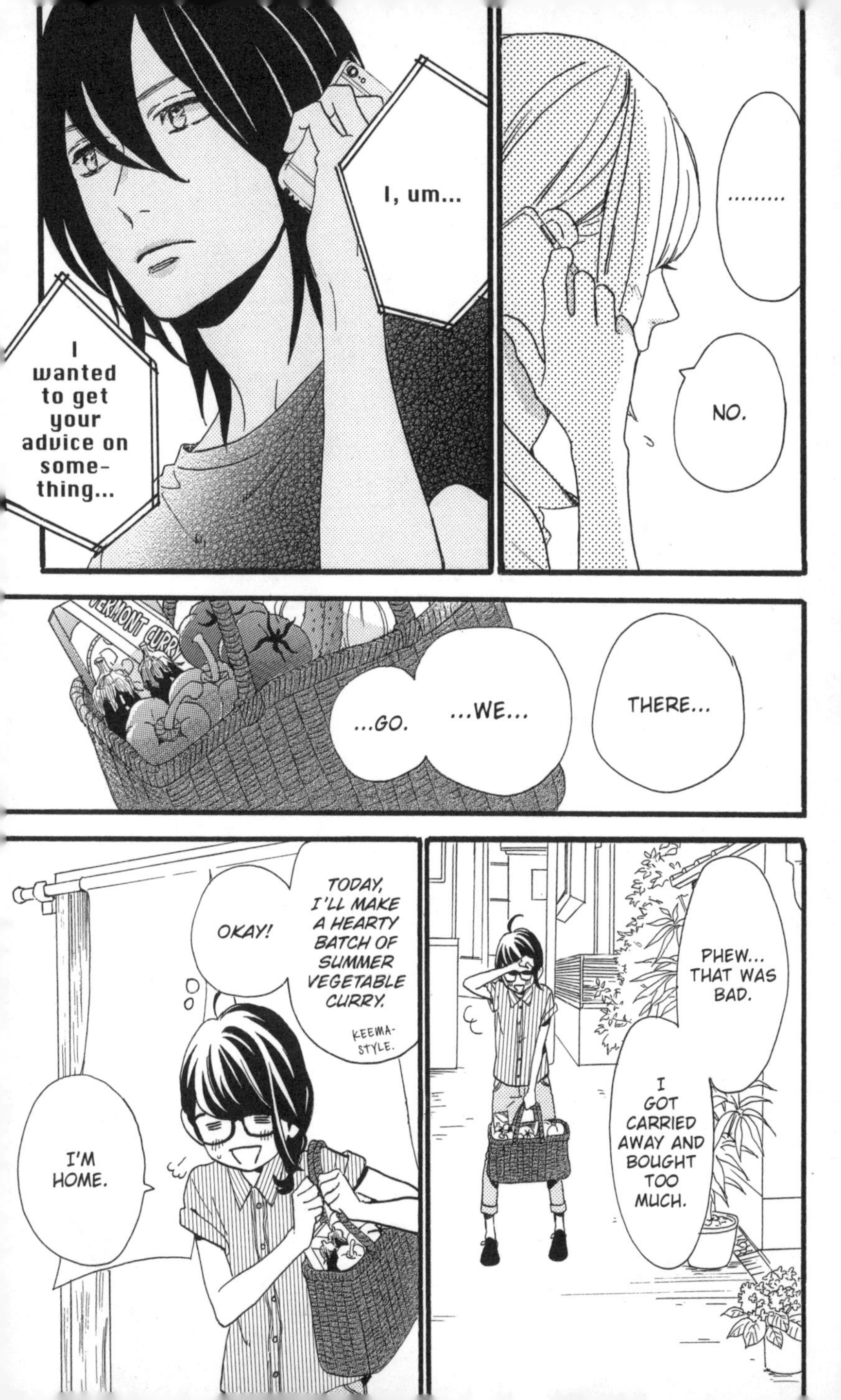
....
NO.
I, um...
I wanted to get your advice on some-thing...
THERE...
...WE...
...GO.
PHEW... THAT WAS BAD.
I GOT CARRIED AWAY AND BOUGHT TOO MUCH.
TODAY, I'LL MAKE A HEARTY BATCH OF SUMMER VEGETABLE CURRY.
OKAY!
KEEMA-STYLE.
I'M HOME.

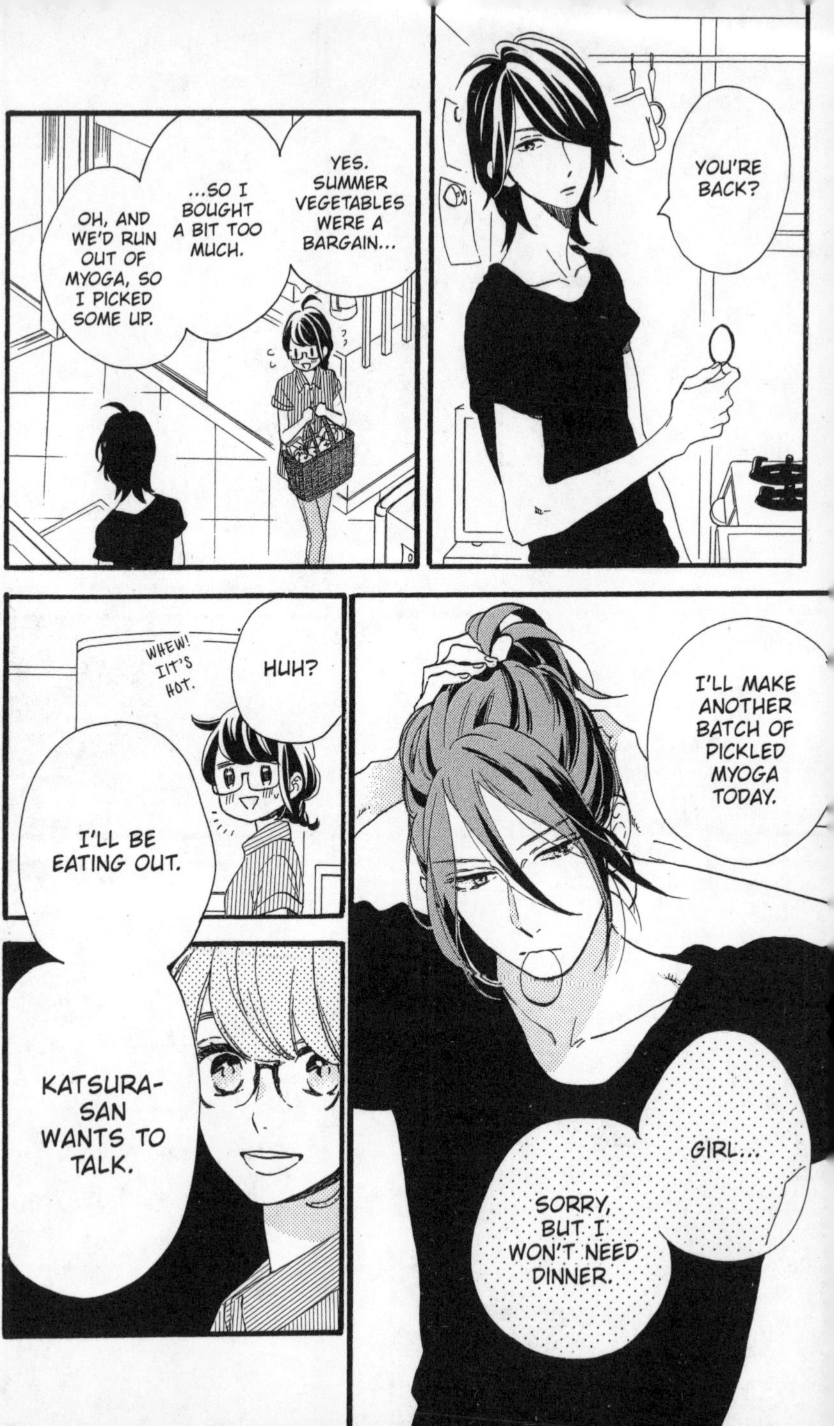
YOU'RE BACK?
YES. SUMMER VEGETABLES WERE A BARGAIN...
...SO I BOUGHT A BIT TOO MUCH.
OH, AND WE'D RUN OUT OF MYOGA, SO I PICKED SOME UP.
I'LL MAKE ANOTHER BATCH OF PICKLED MYOGA TODAY.
GIRL...
SORRY, BUT I WON'T NEED DINNER.
HUH?
WHEW! IT'S HOT.
I'LL BE EATING OUT.
KATSURA-SAN WANTS TO TALK.

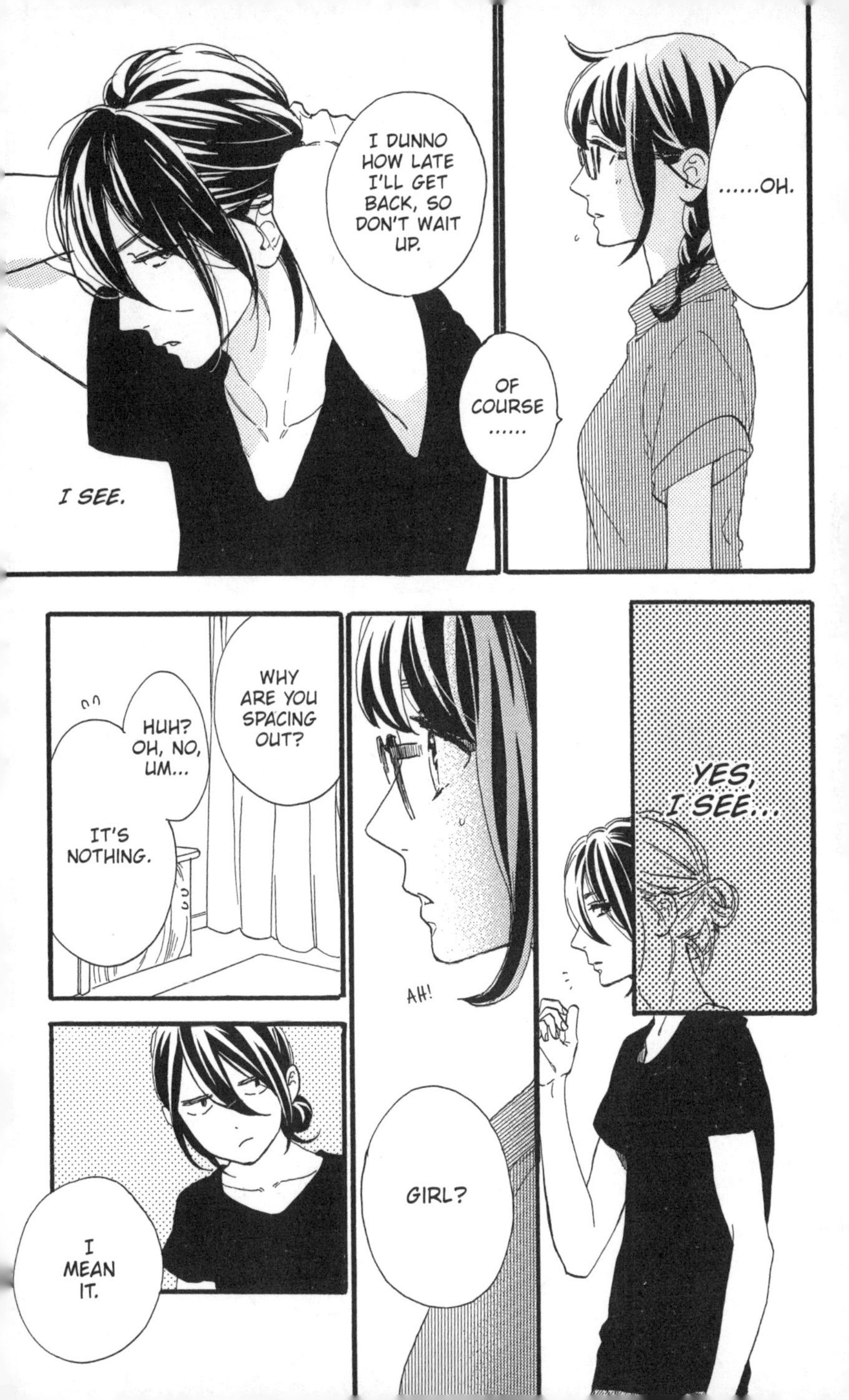
......OH.
OF COURSE ......
I DUNNO HOW LATE I'LL GET BACK, SO DON'T WAIT UP.
I SEE.
YES, I SEE...
AH!
GIRL?
WHY ARE YOU SPACING OUT?
HUH? OH, NO, UM...
IT'S NOTHING.
I MEAN IT.

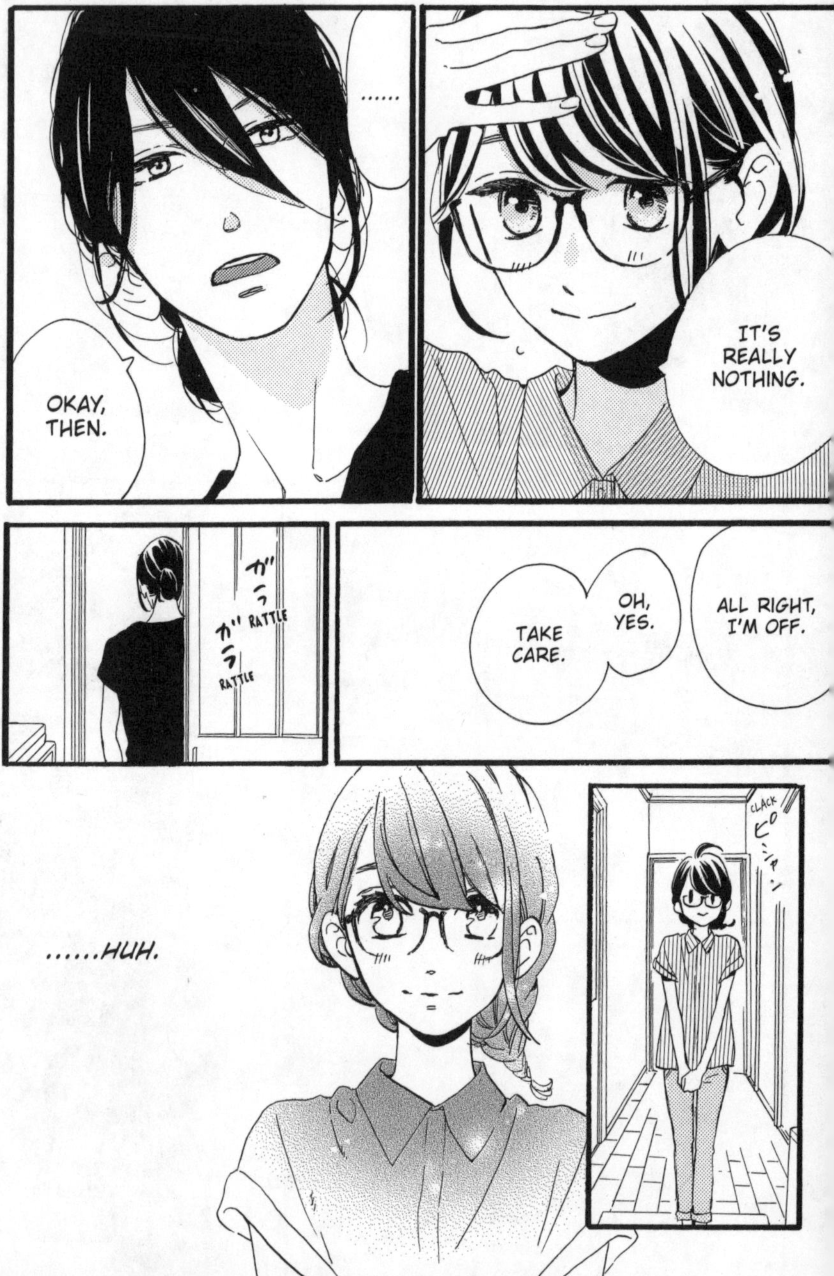
IT'S REALLY NOTHING.
......
OKAY, THEN.
ALL RIGHT, I'M OFF.
OH, YES.
TAKE CARE.
ガラ RATTLE
ガラ RATTLE
CLACK ピシャン
......HUH.

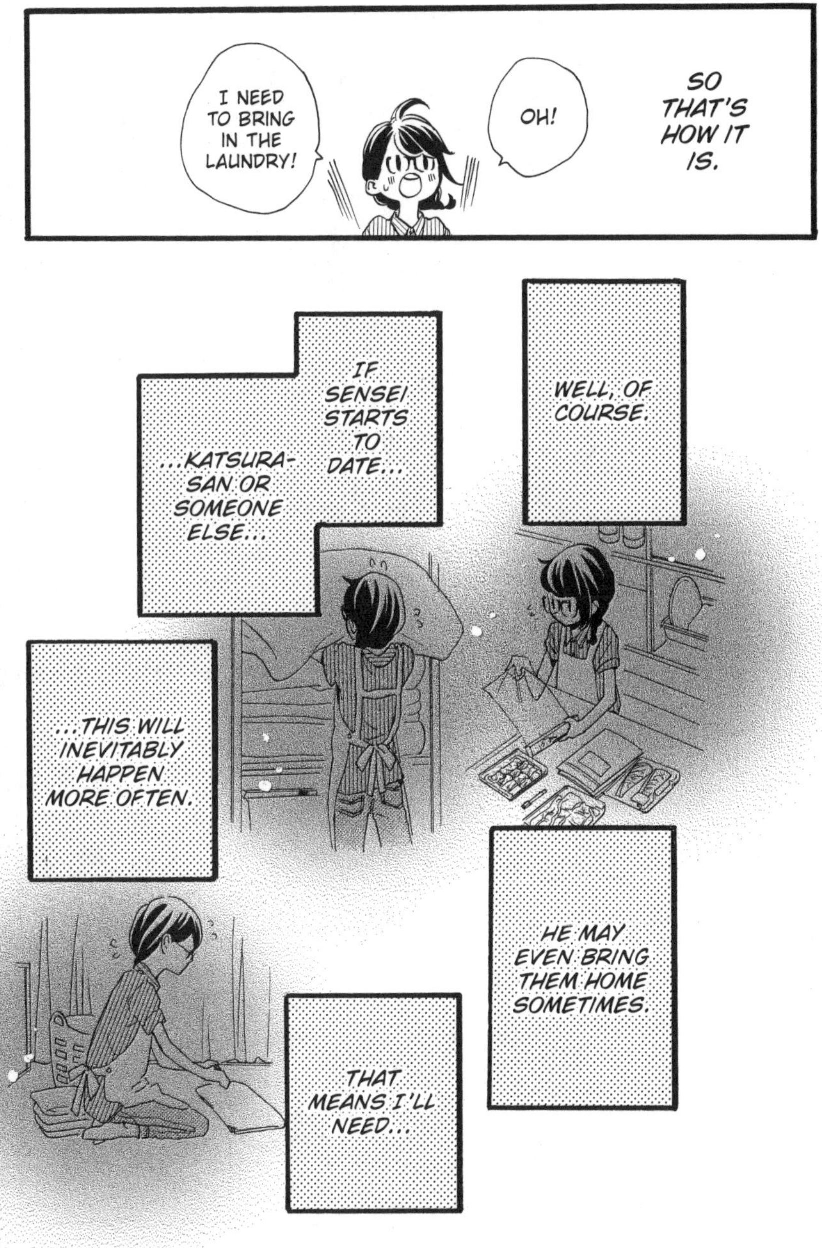
SO THAT'S HOW IT IS.
OH!
I NEED TO BRING IN THE LAUNDRY!
WELL, OF COURSE.
IF SENSEI STARTS TO DATE...
...KATSURA-SAN OR SOMEONE ELSE...
...THIS WILL INEVITABLY HAPPEN MORE OFTEN.
HE MAY EVEN BRING THEM HOME SOMETIMES.
THAT MEANS I'LL NEED...

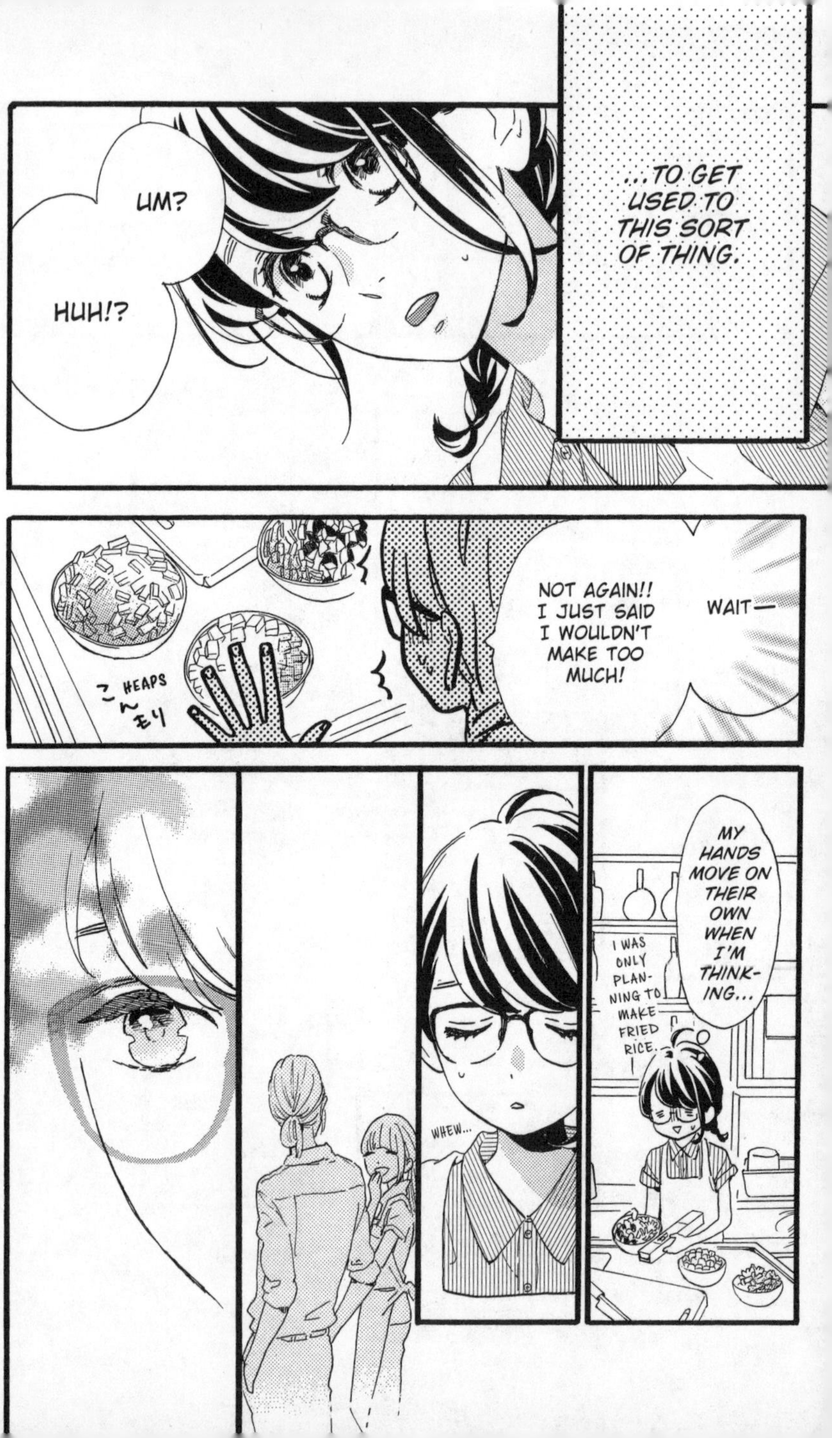
...TO GET USED TO THIS SORT OF THING.
UM?
HUH!?
WAIT—
NOT AGAIN!! I JUST SAID I WOULDN'T MAKE TOO MUCH!
HEAPS
MY HANDS MOVE ON THEIR OWN WHEN I'M THINK-ING...
I WAS ONLY PLAN-NING TO MAKE FRIED RICE.
WHEW...

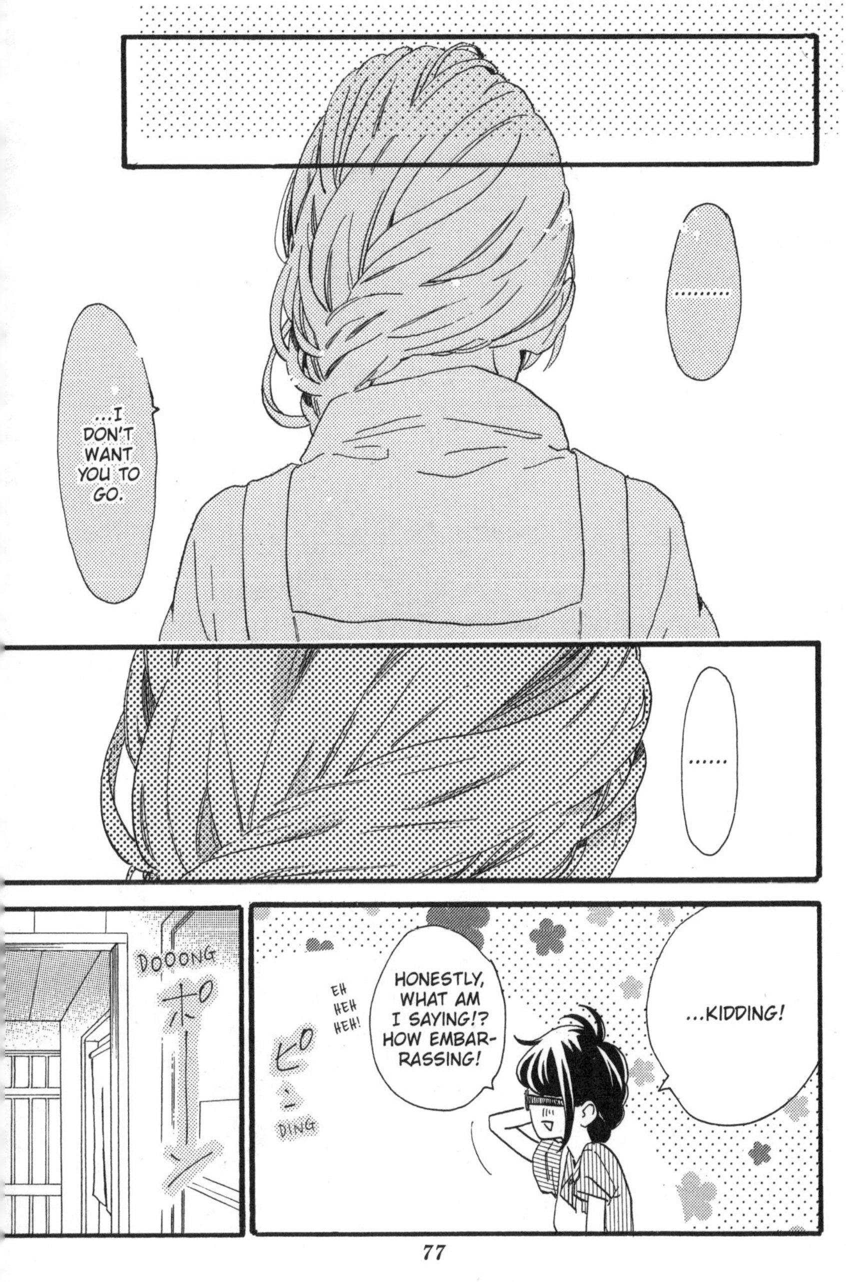
....
...I DON'T WANT YOU TO GO.
......
...KIDDING!
HONESTLY, WHAT AM I SAYING!? HOW EMBARRASSING!
EH HEH HEH!
DING
DOOONG

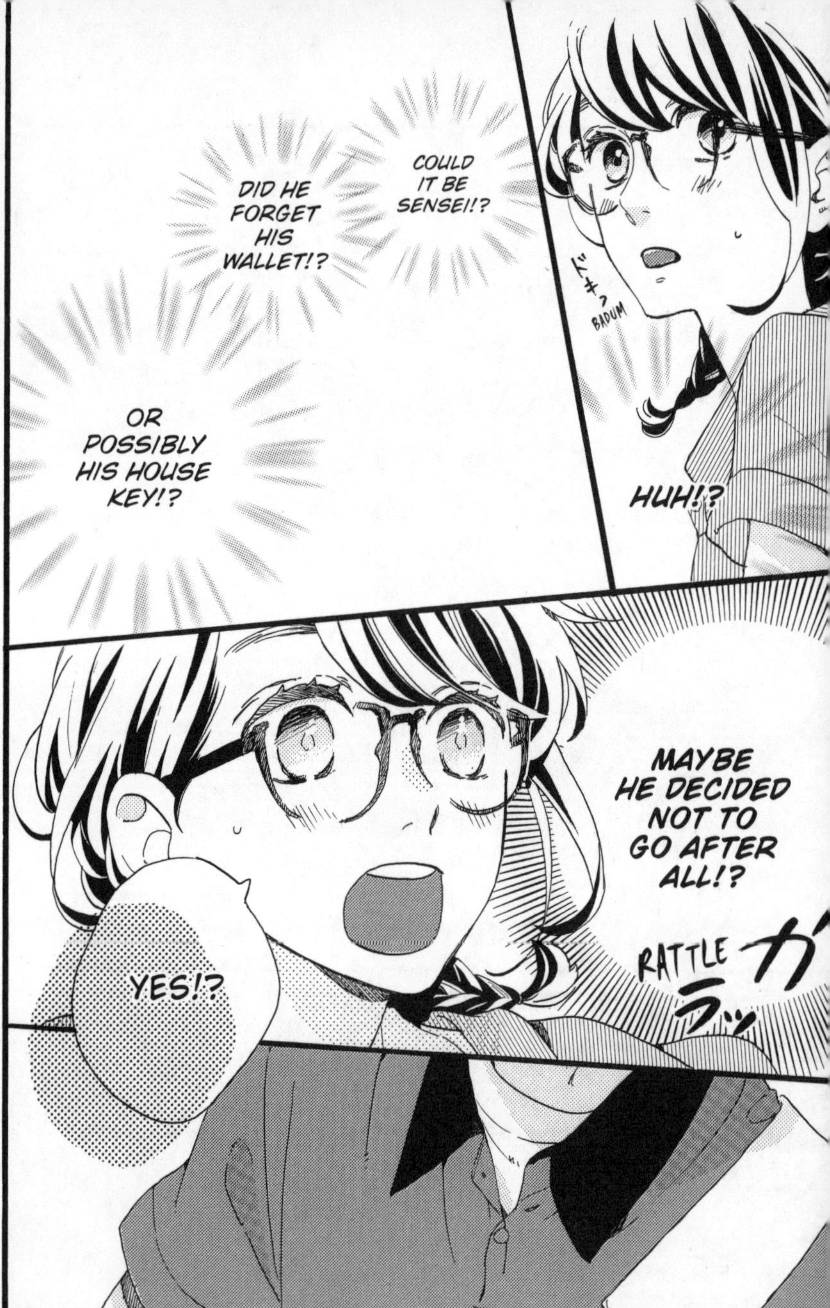
ドキッ
BADUM
HUH!?
COULD IT BE SENSEI!?
DID HE FORGET HIS WALLET!?
OR POSSIBLY HIS HOUSE KEY!?
MAYBE HE DECIDED NOT TO GO AFTER ALL!?
ガラッ
RATTLE
YES!?

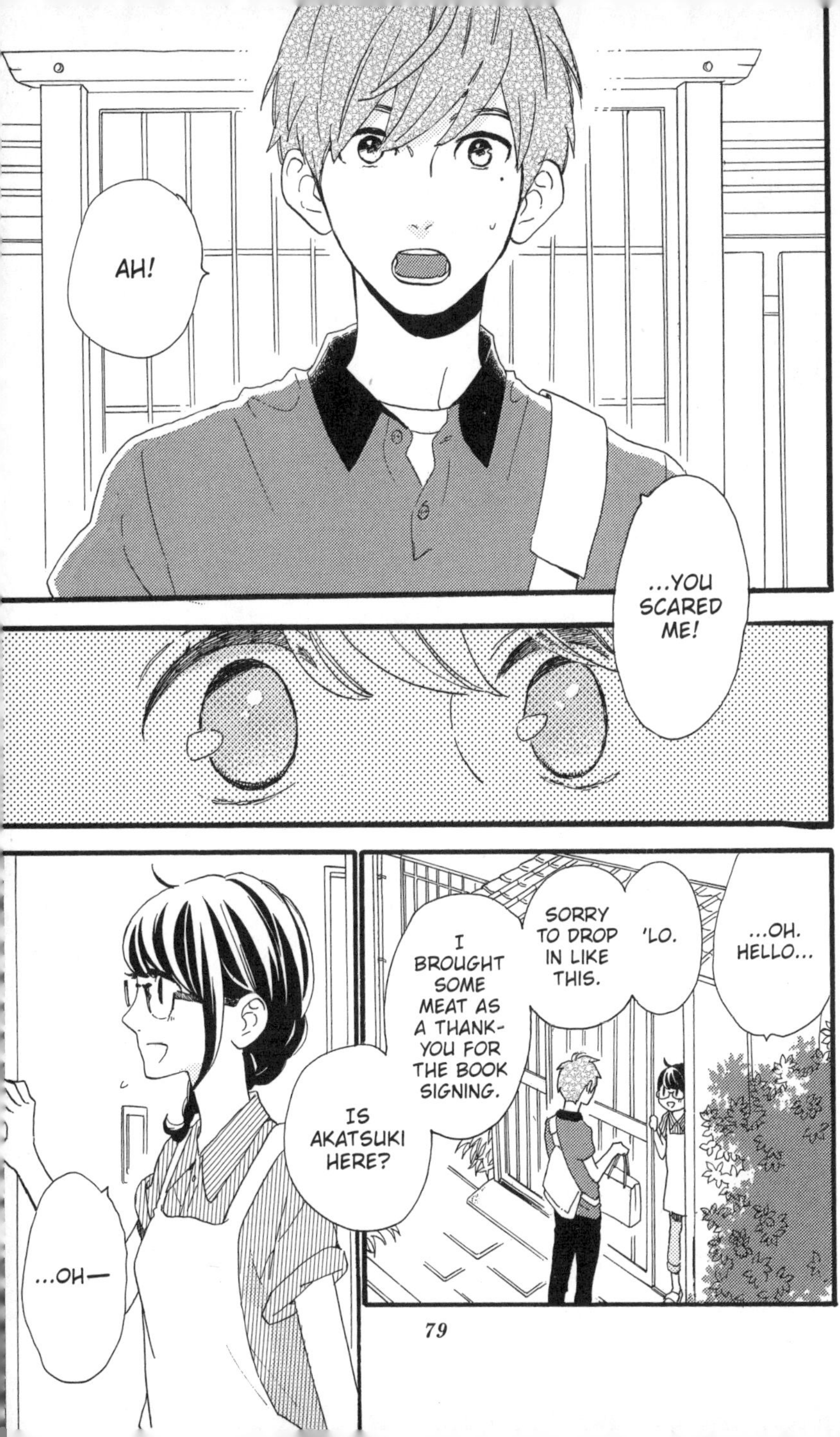
AH!
...YOU SCARED ME!
...OH. HELLO...
'LO.
SORRY TO DROP IN LIKE THIS.
I BROUGHT SOME MEAT AS A THANK-YOU FOR THE BOOK SIGNING.
IS AKATSUKI HERE?
...OH—

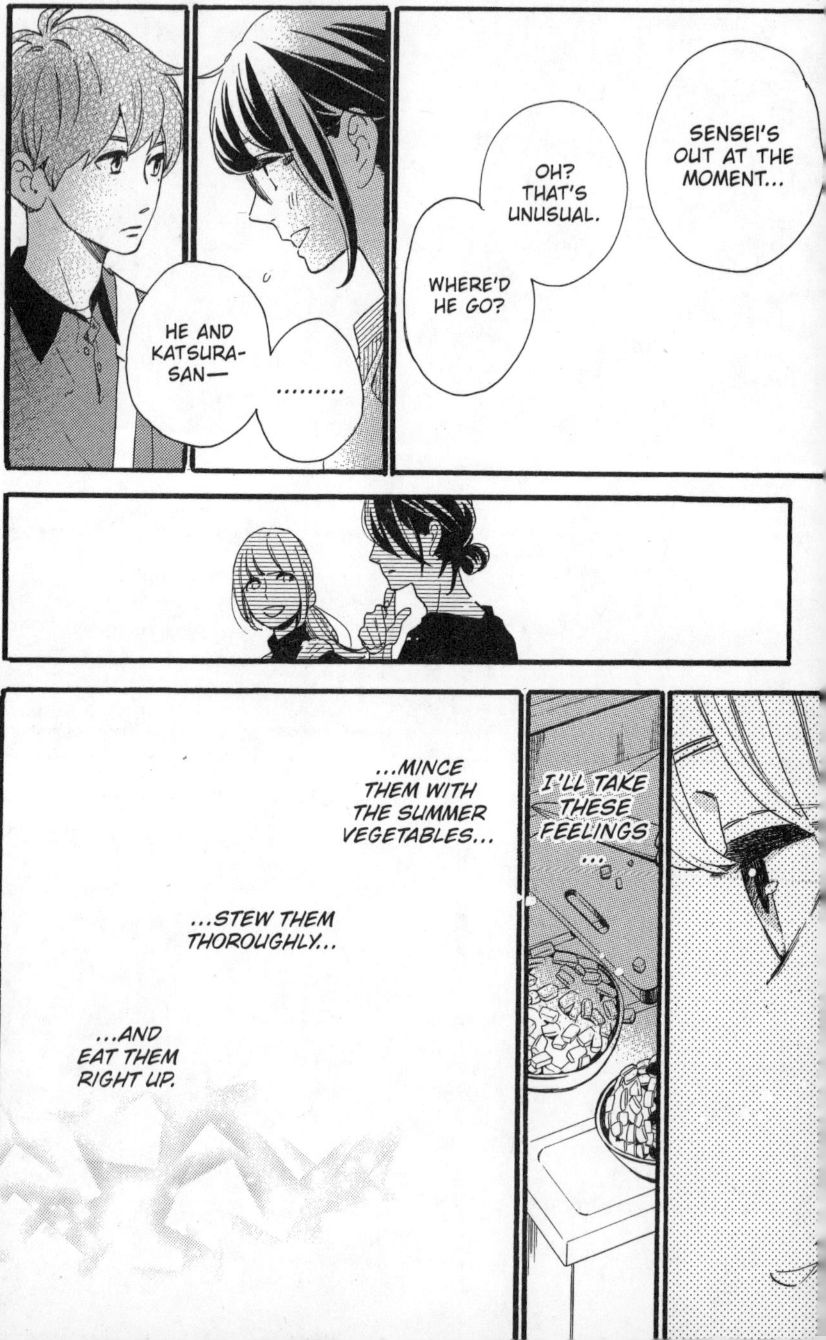
SENSEI'S OUT AT THE MOMENT...
OH? THAT'S UNUSUAL.
WHERE'D HE GO?
HE AND KATSURA-SAN—
....
I'LL TAKE THESE FEELINGS...
...MINCE THEM WITH THE SUMMER VEGETABLES...
...STEW THEM THOROUGHLY...
...AND EAT THEM RIGHT UP.

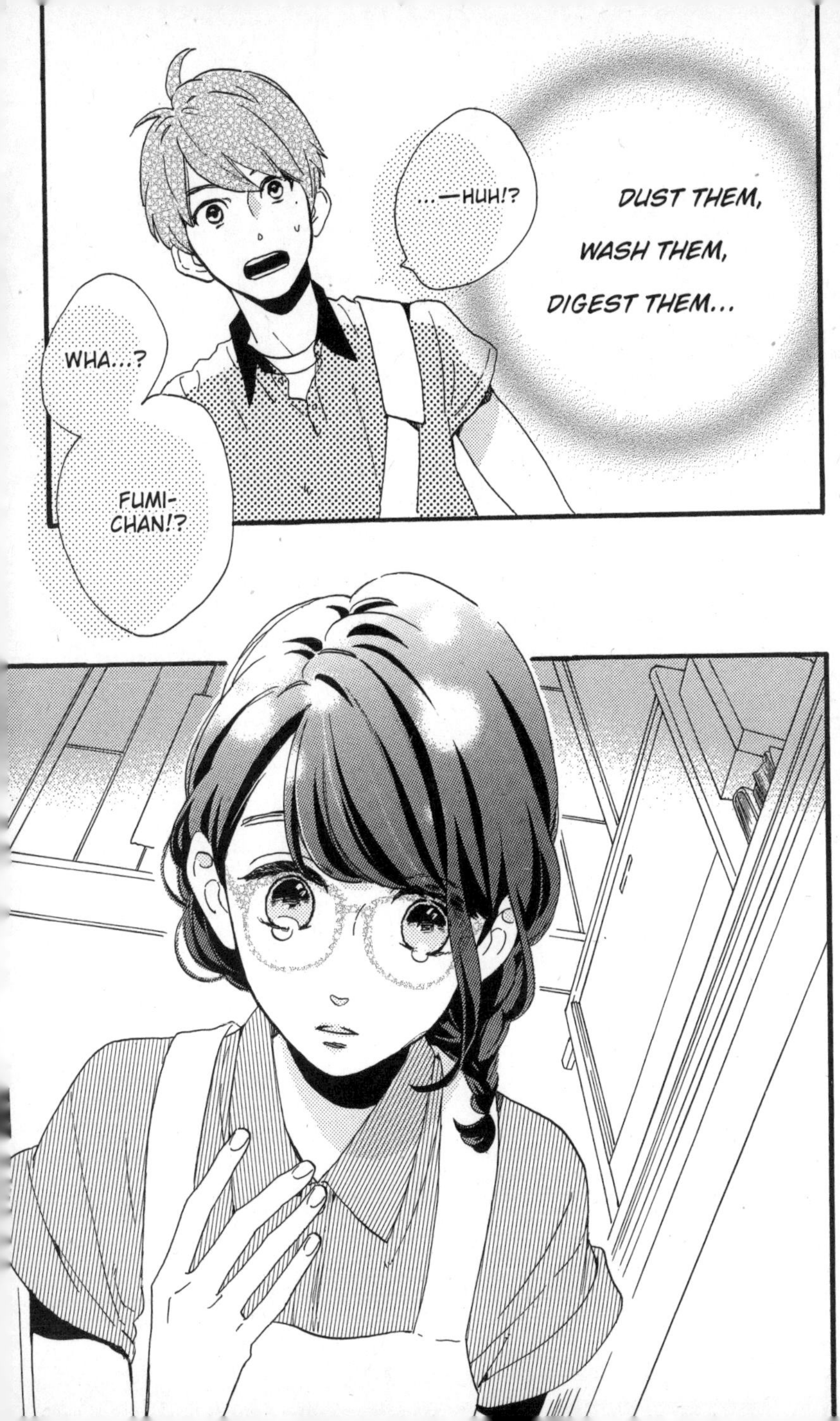
DUST THEM,
WASH THEM,
DIGEST THEM...
...—HUH!?
WHA...?
FUMI-CHAN!?

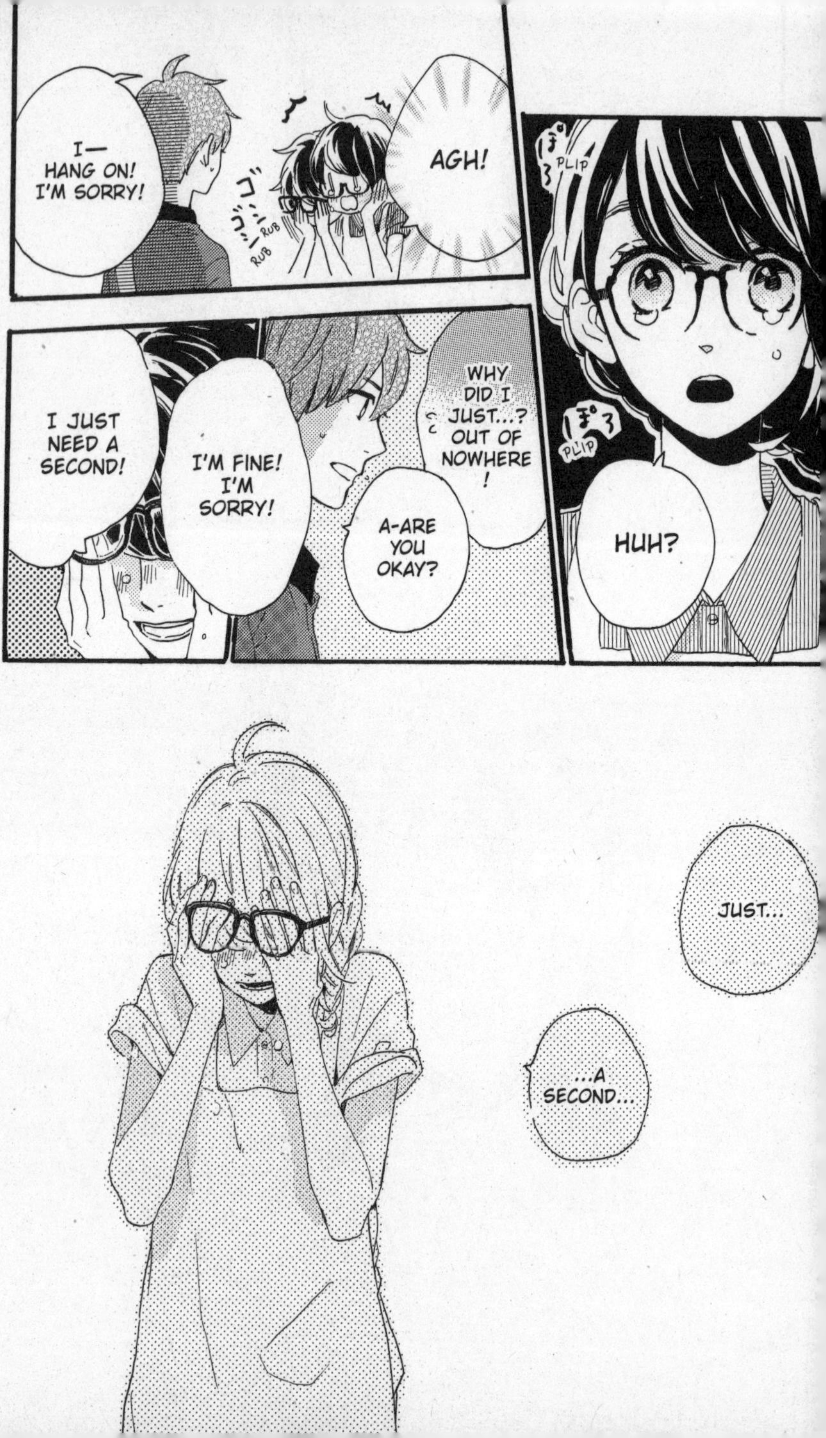
AGH!
ゴシゴシ RUB RUB
I— HANG ON! I'M SORRY!
ぽろ PLIP
ぽろ PLIP
HUH?
WHY DID I JUST...? OUT OF NOWHERE!
A-ARE YOU OKAY?
I'M FINE! I'M SORRY!
I JUST NEED A SECOND!
JUST...
...A SECOND...

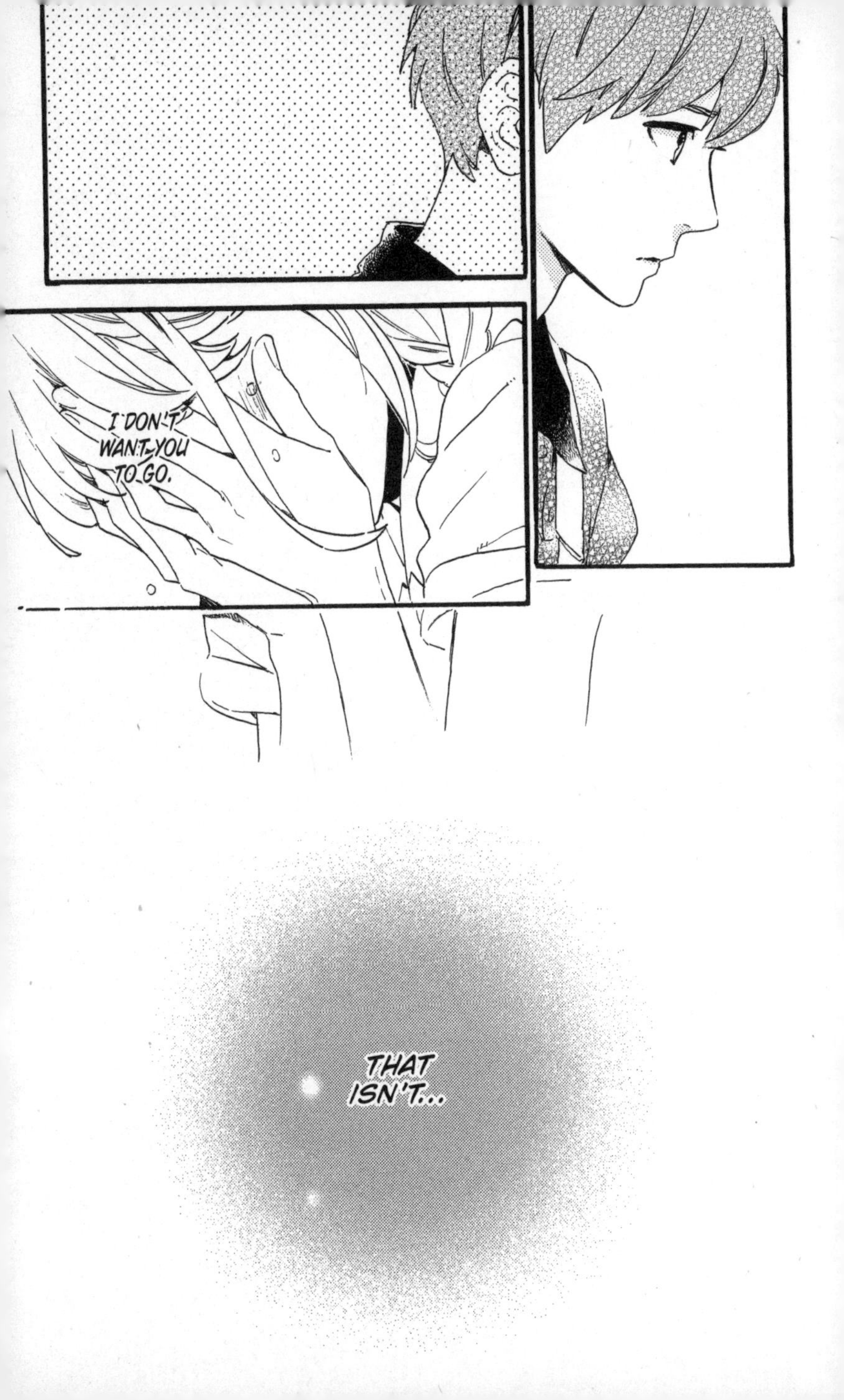
I DON'T WANT YOU TO GO.
THAT ISN'T...

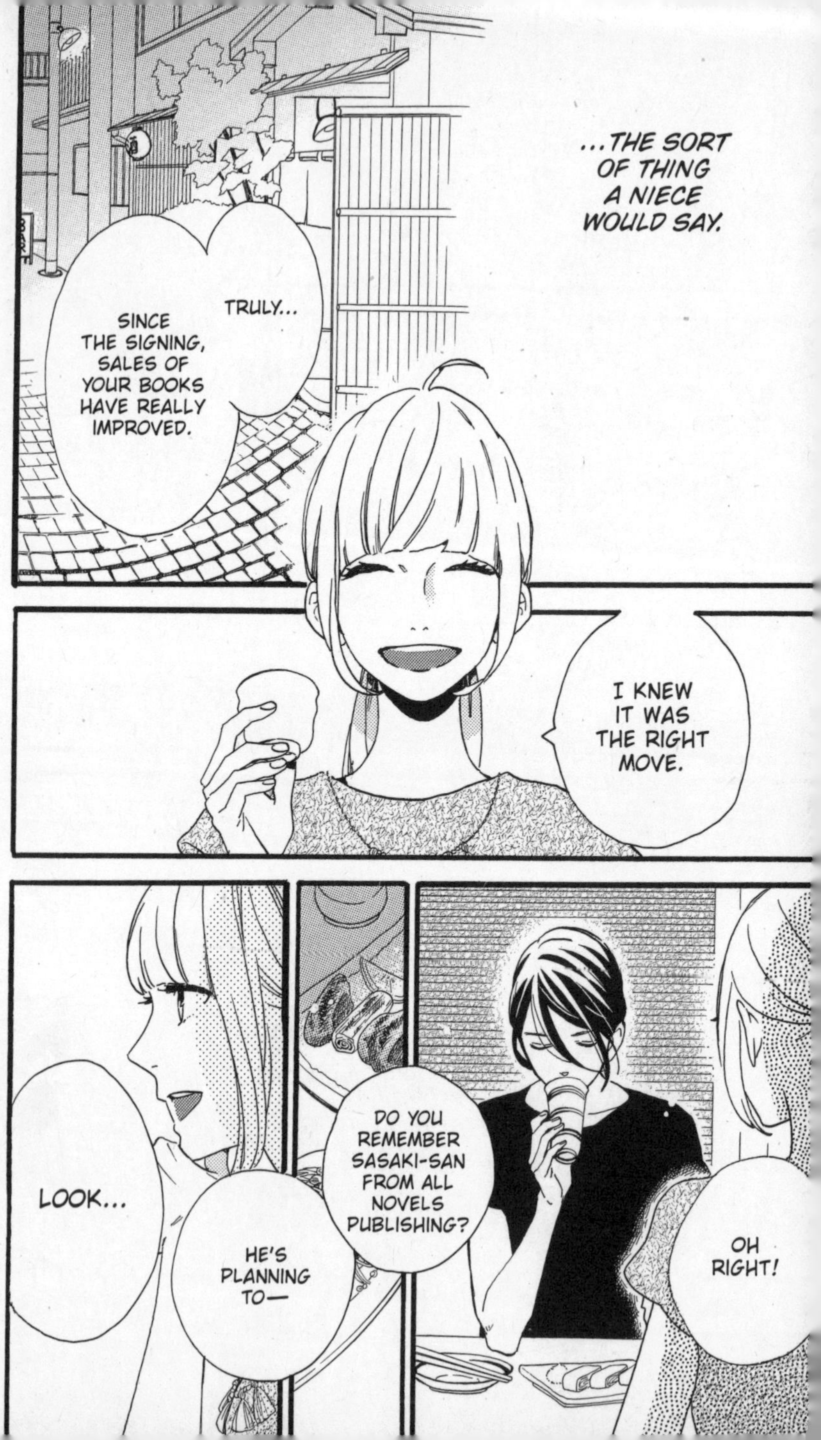
...THE SORT OF THING A NIECE WOULD SAY.
TRULY...
SINCE THE SIGNING, SALES OF YOUR BOOKS HAVE REALLY IMPROVED.
I KNEW IT WAS THE RIGHT MOVE.
DO YOU REMEMBER SASAKI-SAN FROM ALL NOVELS PUBLISHING?
OH RIGHT!
LOOK...
HE'S PLANNING TO—

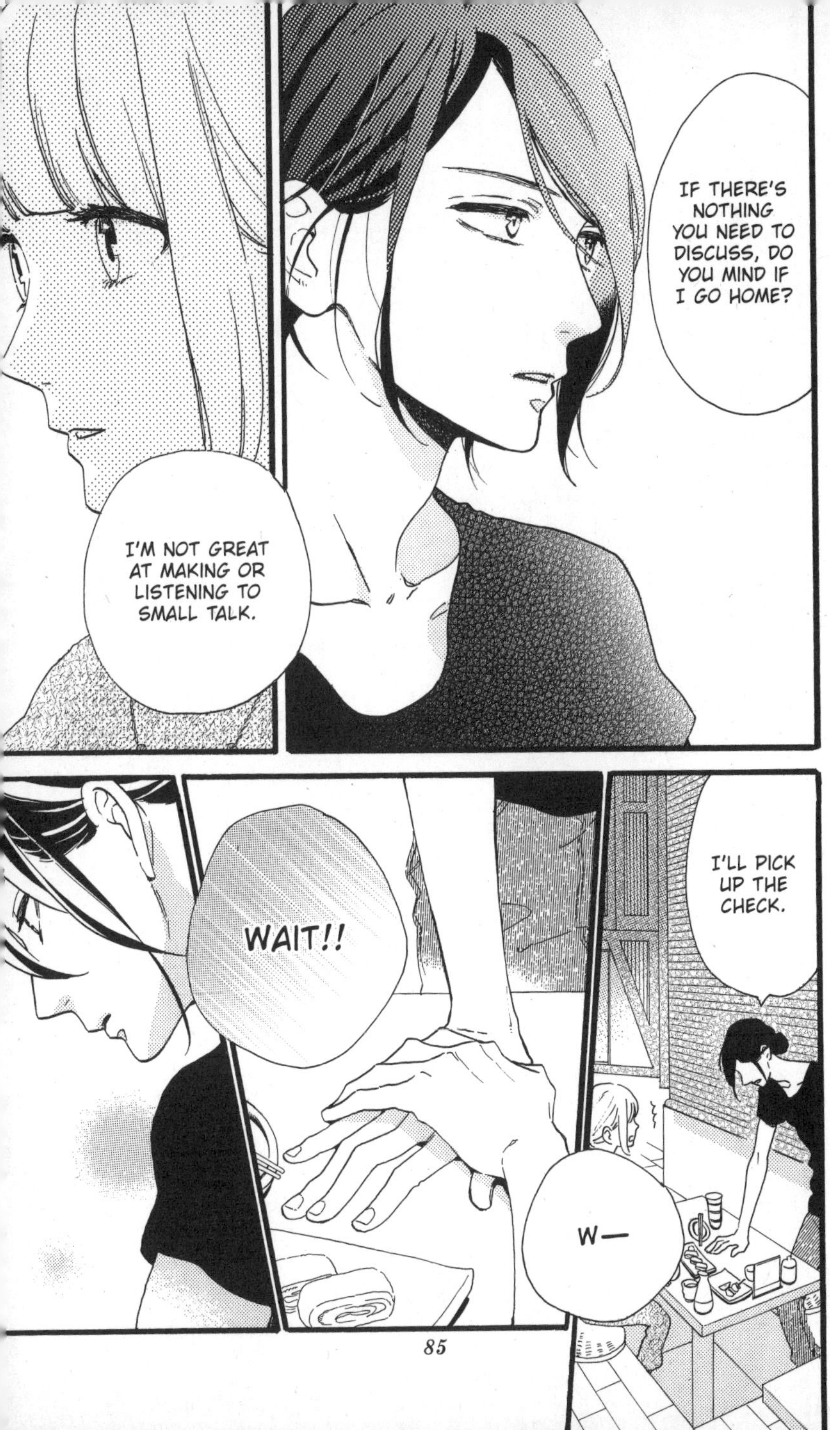
IF THERE'S NOTHING YOU NEED TO DISCUSS, DO YOU MIND IF I GO HOME?
I'M NOT GREAT AT MAKING OR LISTENING TO SMALL TALK.
I'LL PICK UP THE CHECK.
W—
WAIT!!

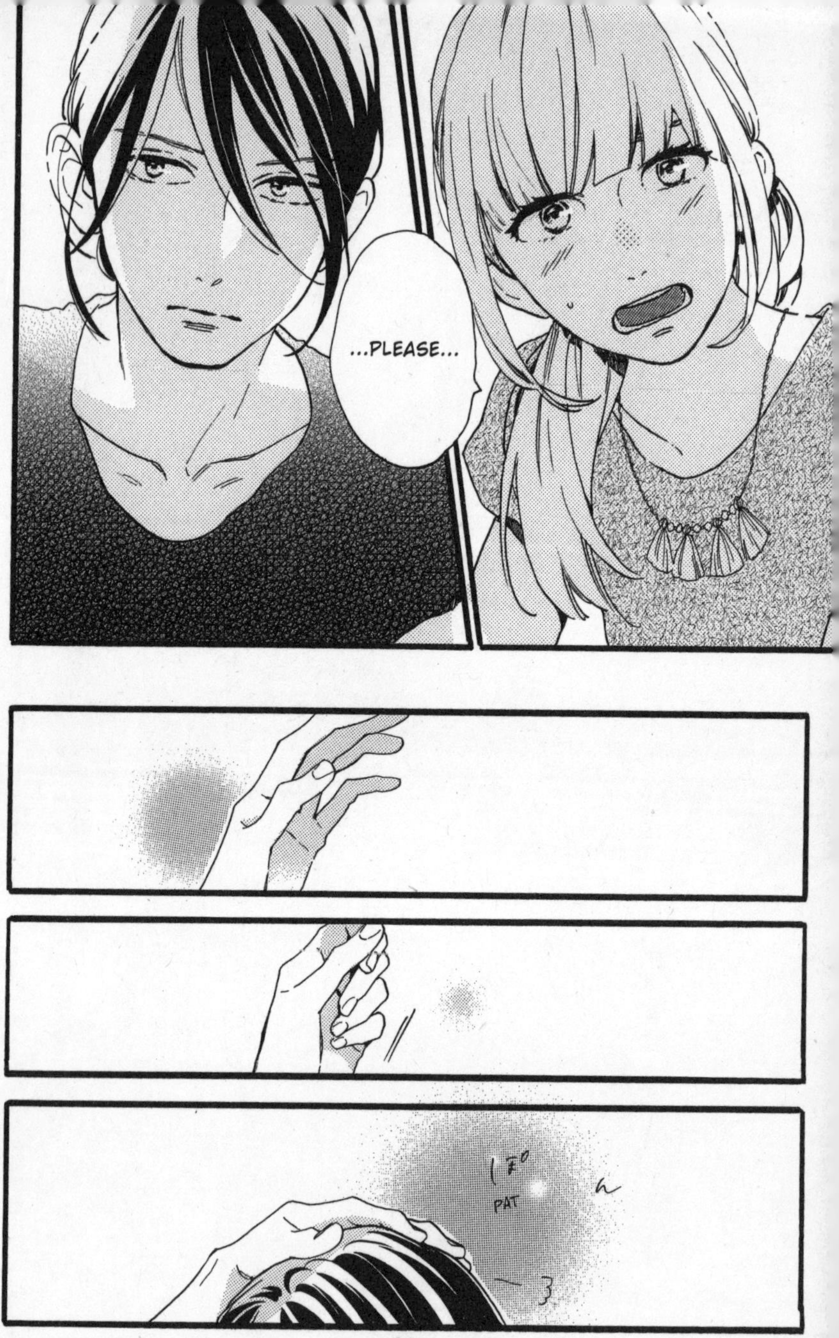
...PLEASE...
PAT

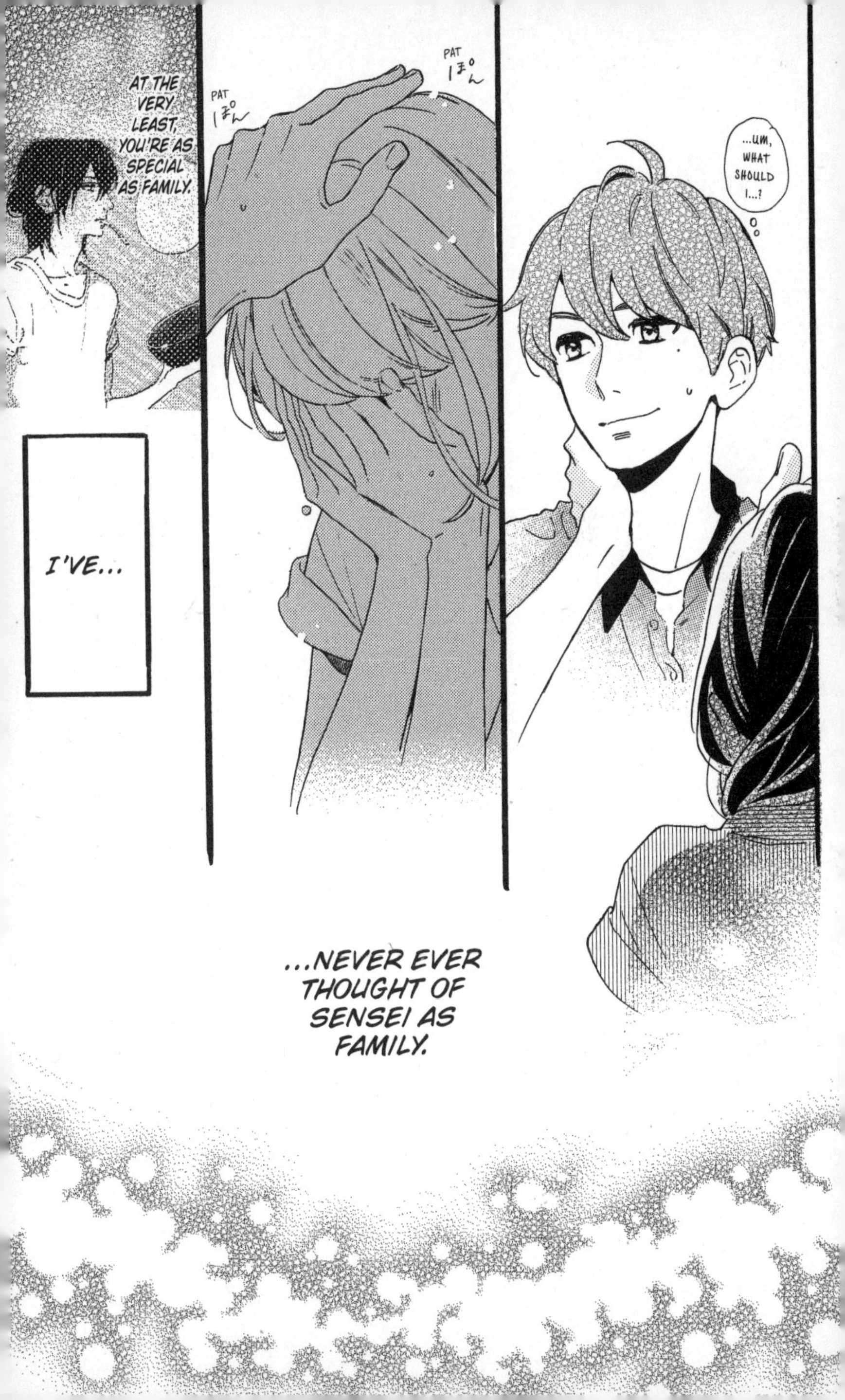
...UM, WHAT SHOULD I...?
PAT ぽん
PAT ぽん
AT THE VERY LEAST, YOU'RE AS SPECIAL AS FAMILY.
I'VE...
...NEVER EVER THOUGHT OF SENSEI AS FAMILY.

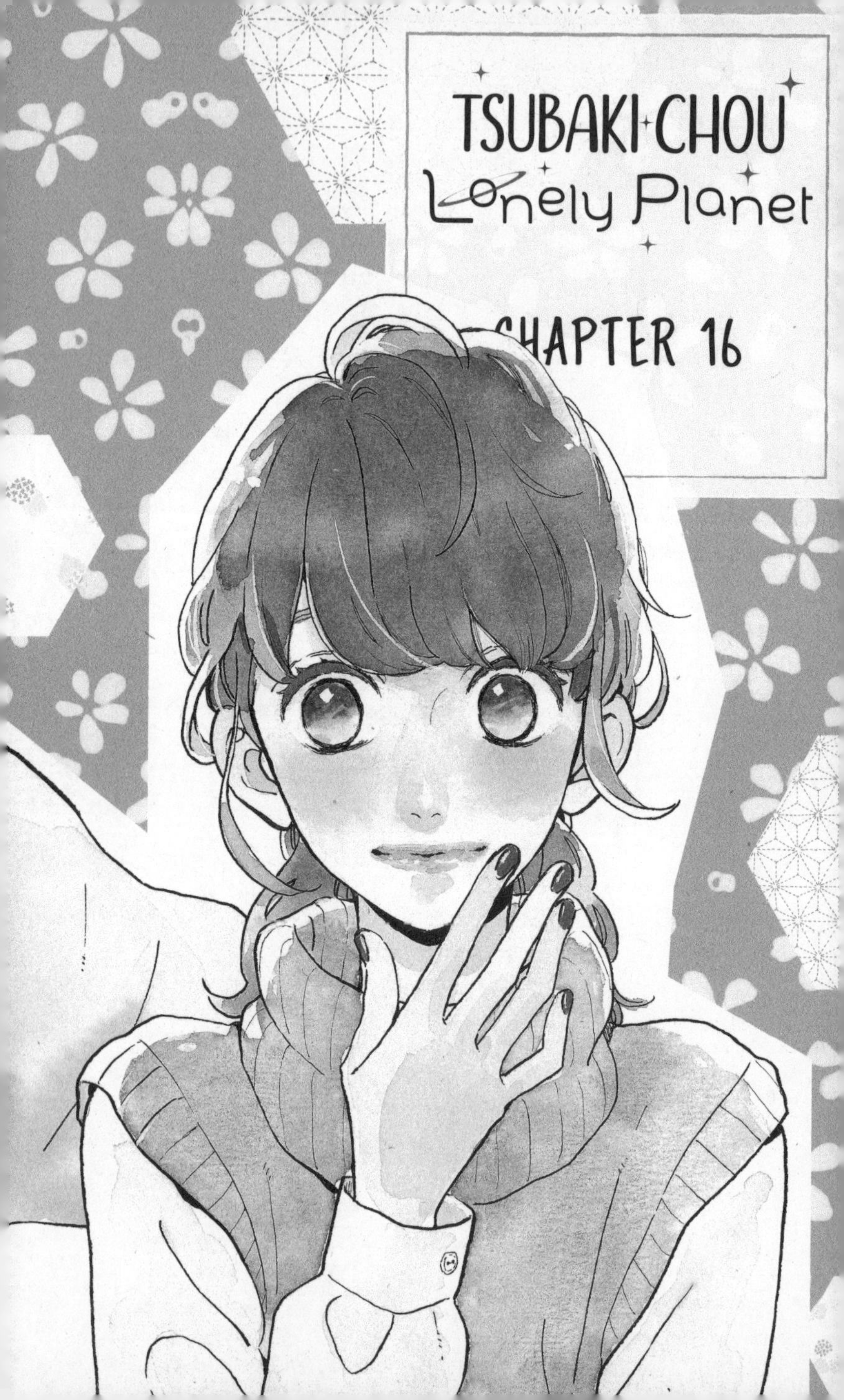
TSUBAKI-CHOU
Lonely Planet
CHAPTER 16

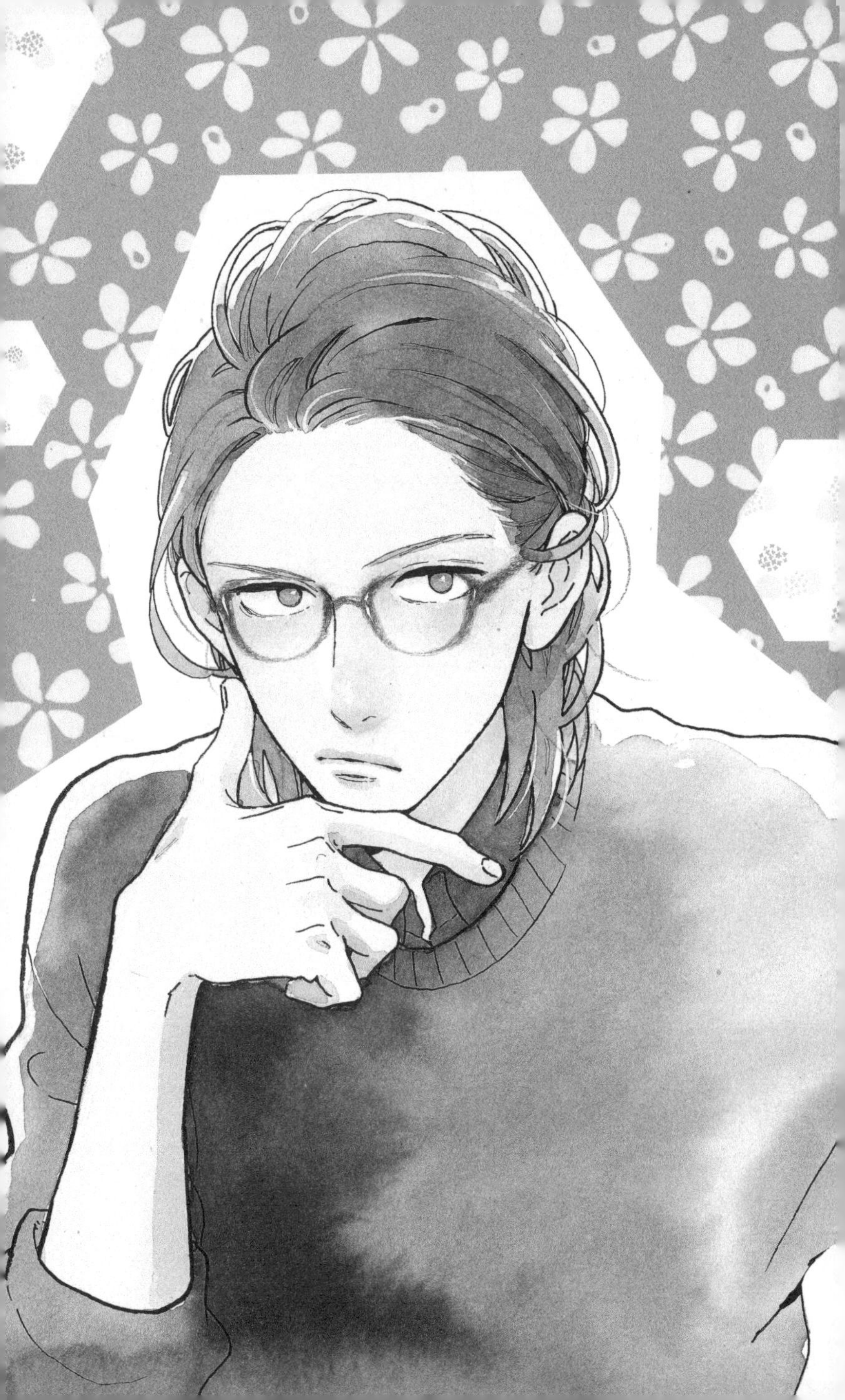

THE MYSTERY OF
THE VANISHING GLASSES
THAT 3-MINUTE
DISAPPEARANCE...!!

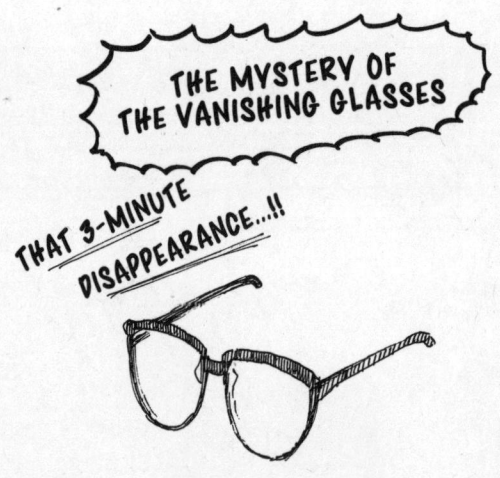

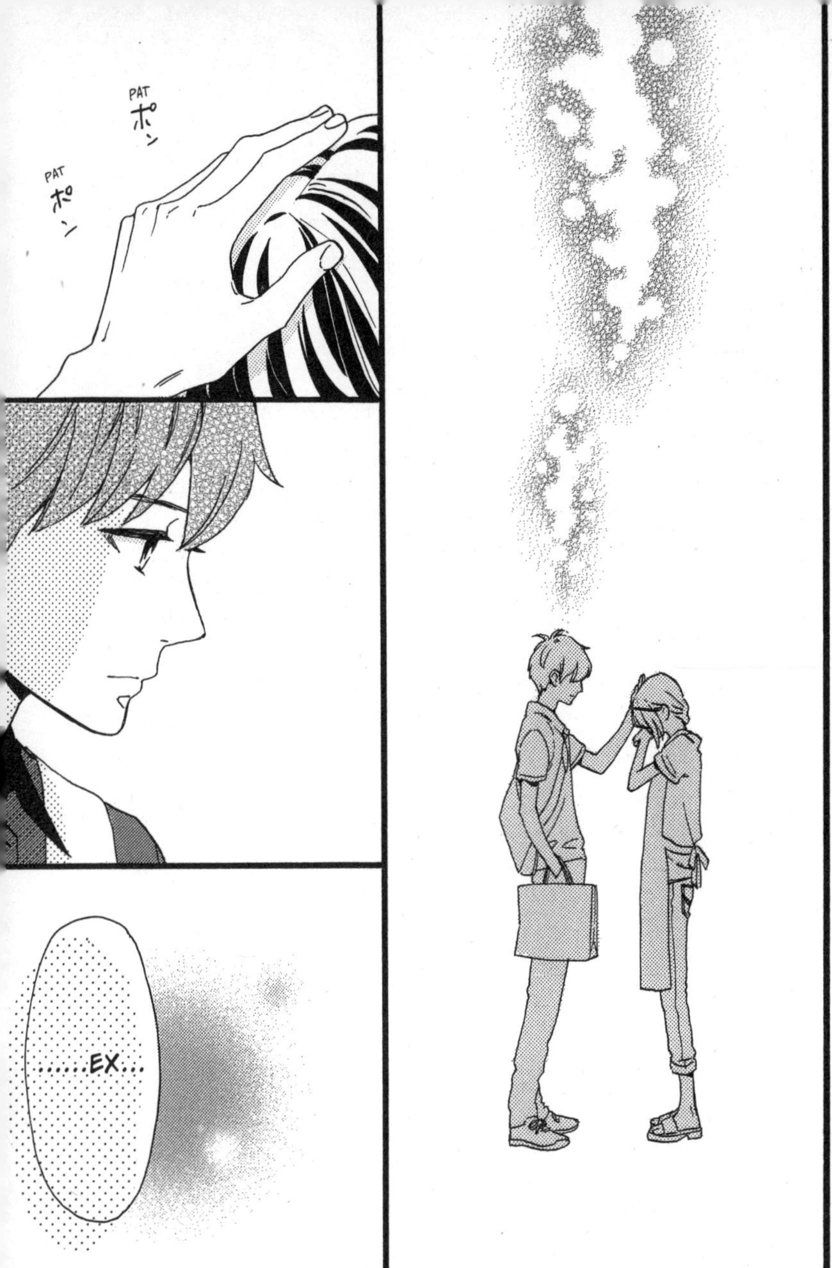
PAT ポン
PAT ポン
......EX...

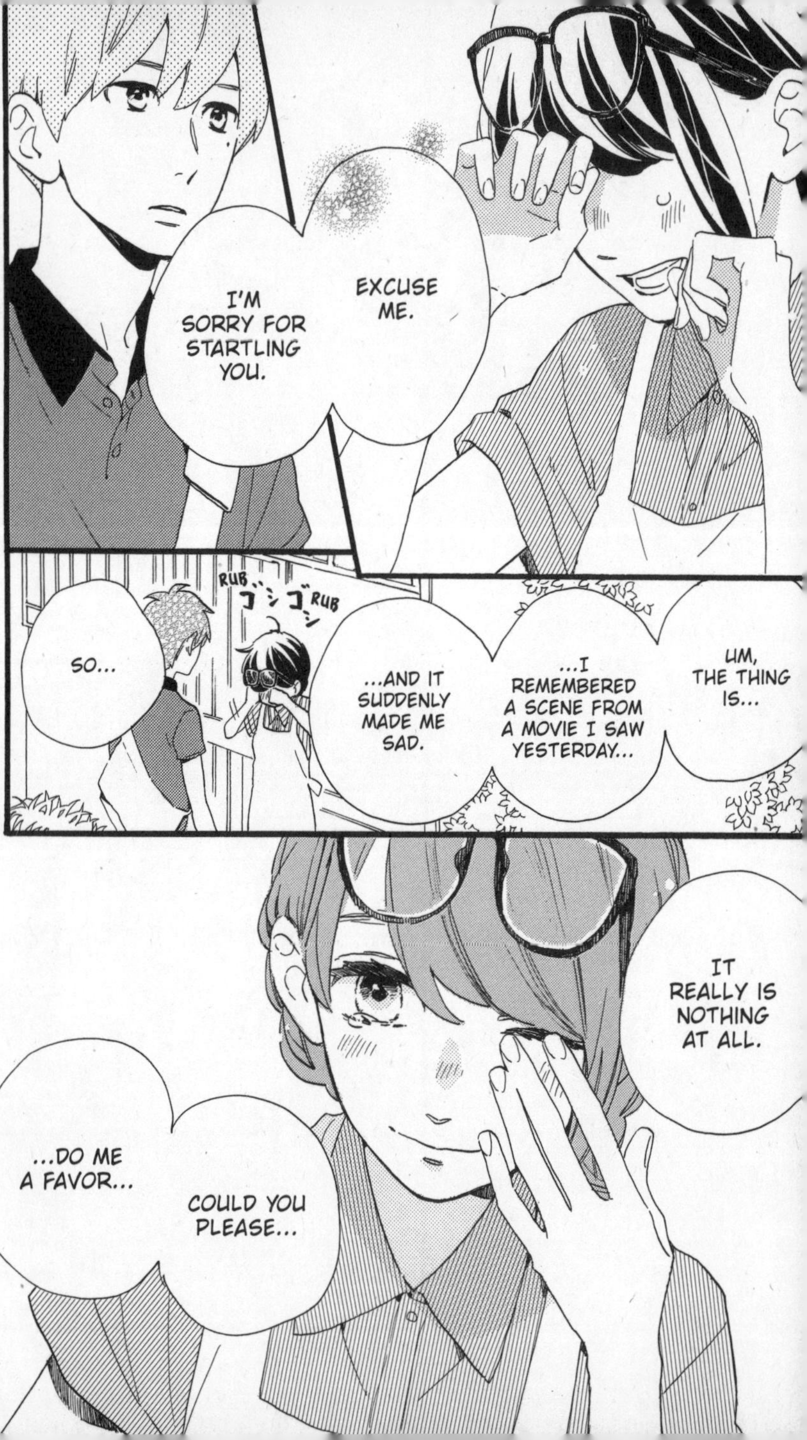
EXCUSE ME.
I'M SORRY FOR STARTLING YOU.
UM, THE THING IS...
...I REMEMBERED A SCENE FROM A MOVIE I SAW YESTERDAY...
...AND IT SUDDENLY MADE ME SAD.
RUB
RUB
SO...
IT REALLY IS NOTHING AT ALL.
COULD YOU PLEASE...
...DO ME A FAVOR...

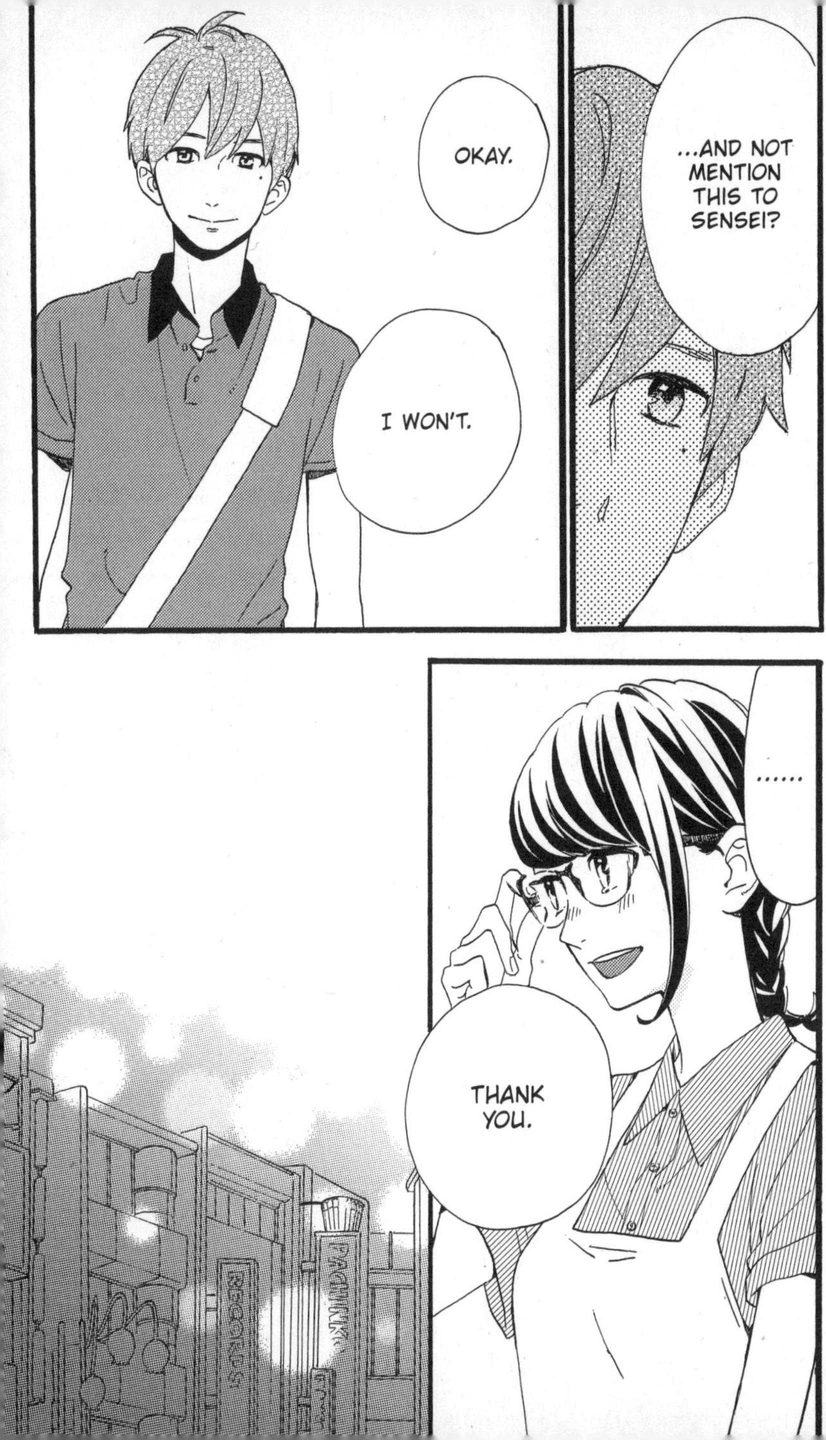
...AND NOT MENTION THIS TO SENSEI?
OKAY.
I WON'T.
......
THANK YOU.

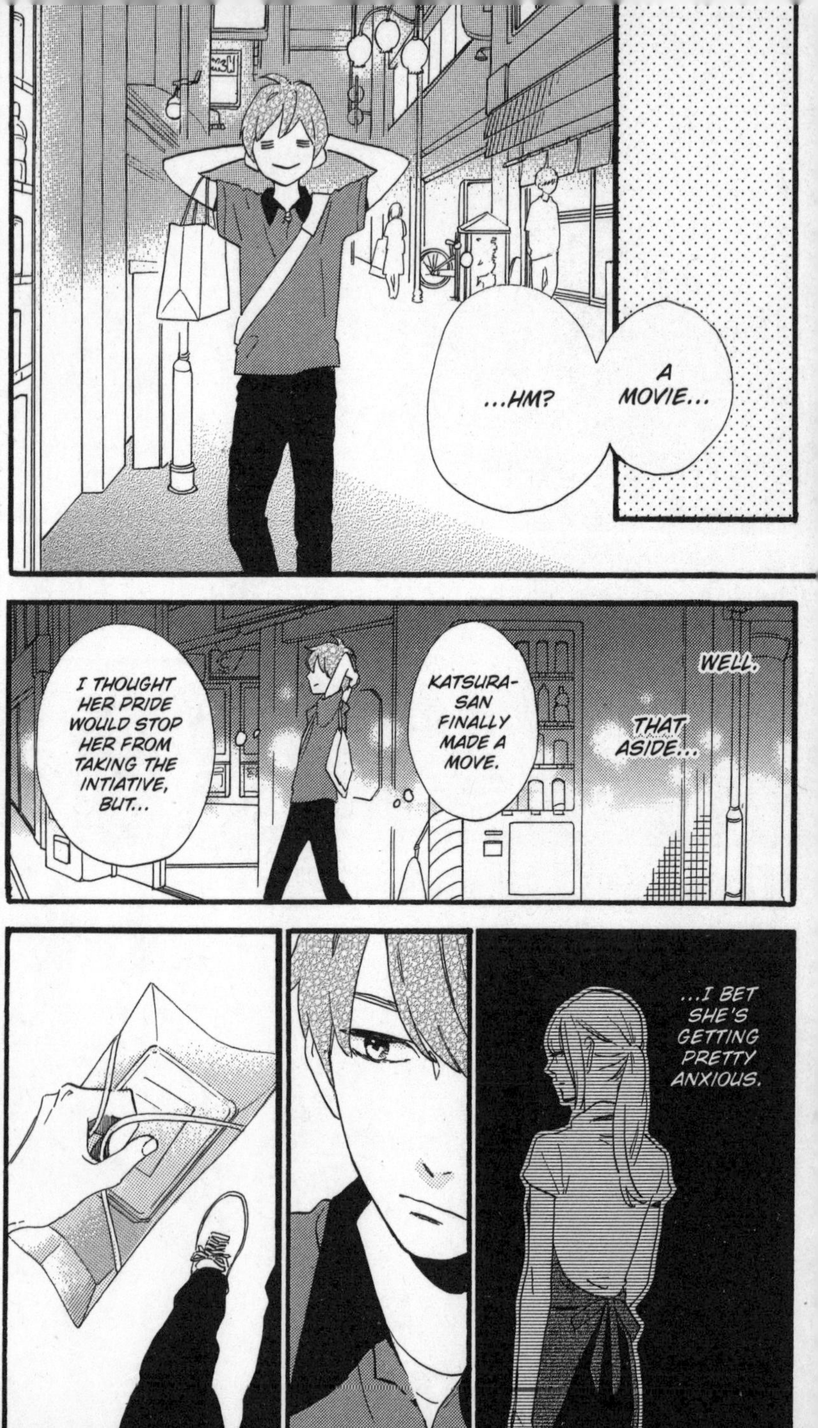
A MOVIE...
...HM?
WELL.
THAT ASIDE...
KATSURA-SAN FINALLY MADE A MOVE.
I THOUGHT HER PRIDE WOULD STOP HER FROM TAKING THE INTIATIVE, BUT...
...I BET SHE'S GETTING PRETTY ANXIOUS.

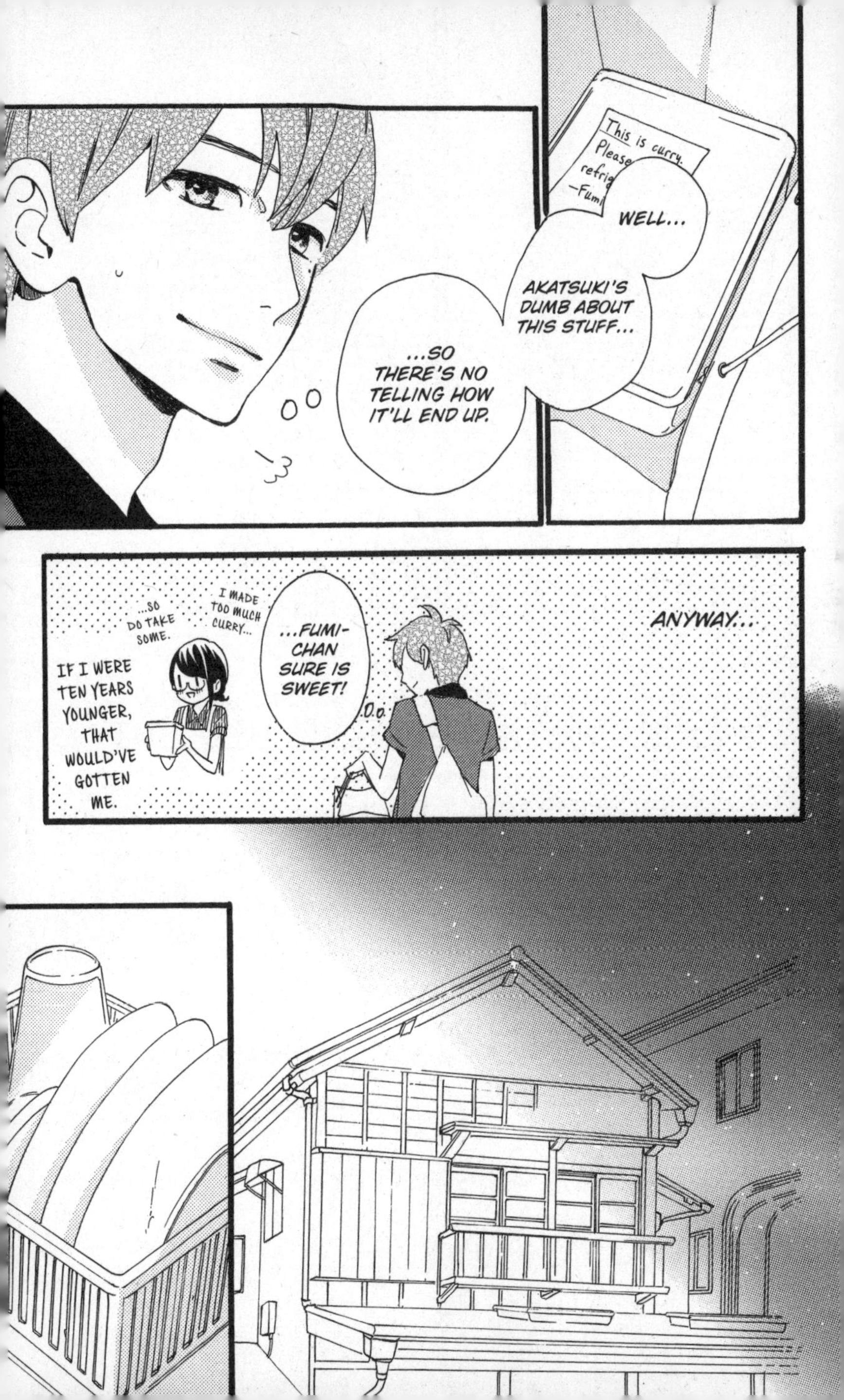
This is curry.
Please
refrig
—Fumi
WELL...
AKATSUKI'S DUMB ABOUT THIS STUFF...
...SO THERE'S NO TELLING HOW IT'LL END UP.
ANYWAY...
...FUMI-CHAN SURE IS SWEET!
O.o
I MADE TOO MUCH CURRY...
...SO DO TAKE SOME.
IF I WERE TEN YEARS YOUNGER, THAT WOULD'VE GOTTEN ME.

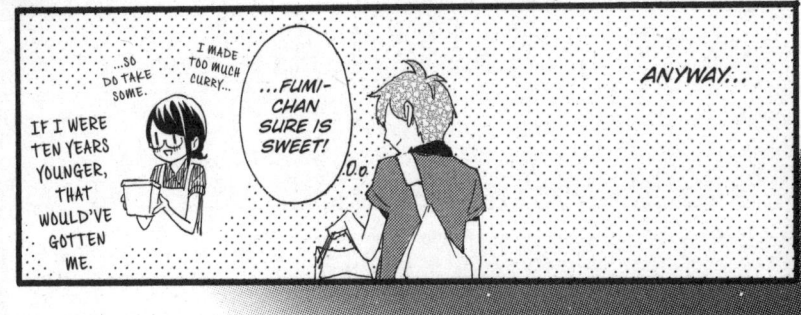

I'VE BEEN TOO PRONE TO TEARS LATELY.

I NEED TO WATCH MYSELF.

CRYING IN FRONT OF SOMEONE IS SOMETHING YOU CAN'T EVER LIVE DOWN......

...... NOW I'VE DONE IT.

BOOONG
ボーン
BOOONG
ボーン

SORRY, BUT COULD I GET SOME TEA?

ORDINARILY, IT WOULD BE...

NINE O'CLOCK...

...ABOUT THAT TIME, BUT—

HAH!

ボーン
BOOONG
BOOONG
ボーン

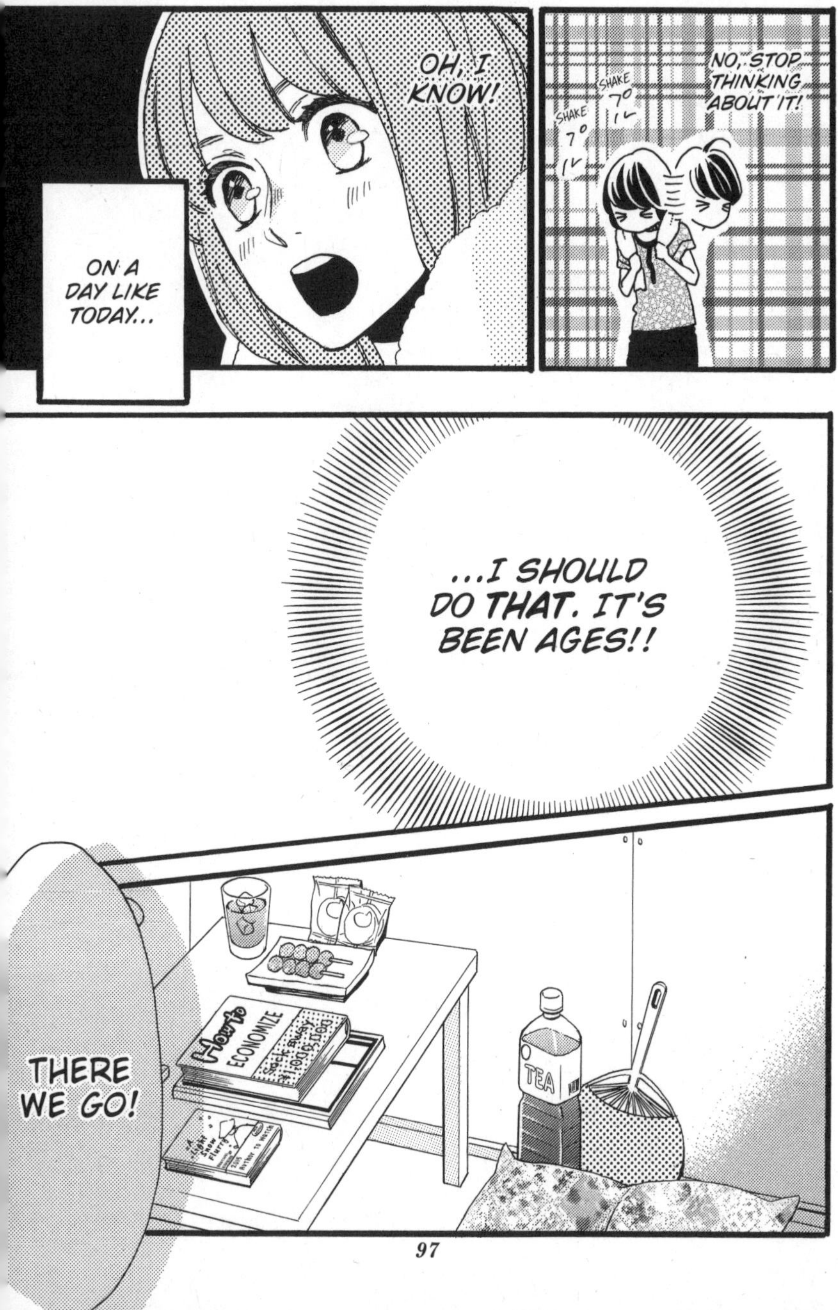
NO, STOP THINKING ABOUT IT!
SHAKE
SHAKE
OH, I KNOW!
ON A DAY LIKE TODAY...
...I SHOULD DO THAT. IT'S BEEN AGES!!
THERE WE GO!
How to ECONOMIZE
TEA

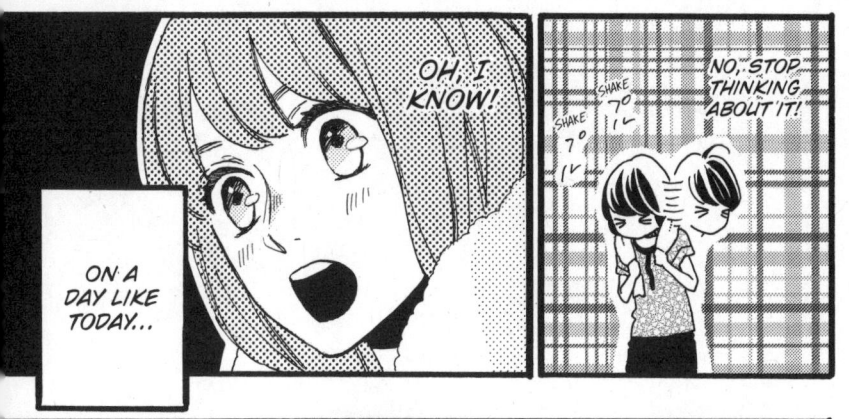

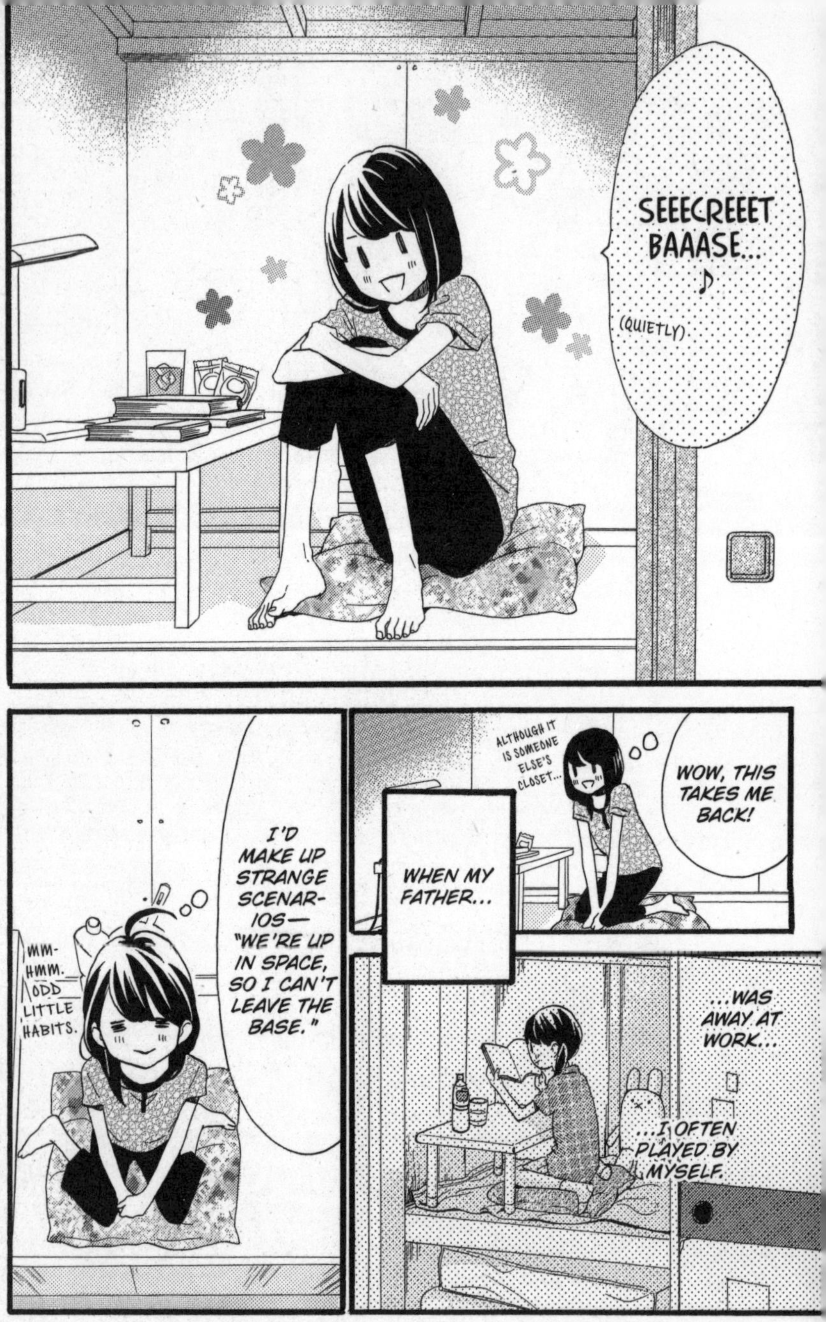
SEEECREEEET BAAASE... ♪
(QUIETLY)
WOW, THIS TAKES ME BACK!
ALTHOUGH IT IS SOMEONE ELSE'S CLOSET...
WHEN MY FATHER...
...WAS AWAY AT WORK...
...I OFTEN PLAYED BY MYSELF.
I'D MAKE UP STRANGE SCENAR-IOS—"WE'RE UP IN SPACE, SO I CAN'T LEAVE THE BASE."
MM-HMM. ODD LITTLE HABITS.

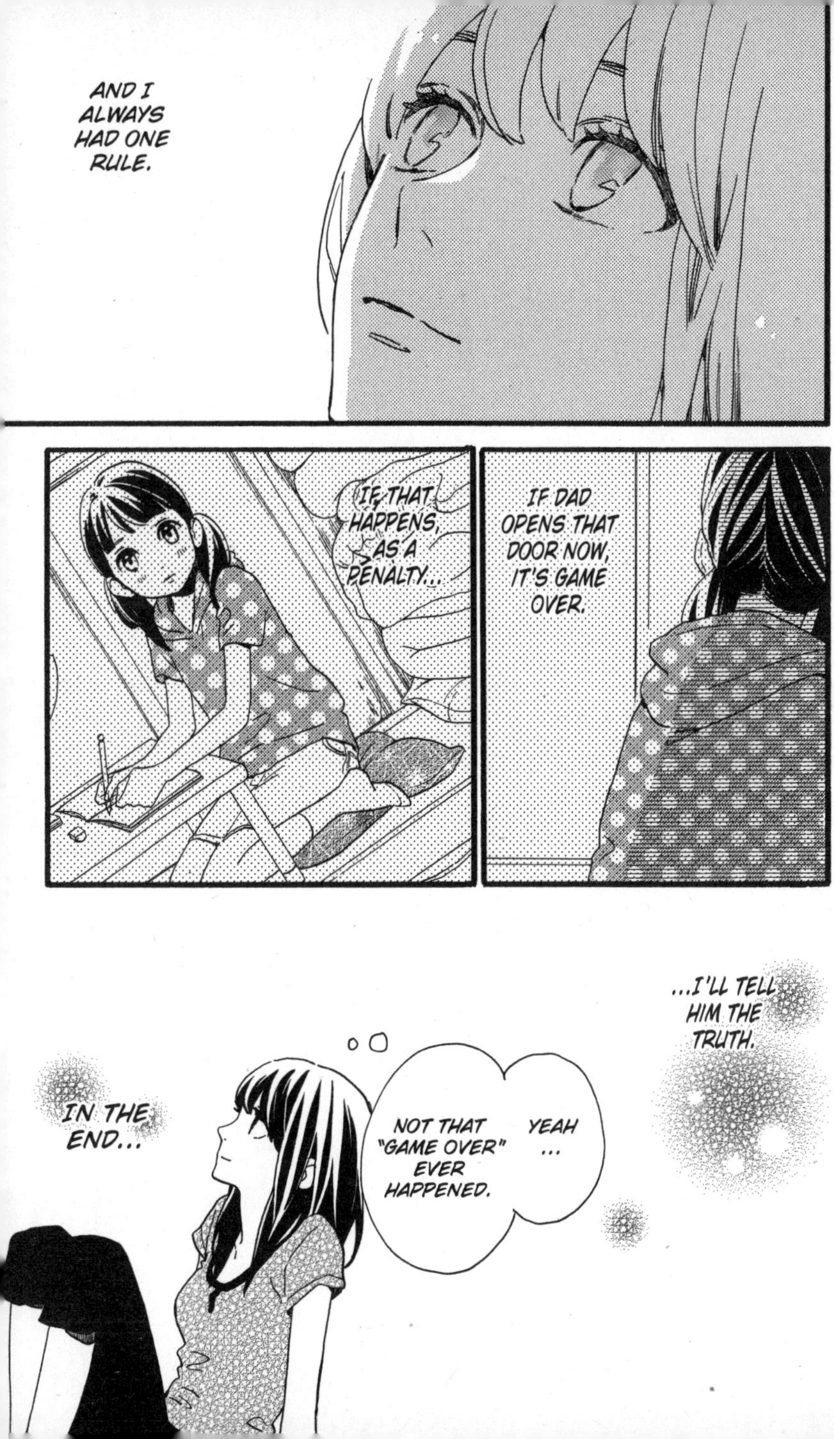
AND I ALWAYS HAD ONE RULE.
IF DAD OPENS THAT DOOR NOW, IT'S GAME OVER.
IF THAT HAPPENS, AS A PENALTY...
...I'LL TELL HIM THE TRUTH.
IN THE END...
NOT THAT "GAME OVER" EVER HAPPENED.
YEAH...

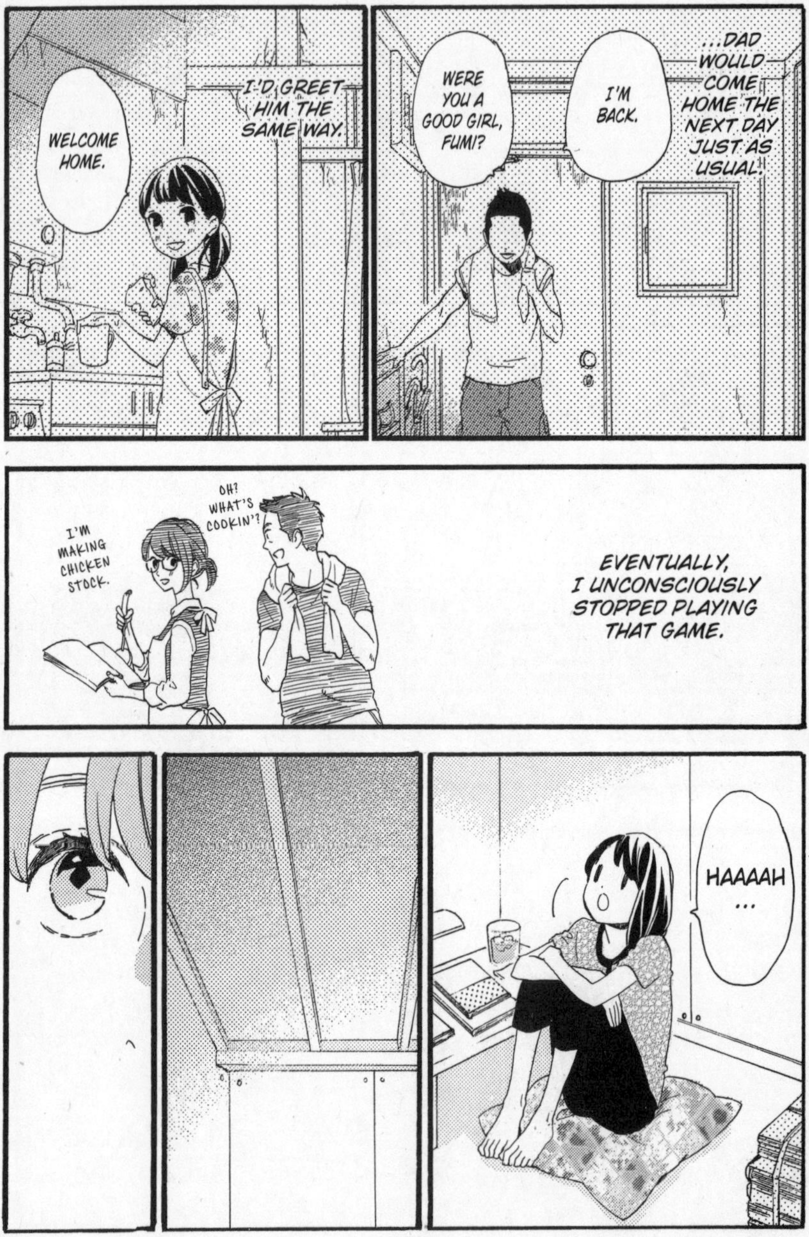
...DAD WOULD COME HOME THE NEXT DAY JUST AS USUAL.
I'M BACK.
WERE YOU A GOOD GIRL, FUMI?
I'D GREET HIM THE SAME WAY.
WELCOME HOME.
EVENTUALLY, I UNCONSCIOUSLY STOPPED PLAYING THAT GAME.
OH? WHAT'S COOKIN'?
I'M MAKING CHICKEN STOCK.
HAAAAH ...

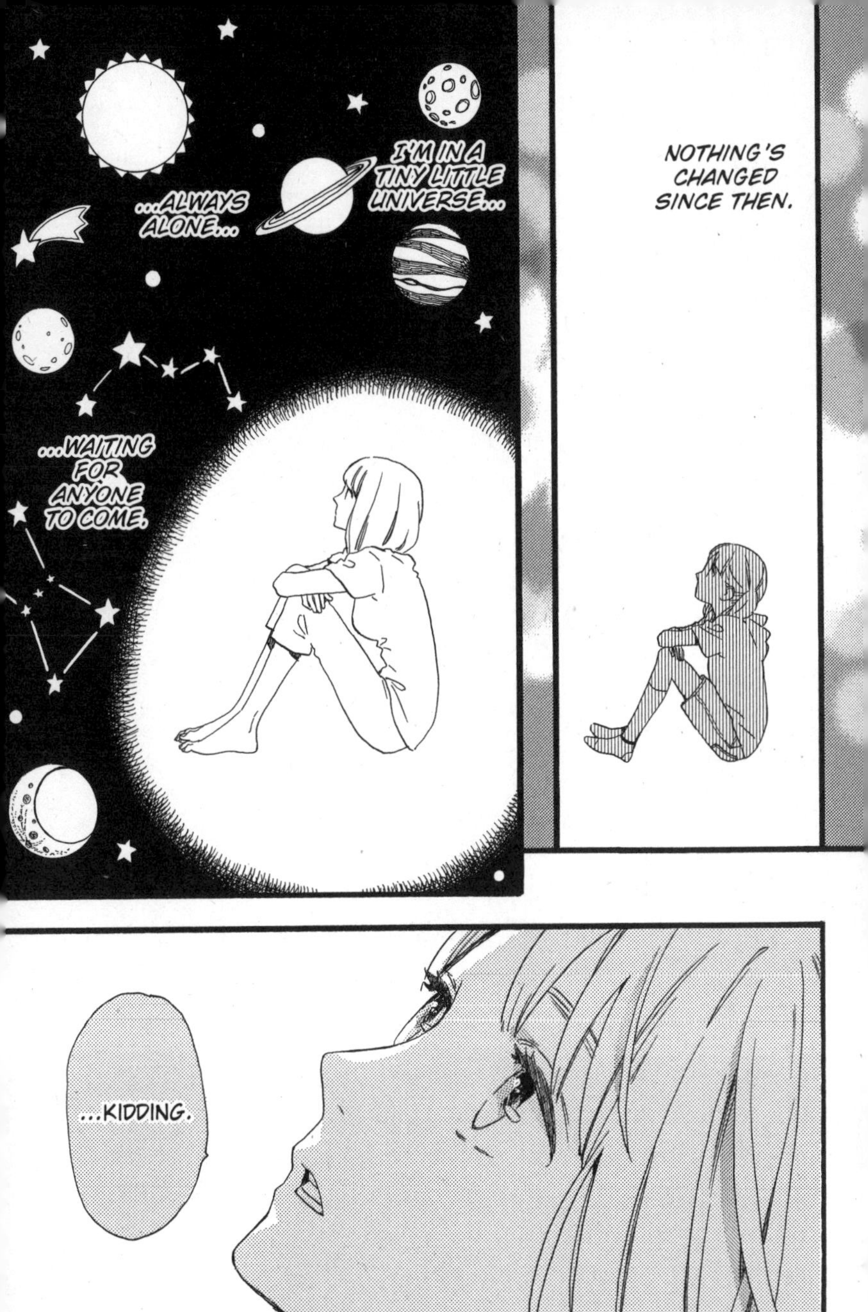
NOTHING'S CHANGED SINCE THEN.
I'M IN A TINY LITTLE UNIVERSE...
...ALWAYS ALONE...
...WAITING FOR ANYONE TO COME.
...KIDDING.

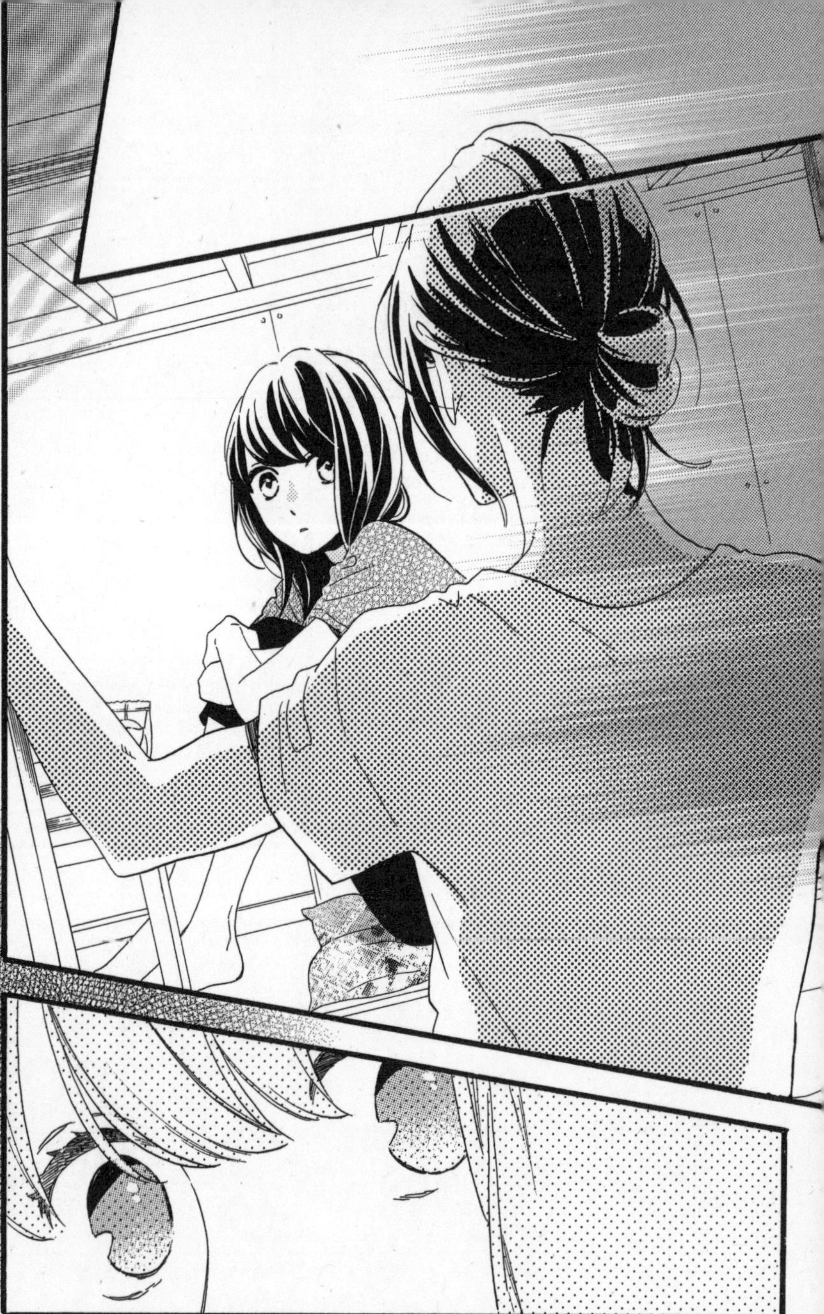

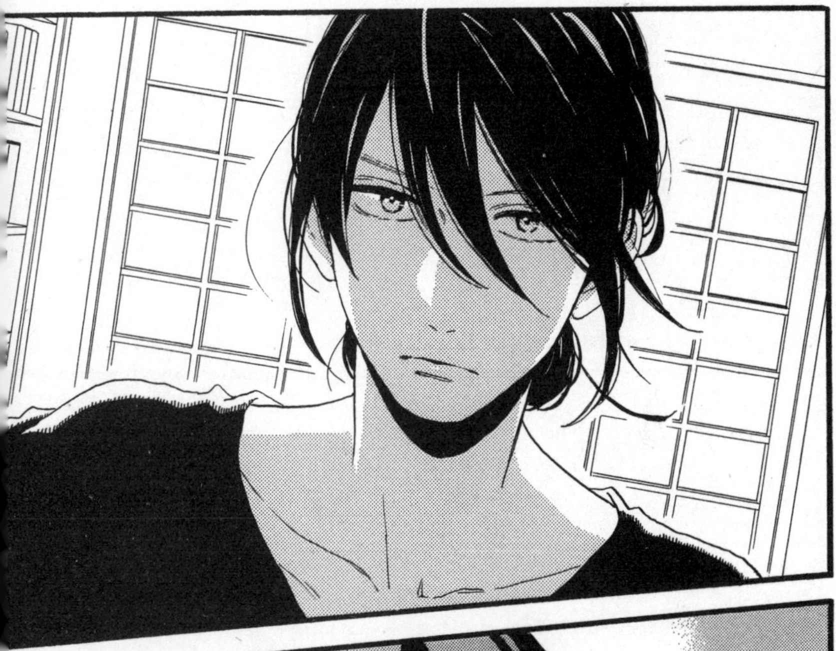
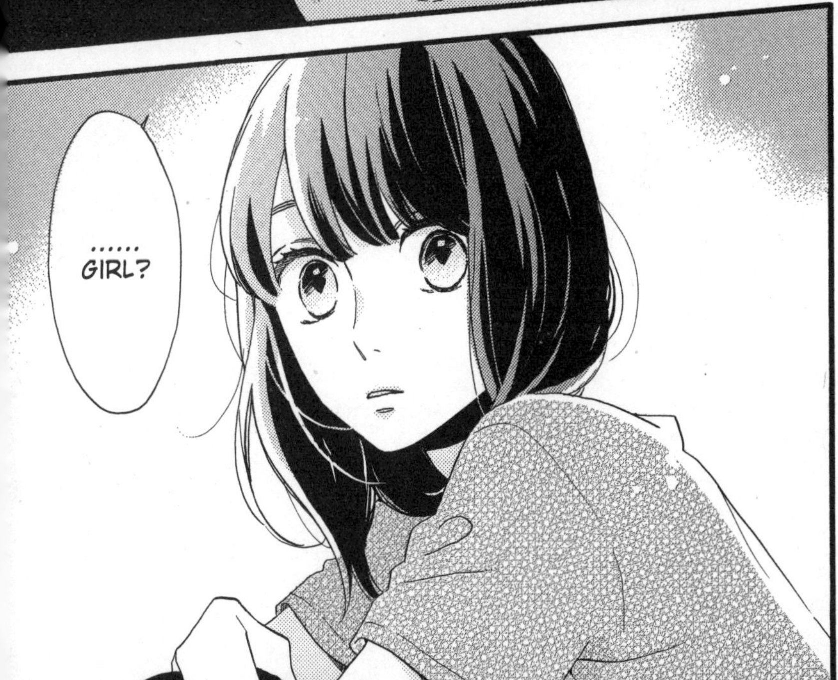
......
GIRL?

... WELCOME HOME......

....

OH...

I'M BACK.

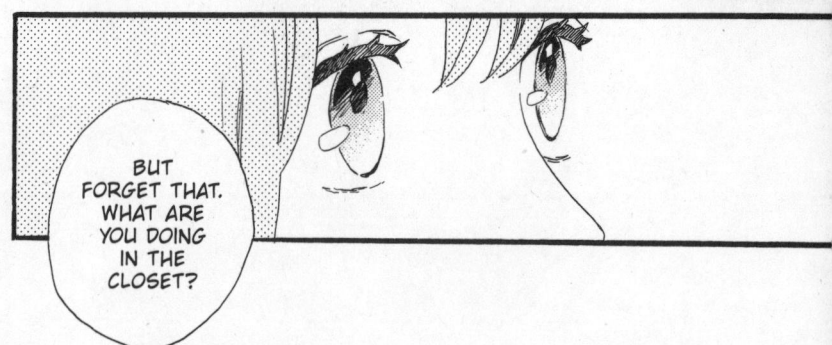

BUT FORGET THAT. WHAT ARE YOU DOING IN THE CLOSET?

OH.

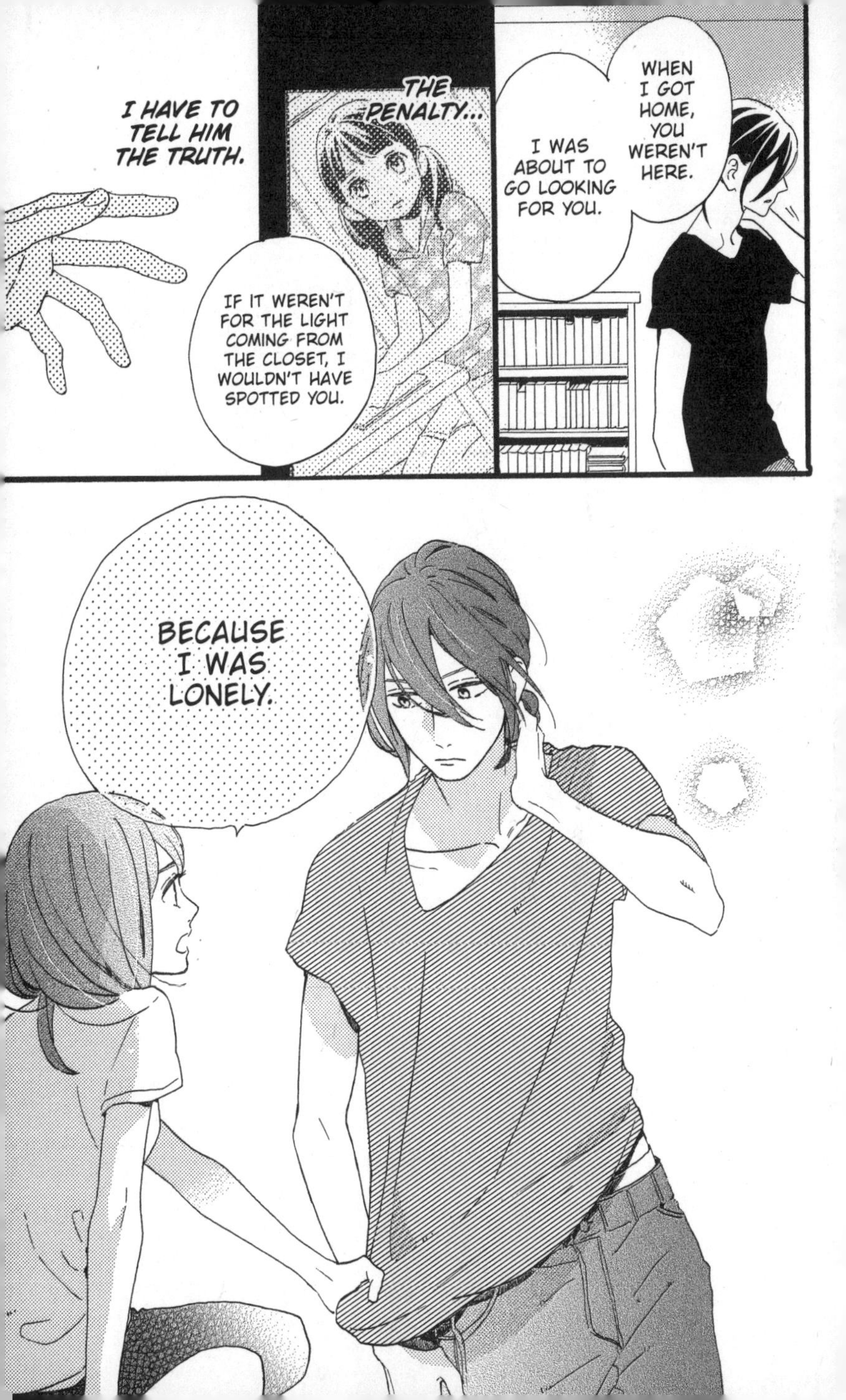
WHEN I GOT HOME, YOU WEREN'T HERE.
I WAS ABOUT TO GO LOOKING FOR YOU.
THE PENALTY...
IF IT WEREN'T FOR THE LIGHT COMING FROM THE CLOSET, I WOULDN'T HAVE SPOTTED YOU.
I HAVE TO TELL HIM THE TRUTH.
BECAUSE I WAS LONELY.

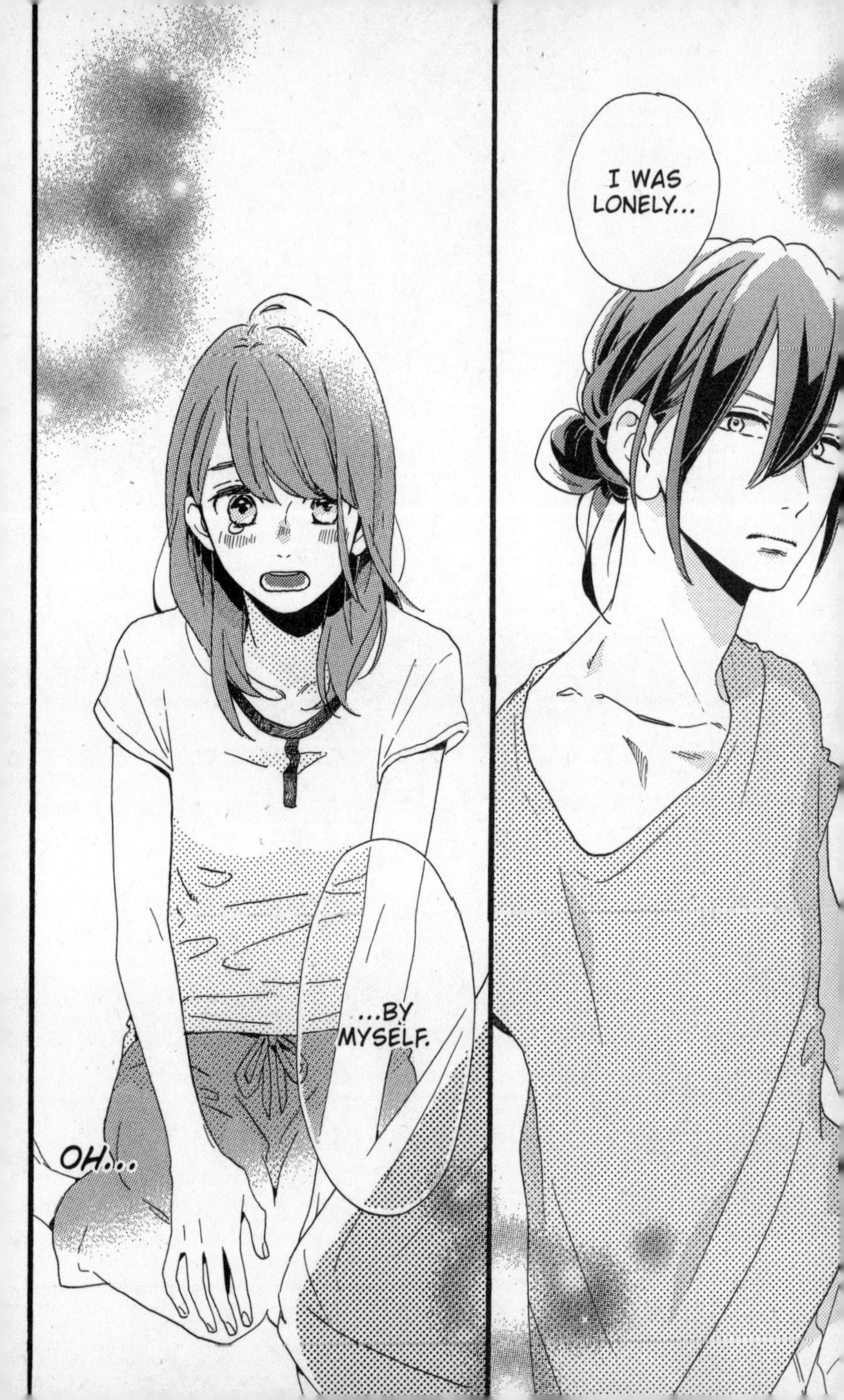
I WAS LONELY...
...BY MYSELF.
OH...

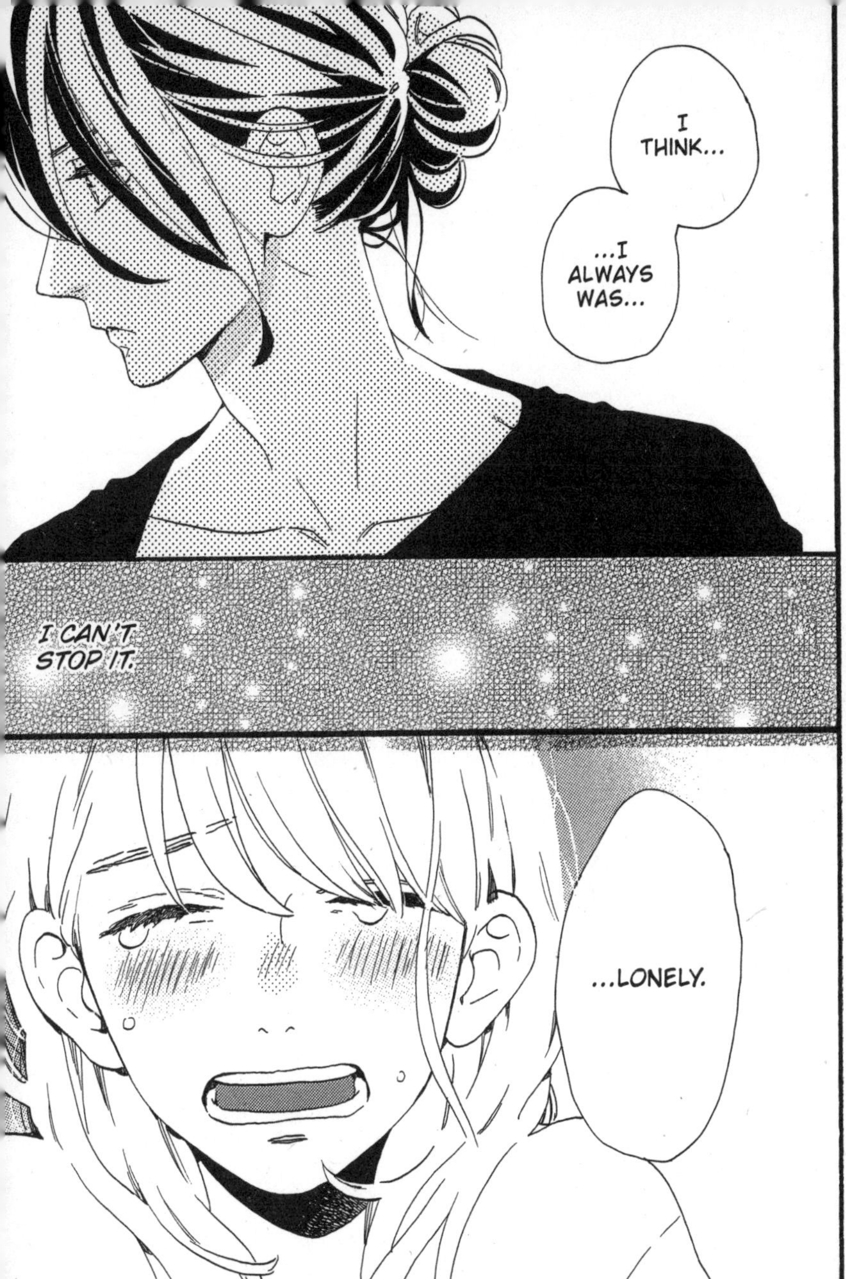
I THINK...
...I ALWAYS WAS...
I CAN'T STOP IT.
...LONELY.

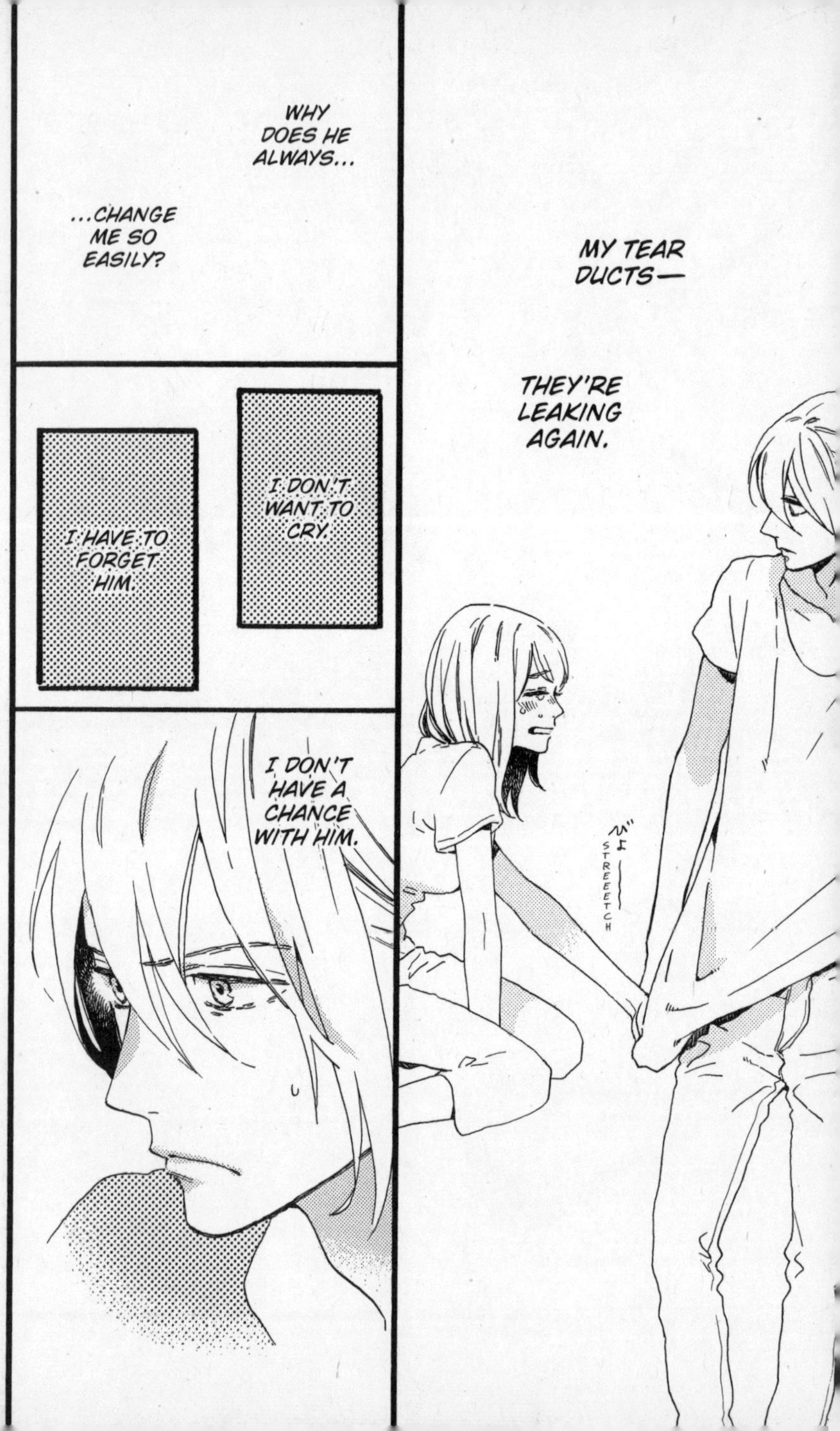
MY TEAR DUCTS—
THEY'RE LEAKING AGAIN.
STREEETCH
WHY DOES HE ALWAYS...
...CHANGE ME SO EASILY?
I DON'T WANT TO CRY.
I HAVE TO FORGET HIM.
I DON'T HAVE A CHANCE WITH HIM.

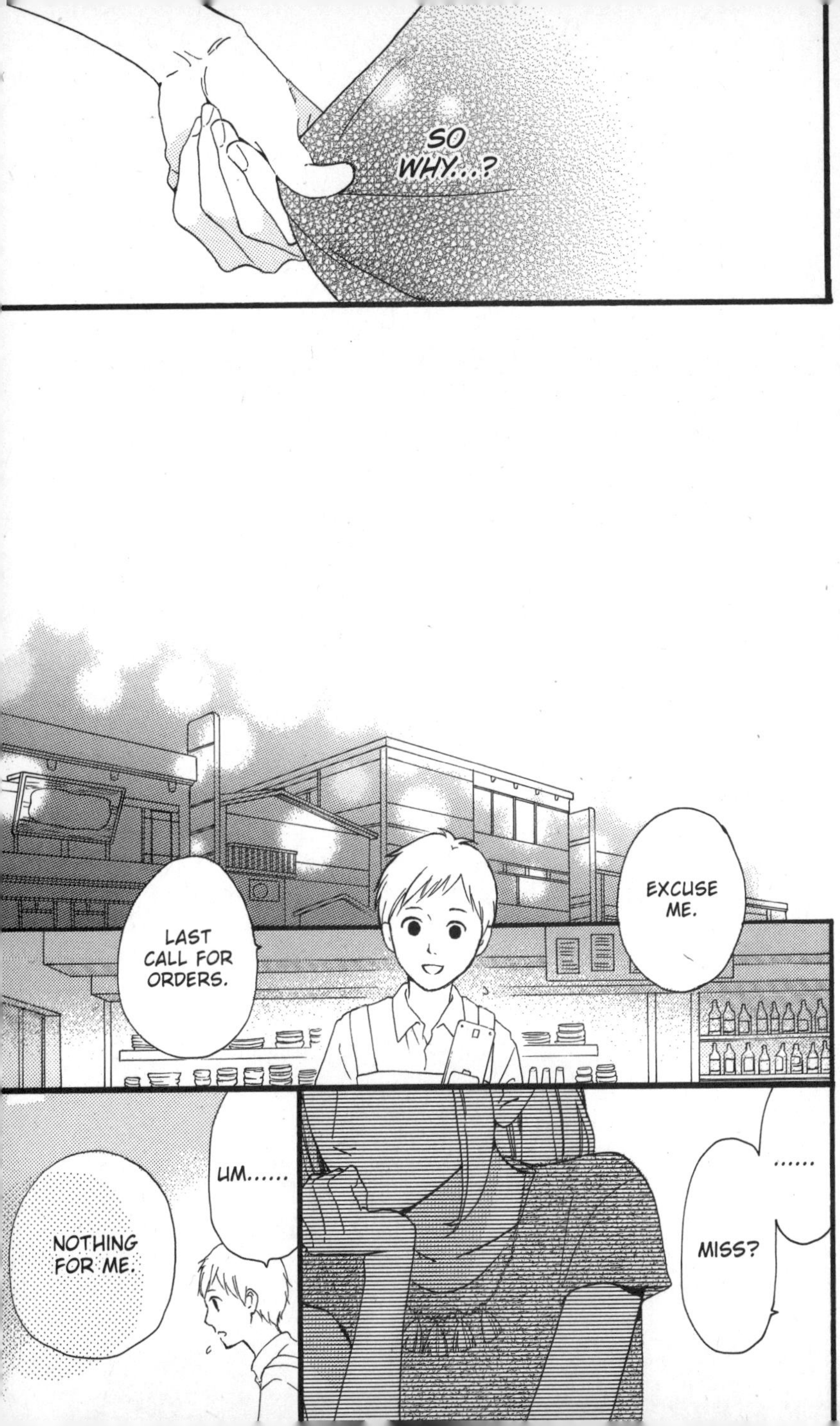
SO WHY...?
EXCUSE ME.
LAST CALL FOR ORDERS.
......
MISS?
UM......
NOTHING FOR ME.

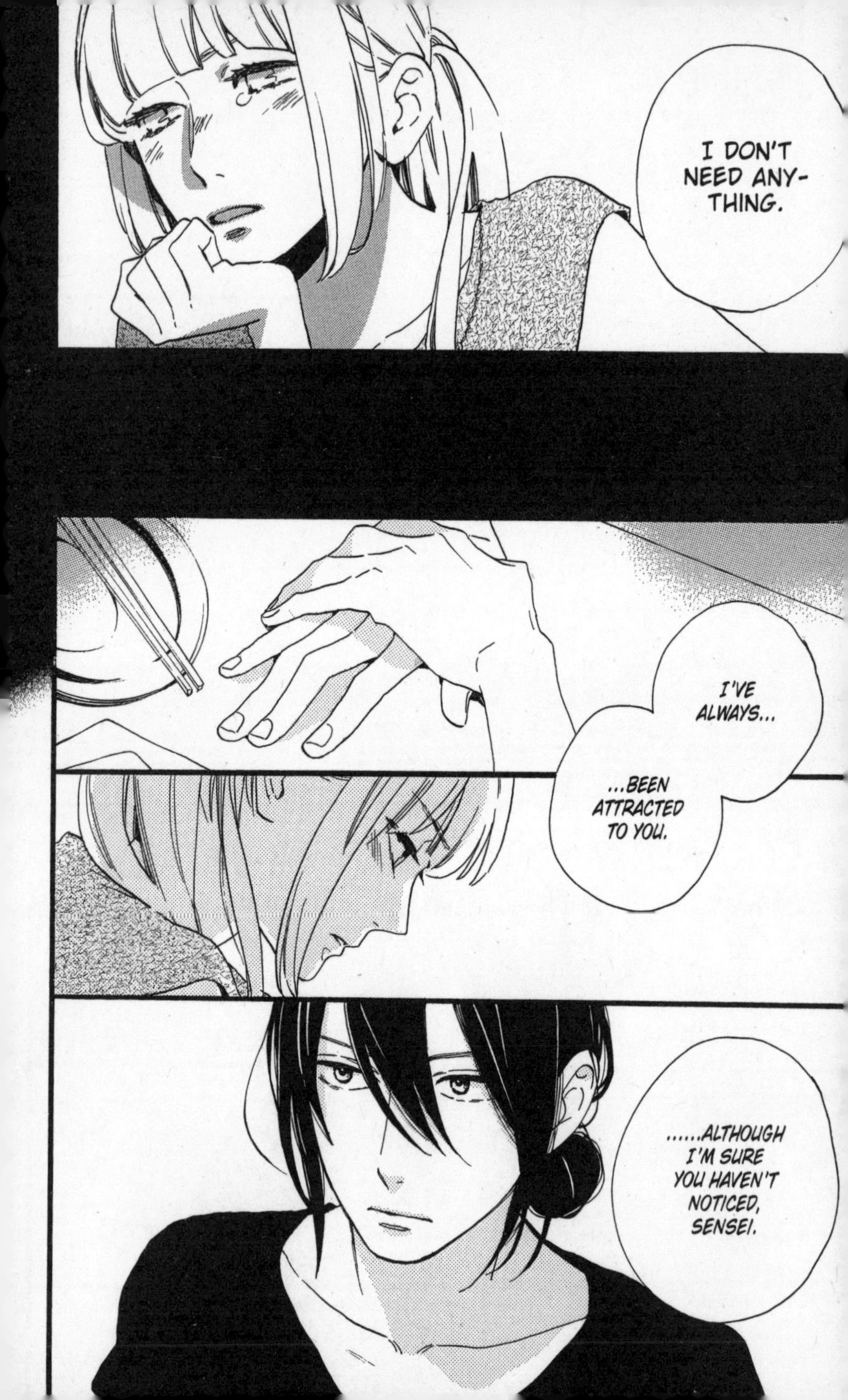
I DON'T NEED ANY-THING.
I'VE ALWAYS...
...BEEN ATTRACTED TO YOU.
......ALTHOUGH I'M SURE YOU HAVEN'T NOTICED, SENSEI.

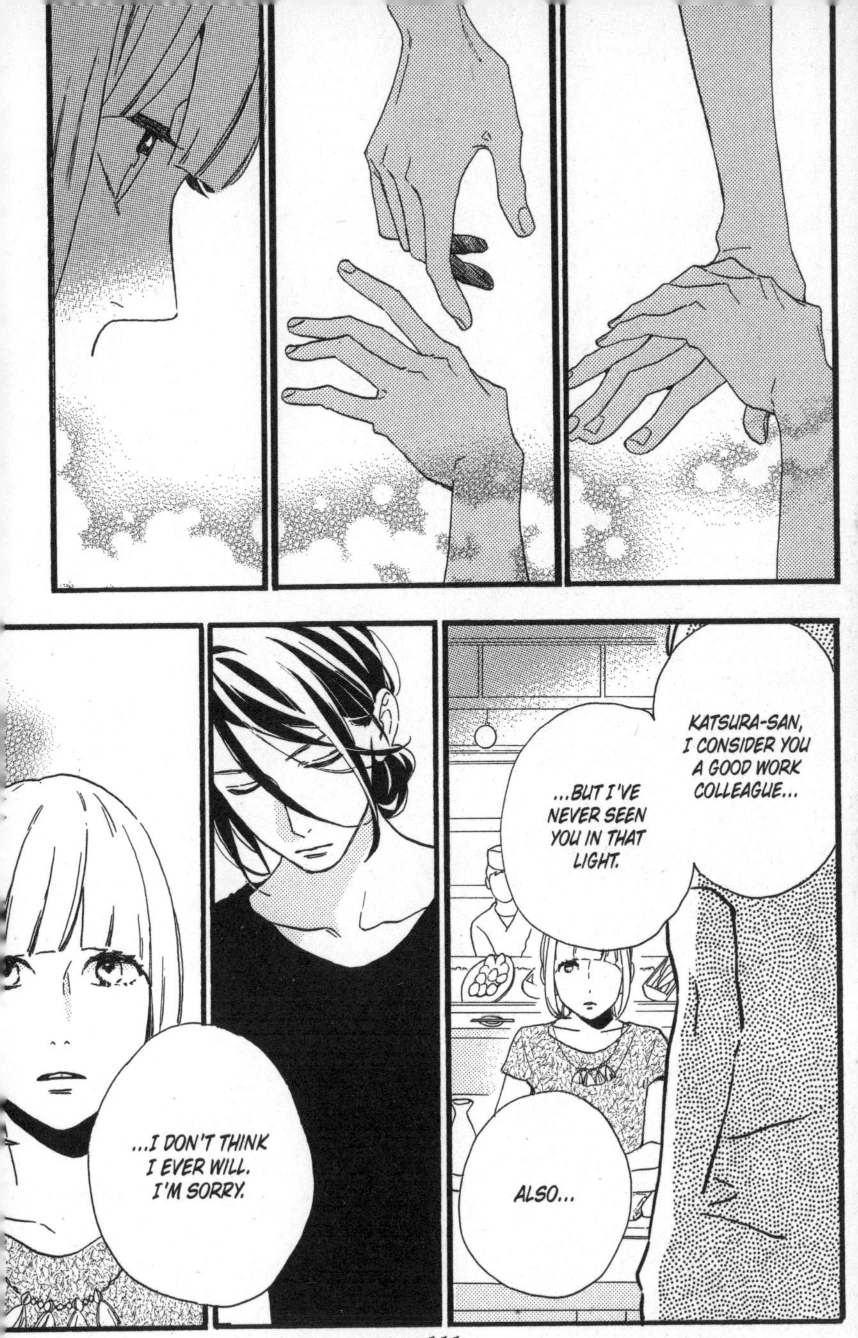
KATSURA-SAN, I CONSIDER YOU A GOOD WORK COLLEAGUE...
...BUT I'VE NEVER SEEN YOU IN THAT LIGHT.
ALSO...
...I DON'T THINK I EVER WILL. I'M SORRY.

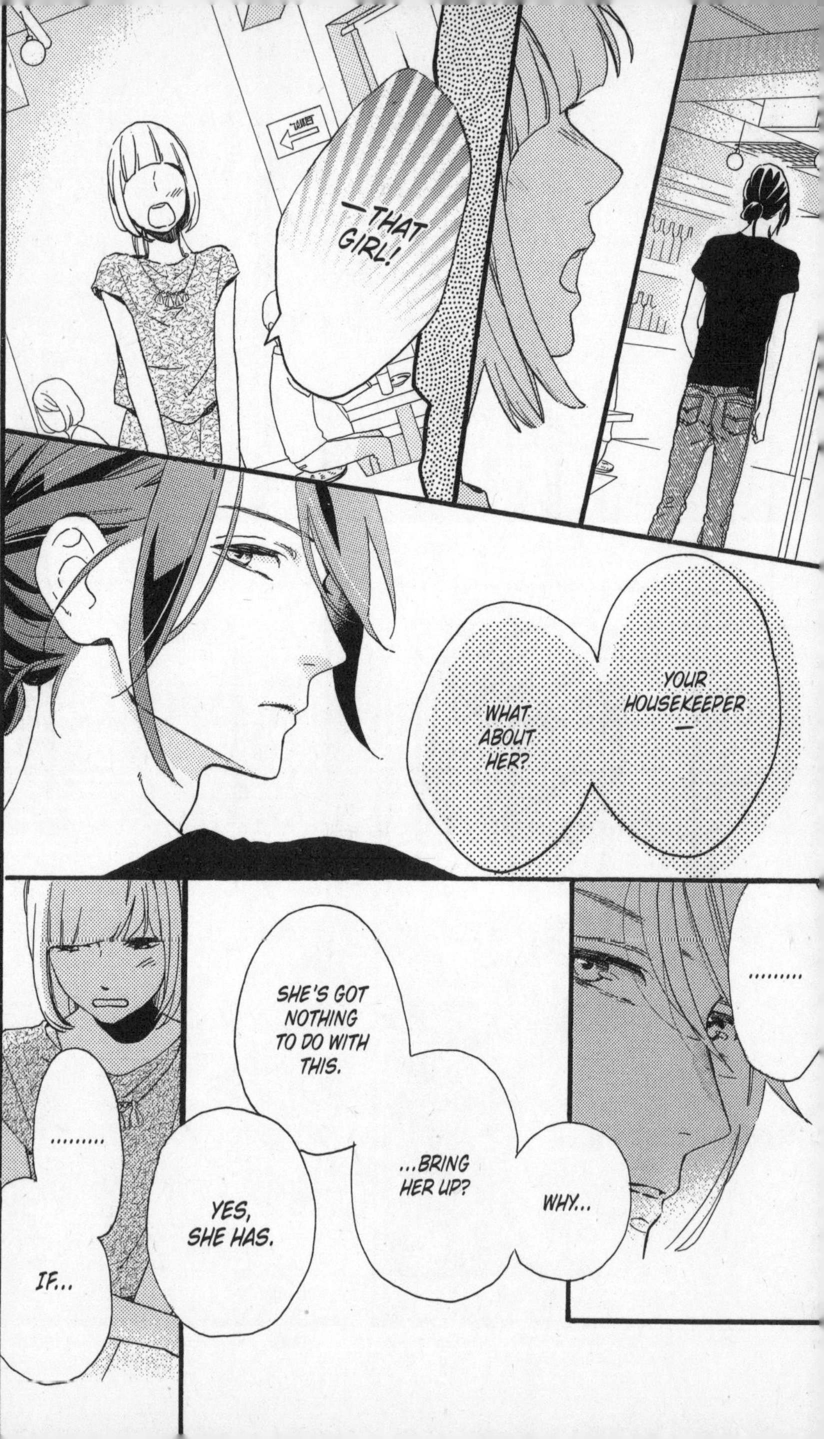
—THAT GIRL!
YOUR HOUSEKEEPER—
WHAT ABOUT HER?
....
WHY...
...BRING HER UP?
SHE'S GOT NOTHING TO DO WITH THIS.
YES, SHE HAS.
....
IF...

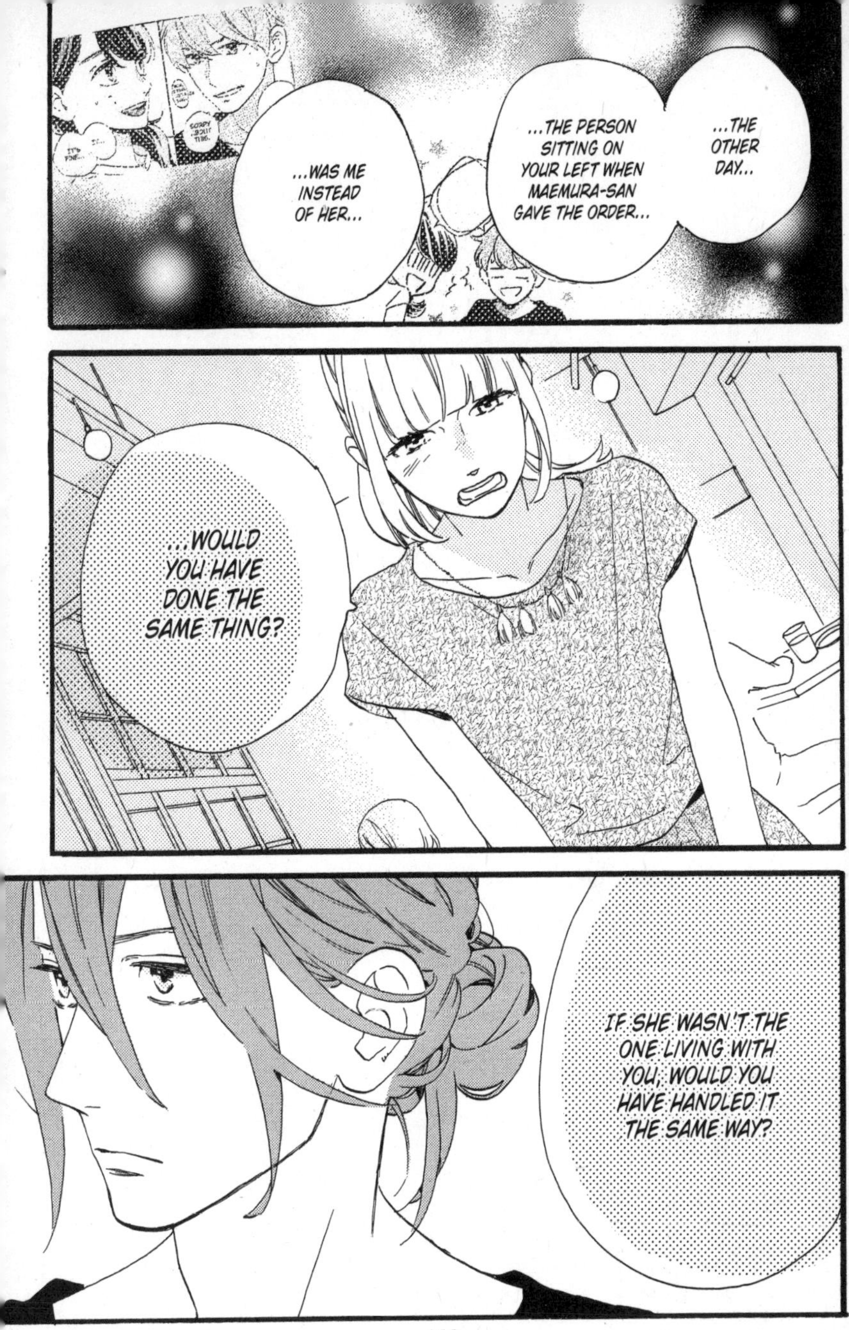
...THE OTHER DAY...
...THE PERSON SITTING ON YOUR LEFT WHEN MAEMURA-SAN GAVE THE ORDER...
...WAS ME INSTEAD OF HER...
SORRY ABOUT THIS.
I...
IT'S FINE...
...WOULD YOU HAVE DONE THE SAME THING?
IF SHE WASN'T THE ONE LIVING WITH YOU, WOULD YOU HAVE HANDLED IT THE SAME WAY?

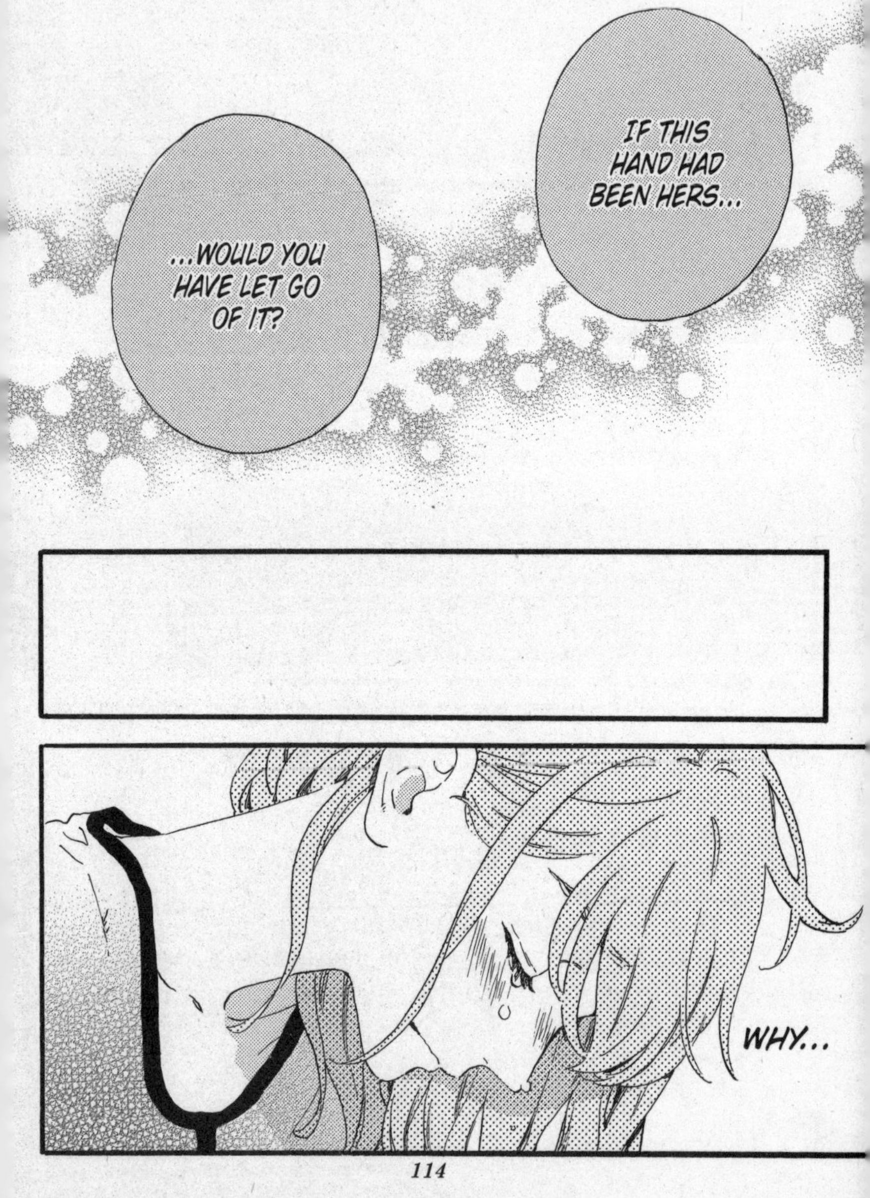
IF THIS HAND HAD BEEN HERS...
...WOULD YOU HAVE LET GO OF IT?
WHY...

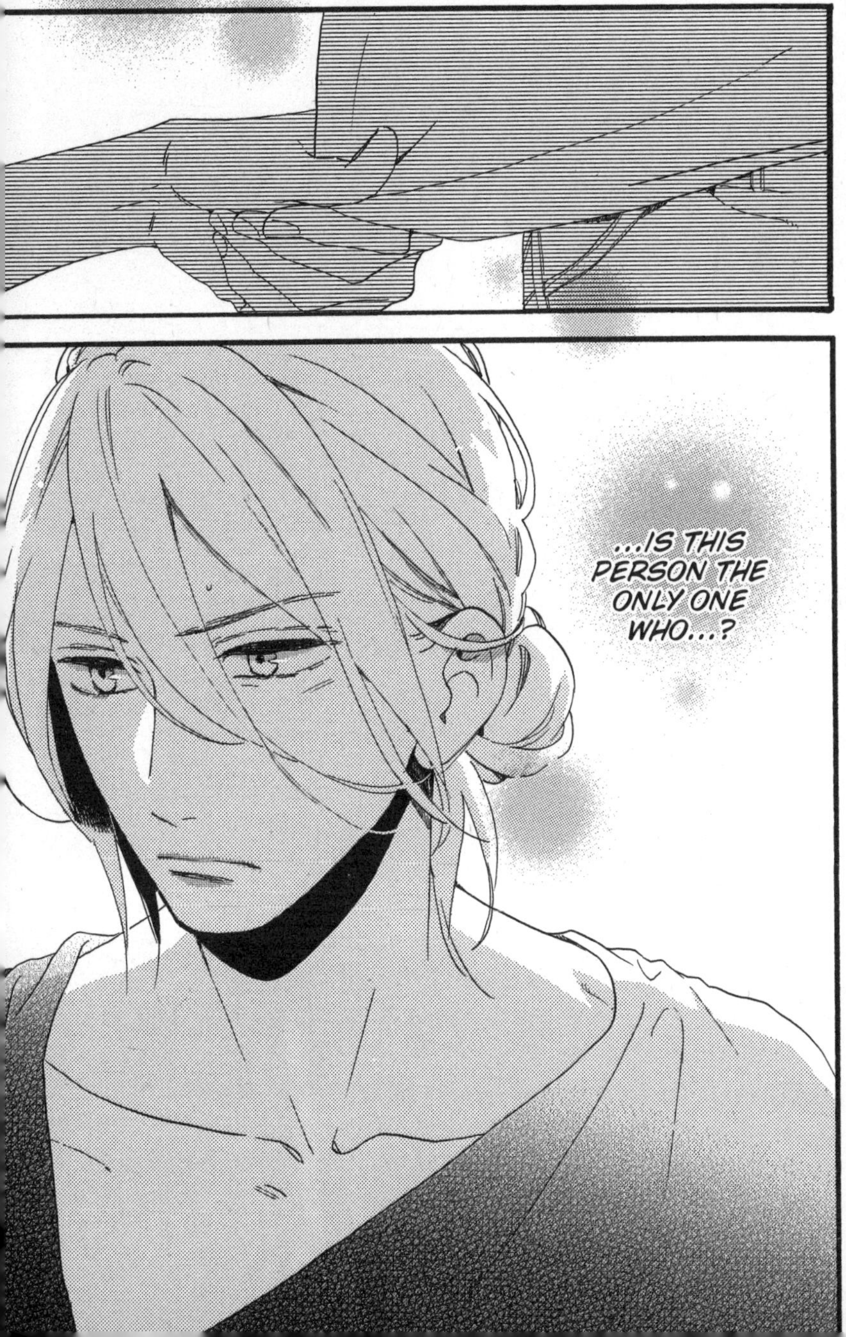
...IS THIS PERSON THE ONLY ONE WHO...?

The glasses were miraculously restored!

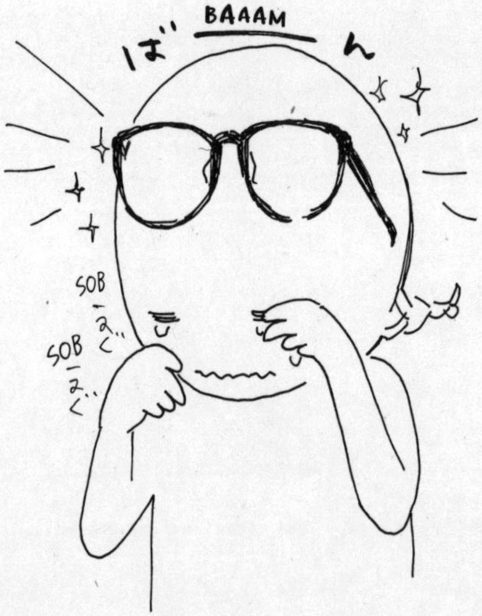
BAAAM
ば―ん
SOB
えぐ
SOB
えぐ

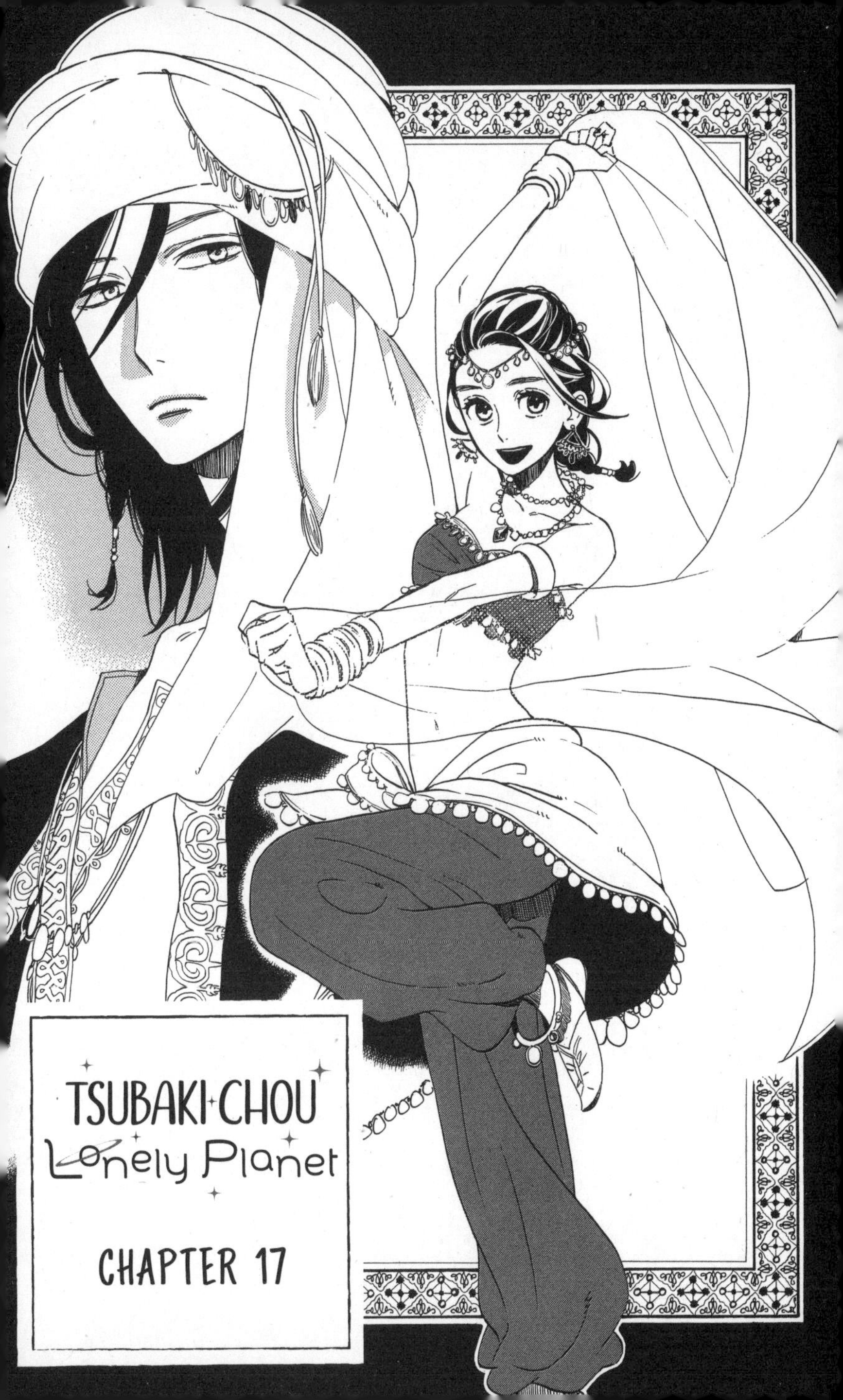
TSUBAKI-CHOU
Lonely Planet
CHAPTER 17

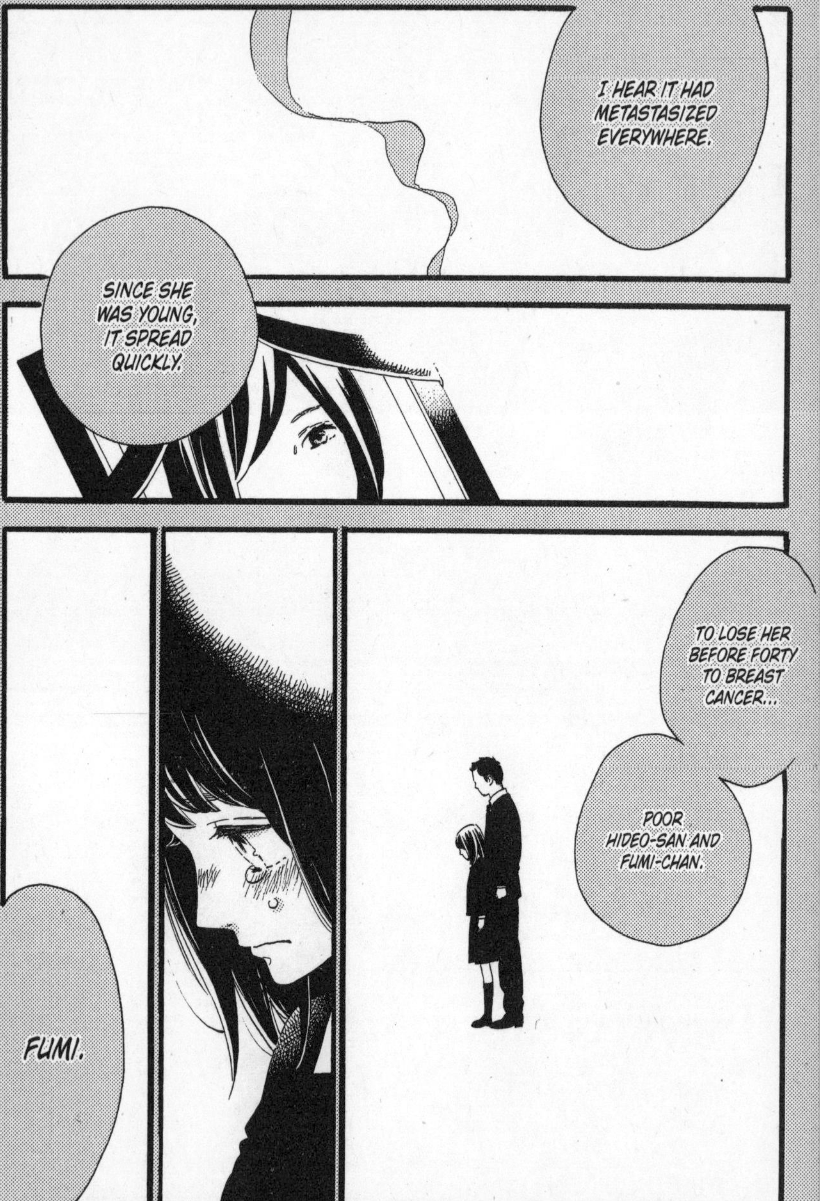
I HEAR IT HAD METASTASIZED EVERYWHERE.
SINCE SHE WAS YOUNG, IT SPREAD QUICKLY.
TO LOSE HER BEFORE FORTY TO BREAST CANCER...
POOR HIDEO-SAN AND FUMI-CHAN.
FUMI.

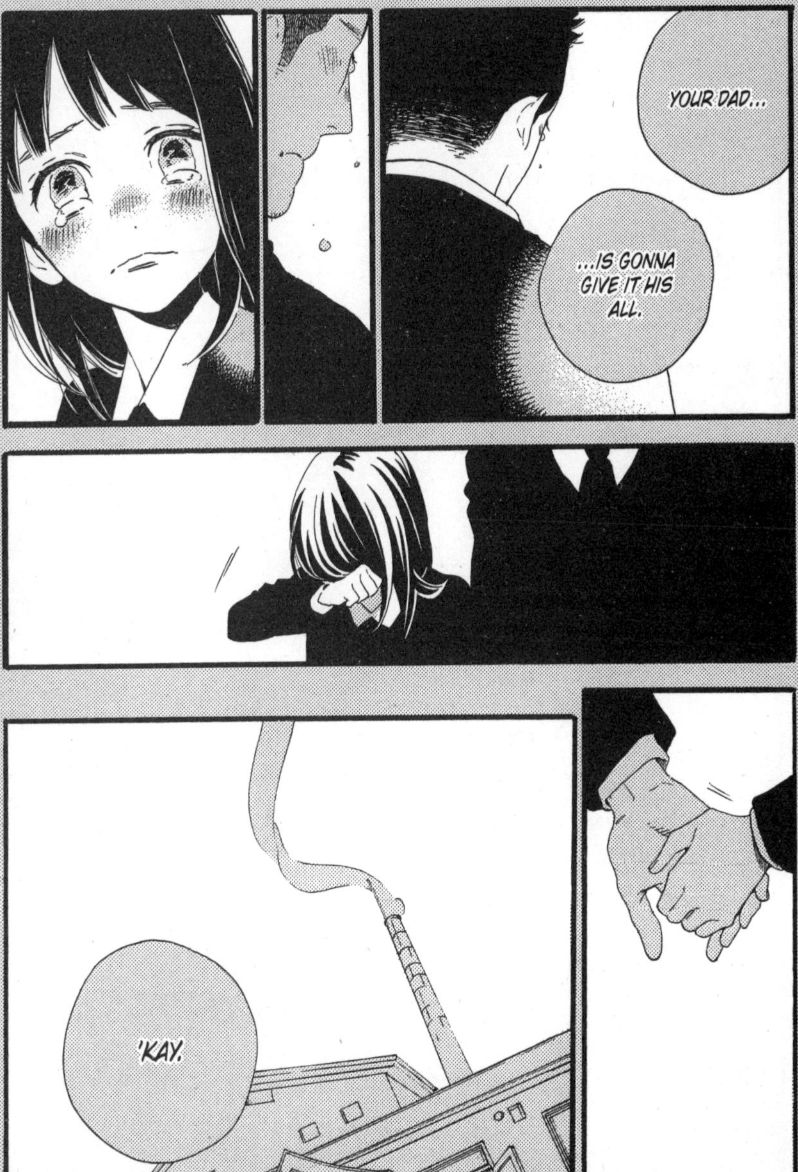
YOUR DAD...
...IS GONNA GIVE IT HIS ALL.
'KAY.

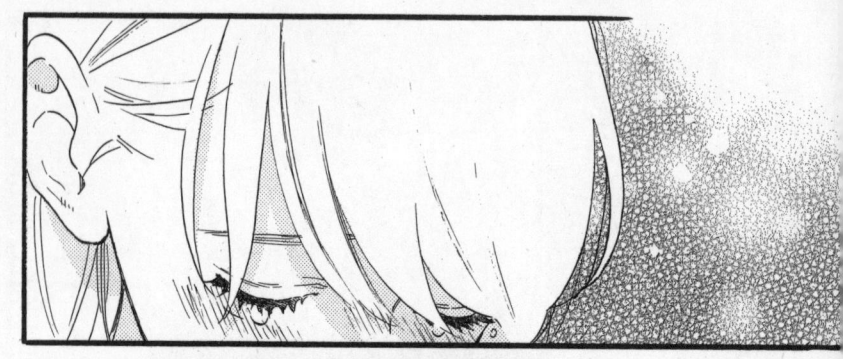

...GIRL?

HEY.

....

WHEN MY
MOTHER...

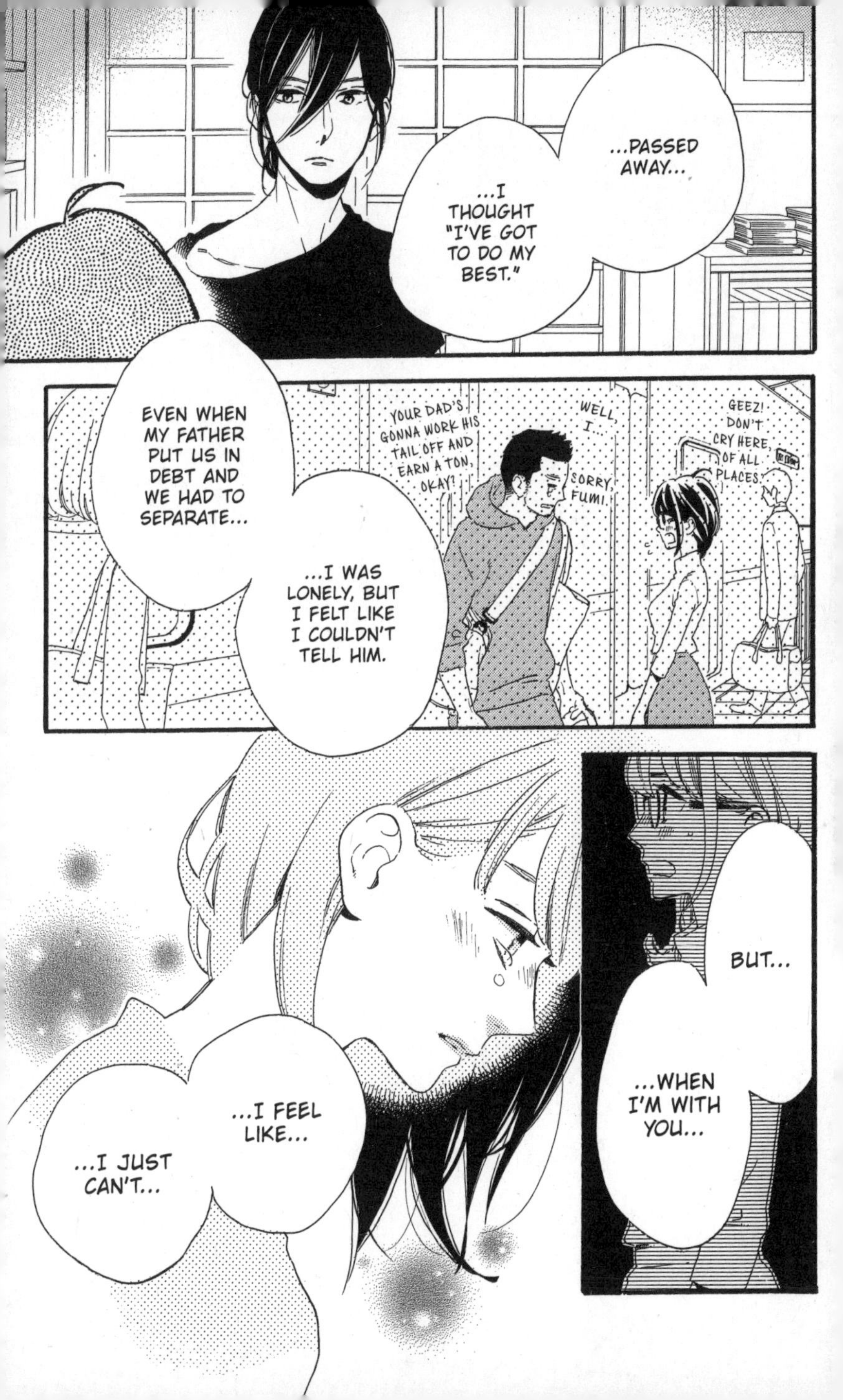
...PASSED AWAY...
...I THOUGHT "I'VE GOT TO DO MY BEST."
GEEZ! DON'T CRY HERE, OF ALL PLACES.
WELL, I...
SORRY, FUMI.
YOUR DAD'S GONNA WORK HIS TAIL OFF AND EARN A TON, OKAY?
EVEN WHEN MY FATHER PUT US IN DEBT AND WE HAD TO SEPARATE...
...I WAS LONELY, BUT I FELT LIKE I COULDN'T TELL HIM.
BUT...
...WHEN I'M WITH YOU...
...I FEEL LIKE...
...I JUST CAN'T...

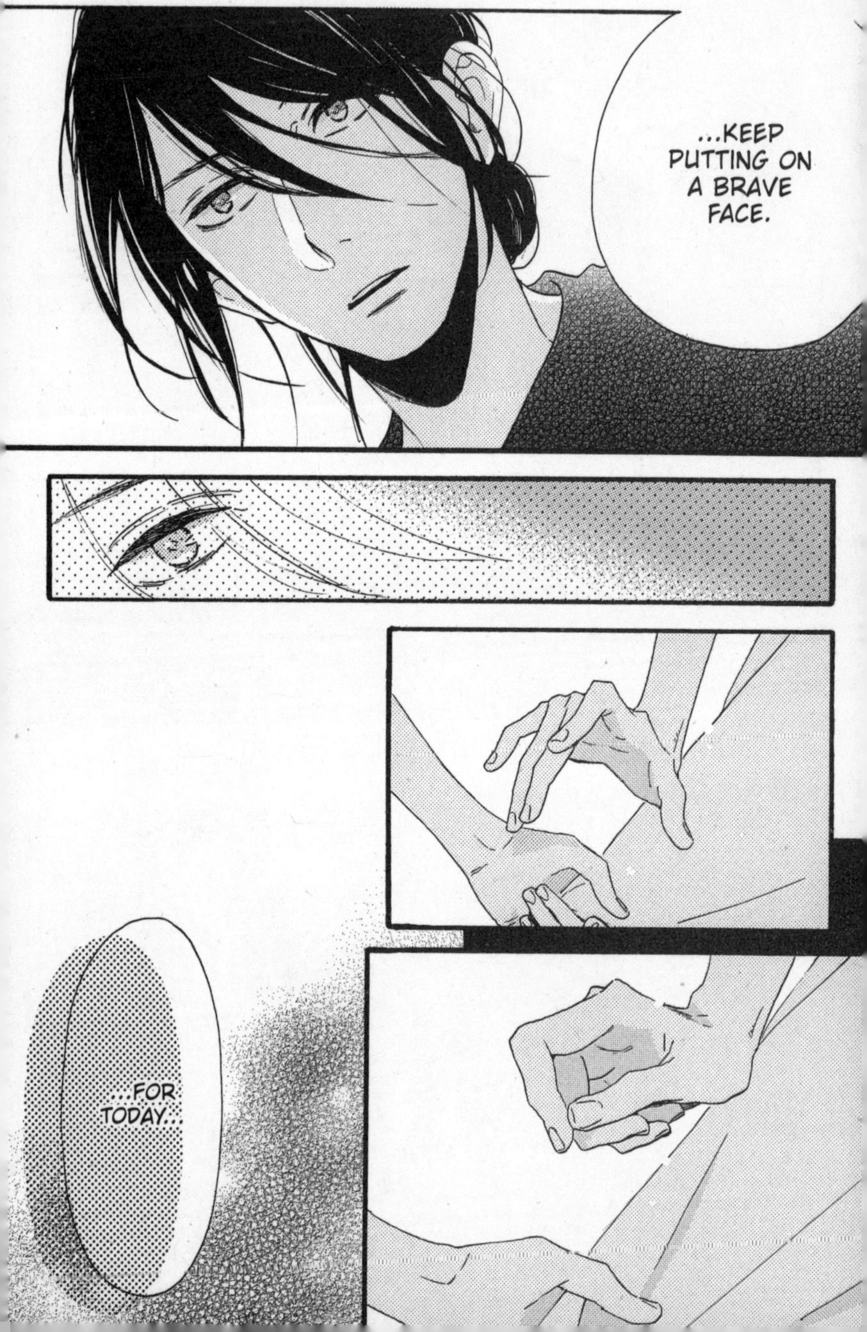
...KEEP PUTTING ON A BRAVE FACE.
...FOR TODAY...

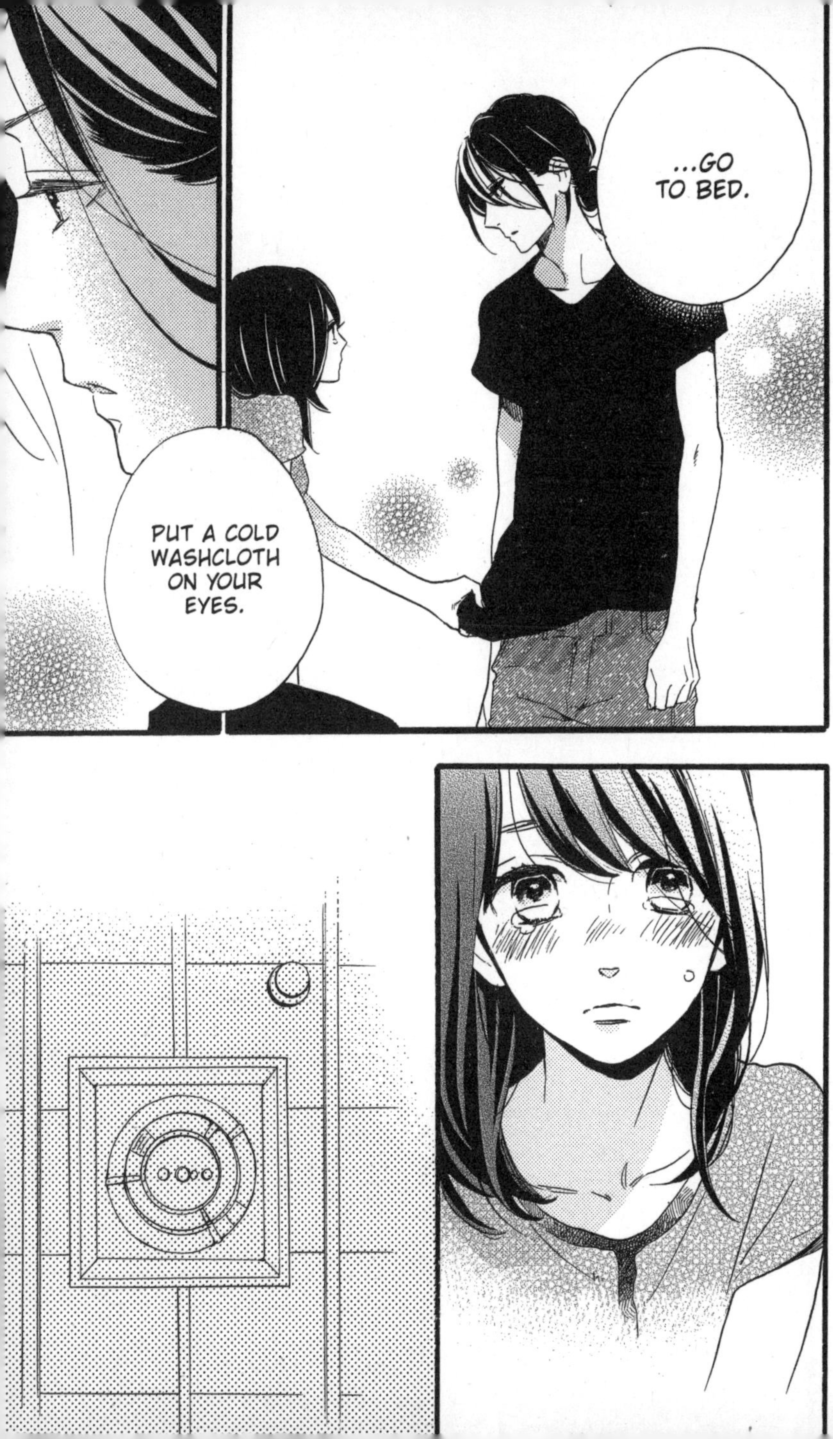
...GO TO BED.
PUT A COLD WASHCLOTH ON YOUR EYES.

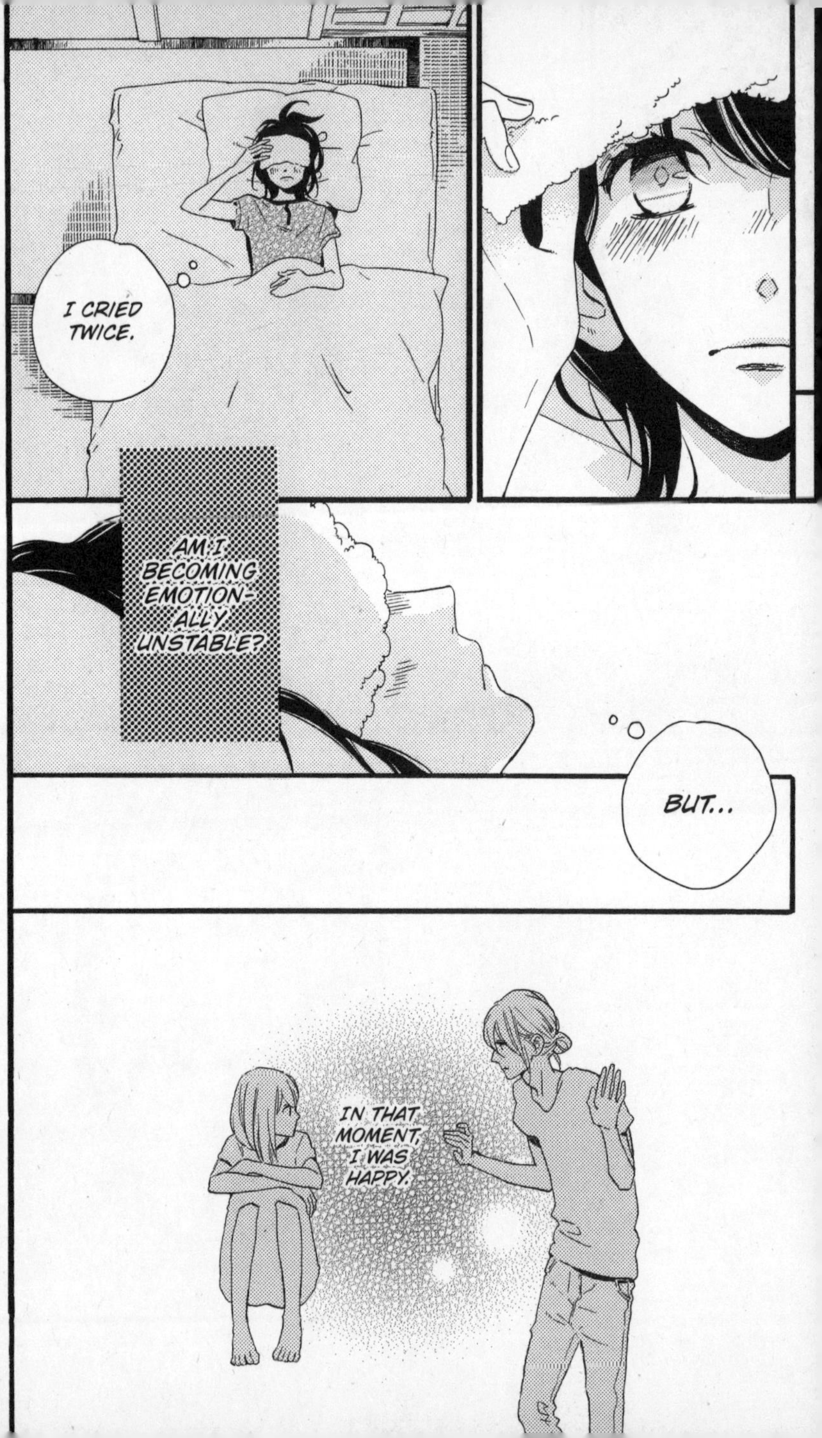
I CRIED TWICE.
AM I BECOMING EMOTION-ALLY UNSTABLE?
BUT...
IN THAT MOMENT, I WAS HAPPY.

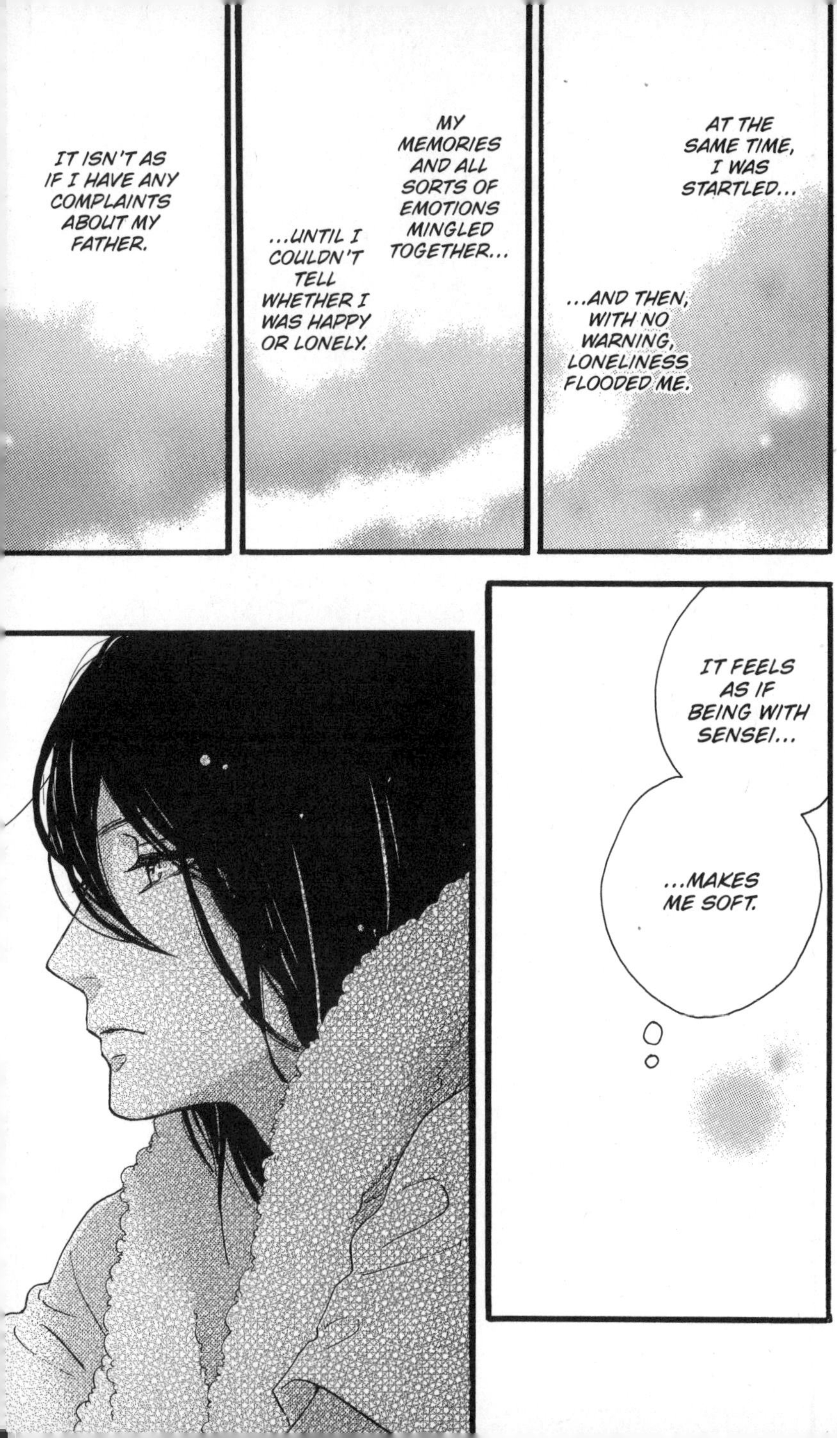
AT THE SAME TIME, I WAS STARTLED...
...AND THEN, WITH NO WARNING, LONELINESS FLOODED ME.
MY MEMORIES AND ALL SORTS OF EMOTIONS MINGLED TOGETHER...
...UNTIL I COULDN'T TELL WHETHER I WAS HAPPY OR LONELY.
IT ISN'T AS IF I HAVE ANY COMPLAINTS ABOUT MY FATHER.
IT FEELS AS IF BEING WITH SENSEI...
...MAKES ME SOFT.

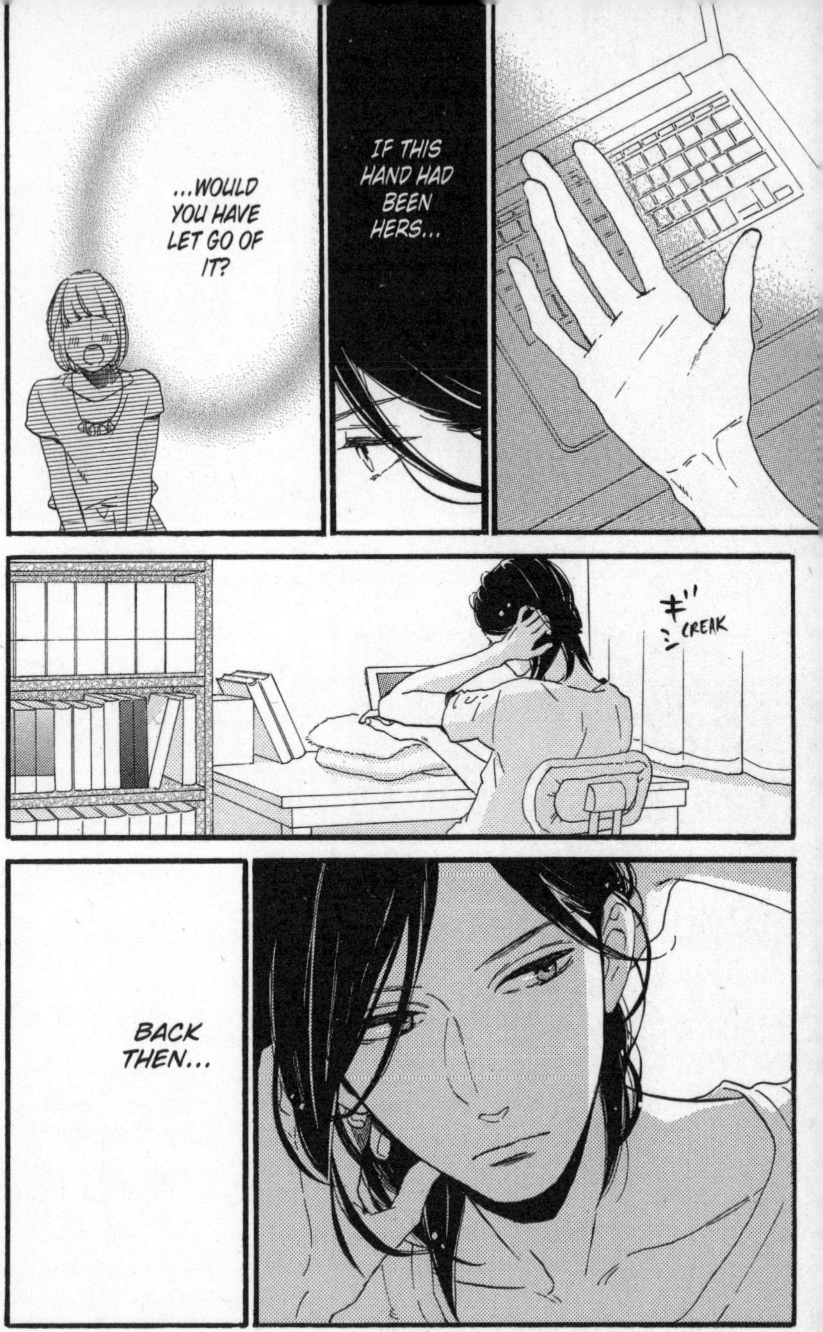
IF THIS HAND HAD BEEN HERS...
...WOULD YOU HAVE LET GO OF IT?
ギ CREAK
BACK THEN...

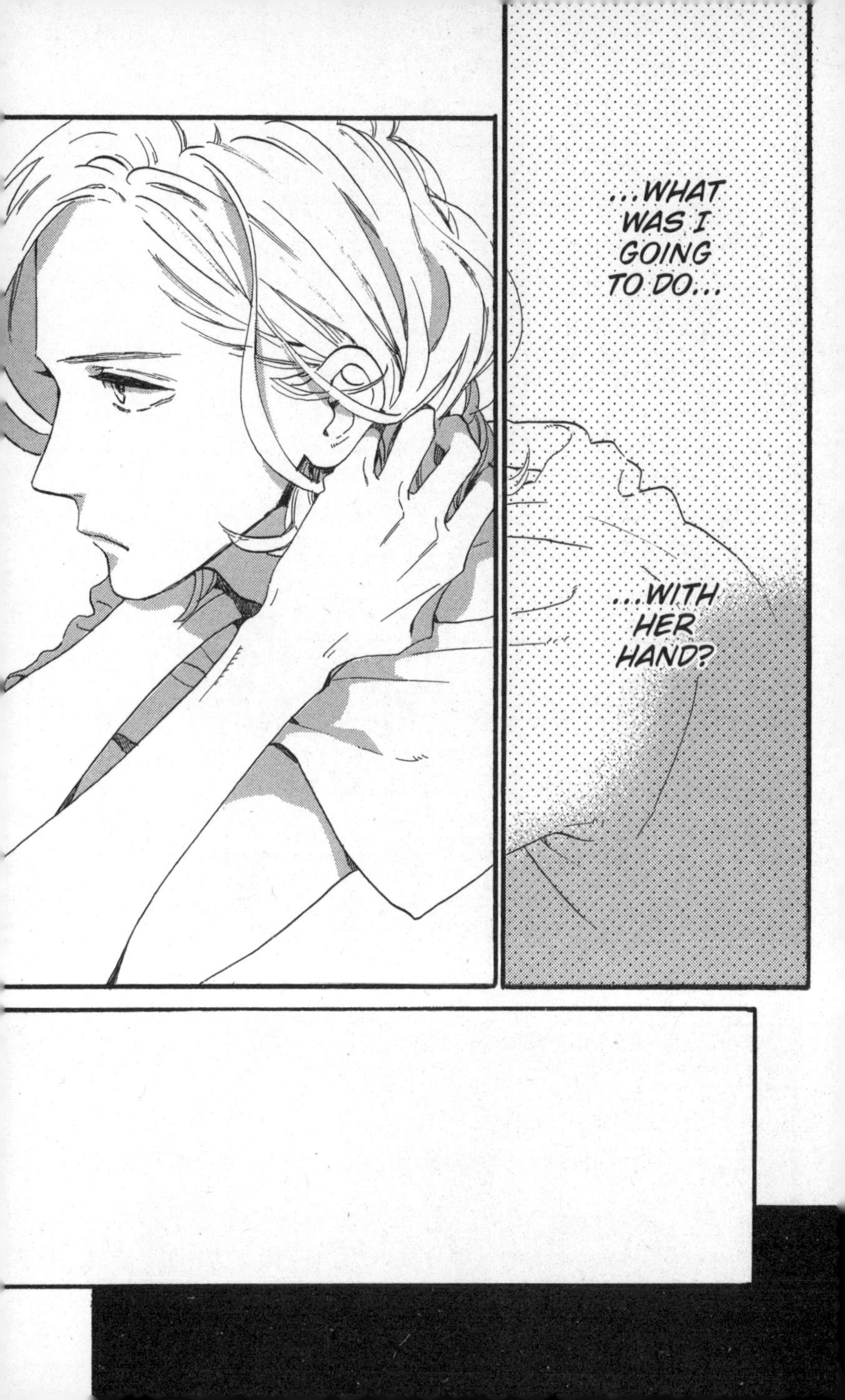
...WHAT WAS I GOING TO DO...
...WITH HER HAND?

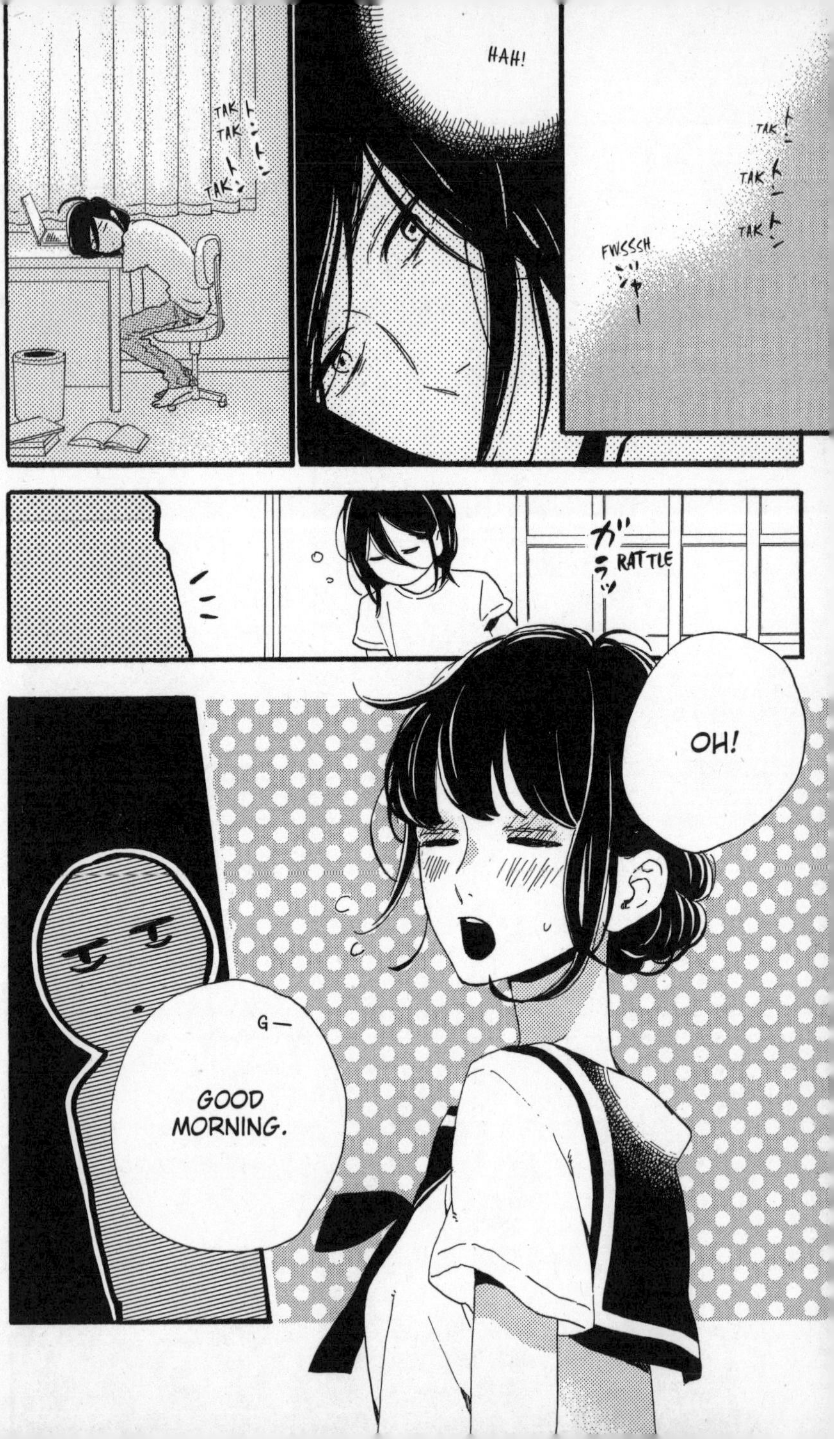
TAK
TAK
TAK
FWSSSH ジャー
HAH!
TAK
TAK
TAK
ガラッ RATTLE
OH!
G—
GOOD MORNING.

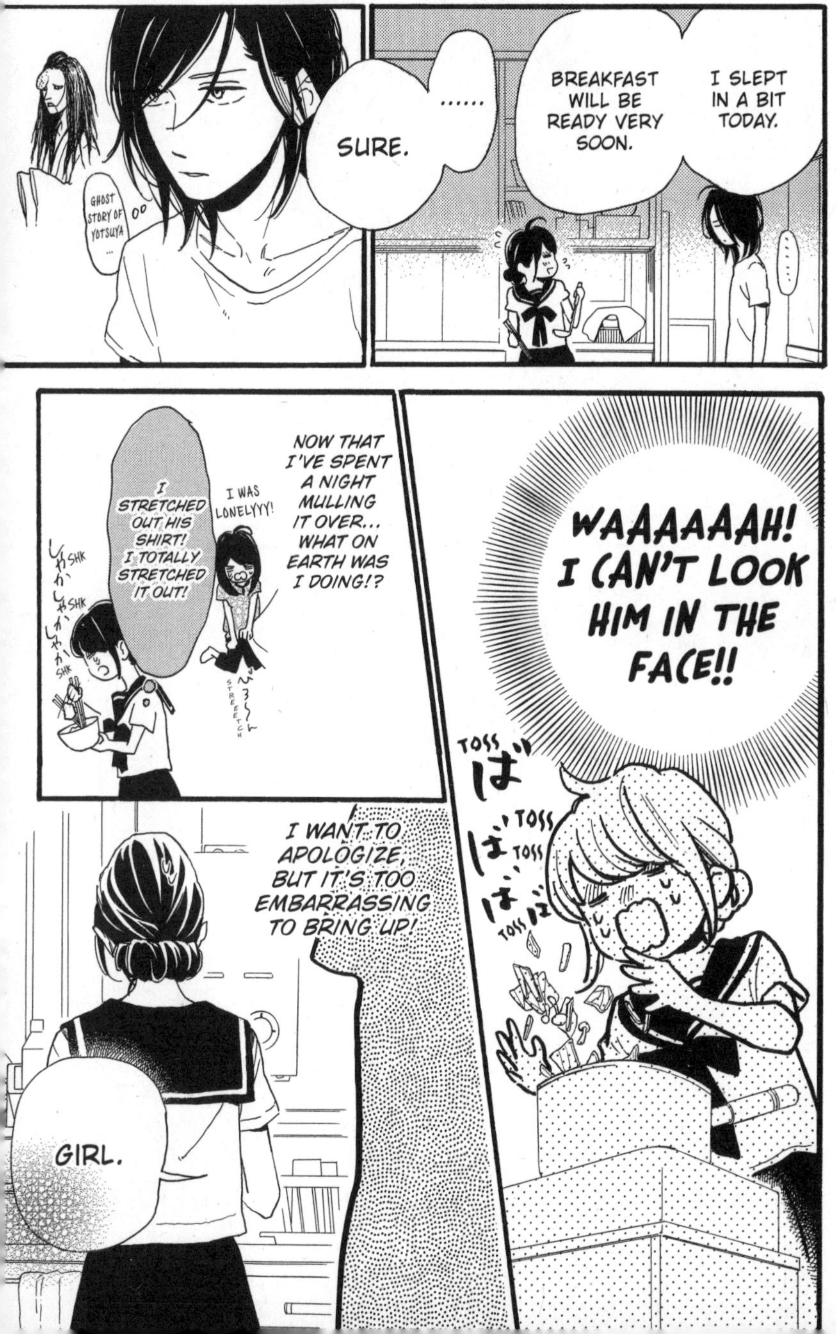
I SLEPT IN A BIT TODAY.
BREAKFAST WILL BE READY VERY SOON.
......
......
SURE.
GHOST STORY OF YOTSUYA...
WAAAAAAH! I CAN'T LOOK HIM IN THE FACE!!
TOSS
TOSS
TOSS
TOSS
NOW THAT I'VE SPENT A NIGHT MULLING IT OVER... WHAT ON EARTH WAS I DOING!?
I WAS LONELYYY!
STREEETCH
I STRETCHED OUT HIS SHIRT! I TOTALLY STRETCHED IT OUT!
SHK
SHK
SHK
I WANT TO APOLOGIZE, BUT IT'S TOO EMBARRASSING TO BRING UP!
GIRL.

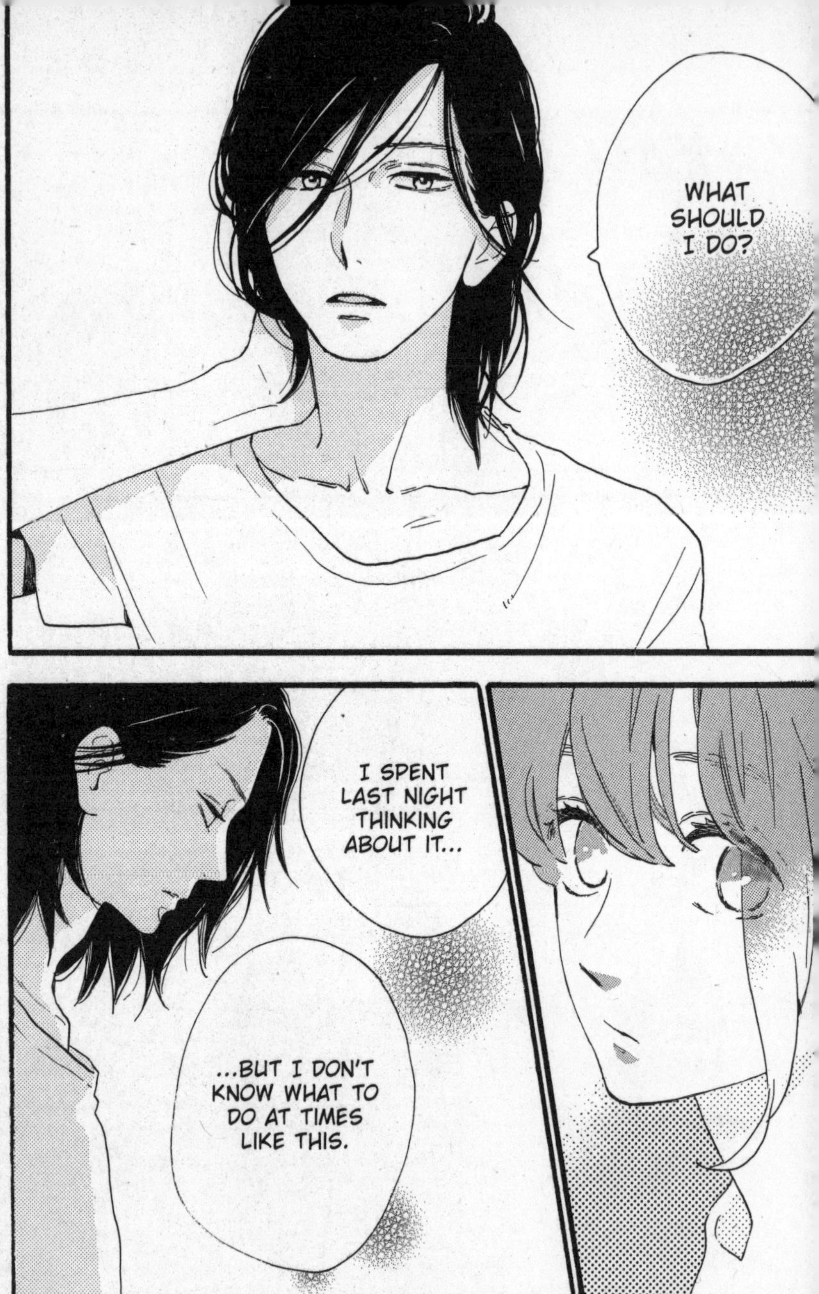
WHAT SHOULD I DO?
I SPENT LAST NIGHT THINKING ABOUT IT...
...BUT I DON'T KNOW WHAT TO DO AT TIMES LIKE THIS.

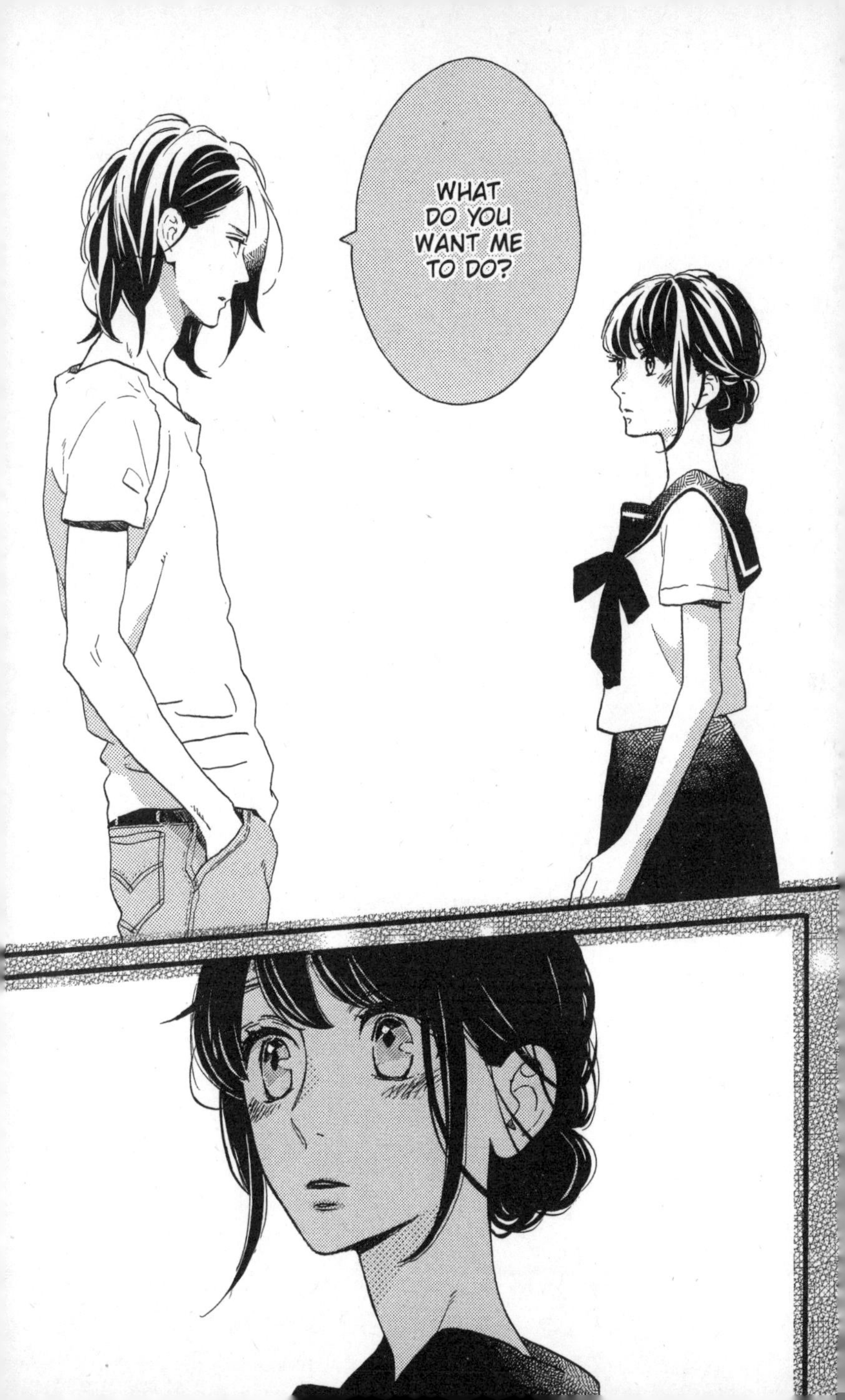
WHAT DO YOU WANT ME TO DO?

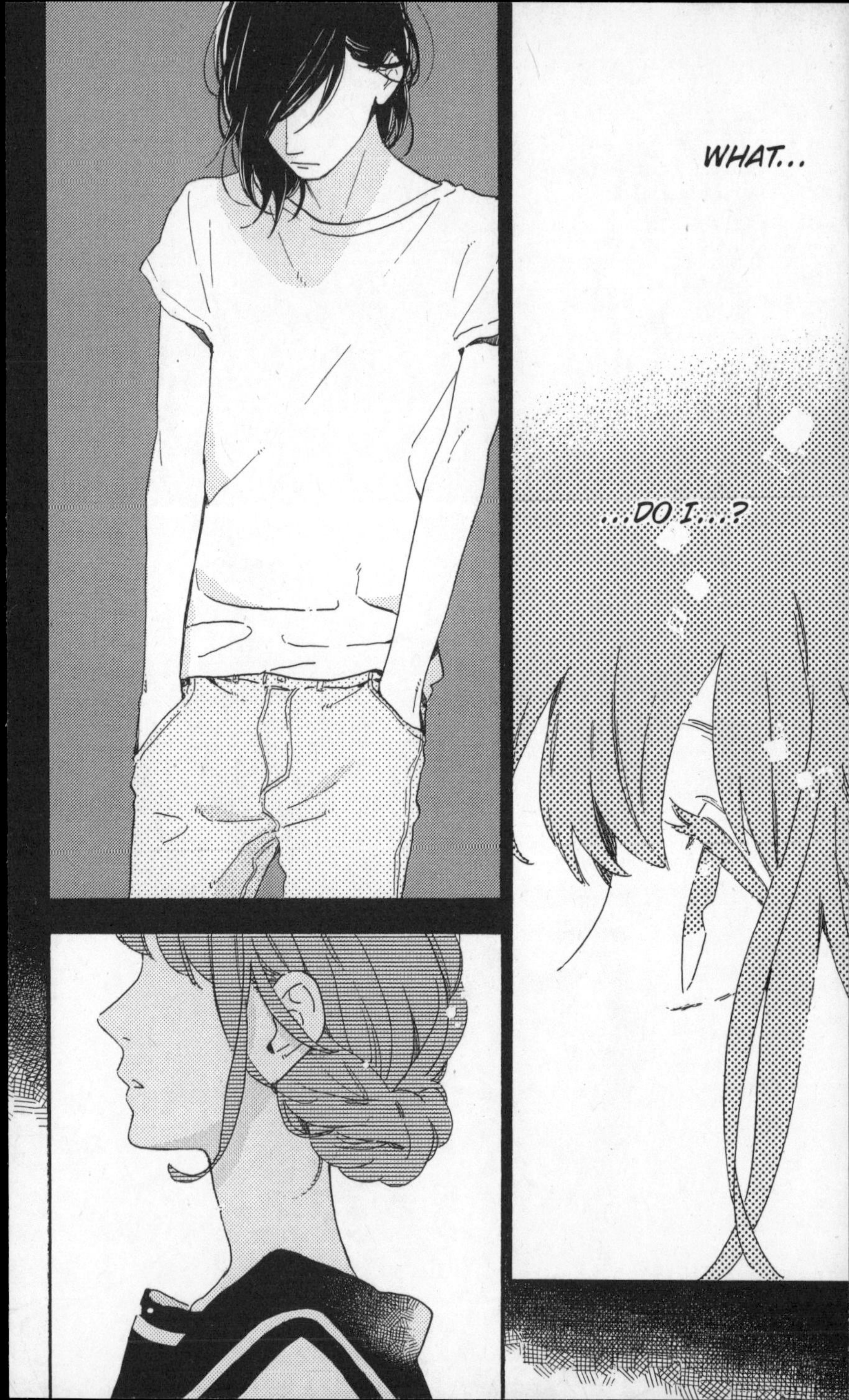
WHAT...
...DO I...?

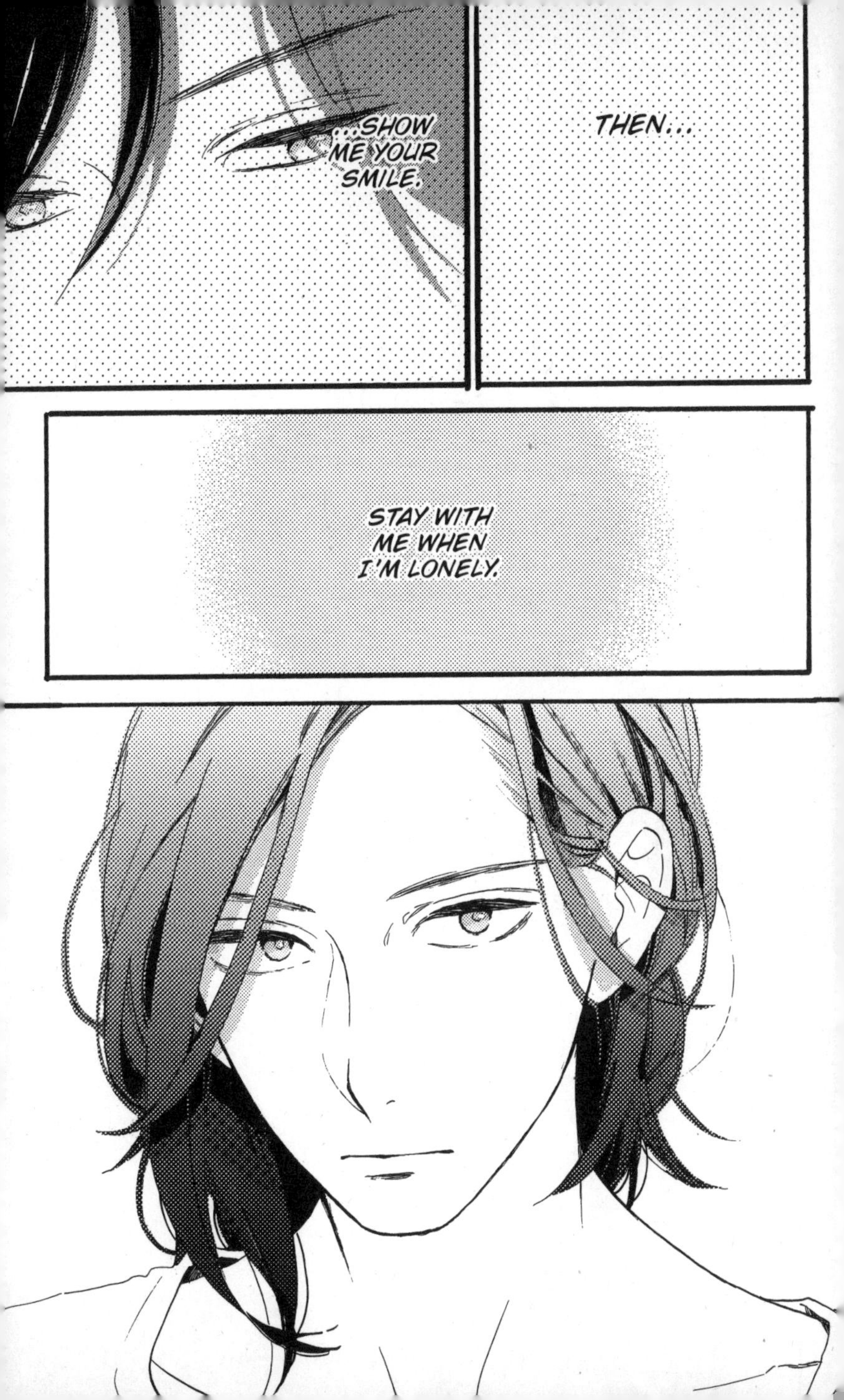
THEN...
...SHOW ME YOUR SMILE.
STAY WITH ME WHEN I'M LONELY.

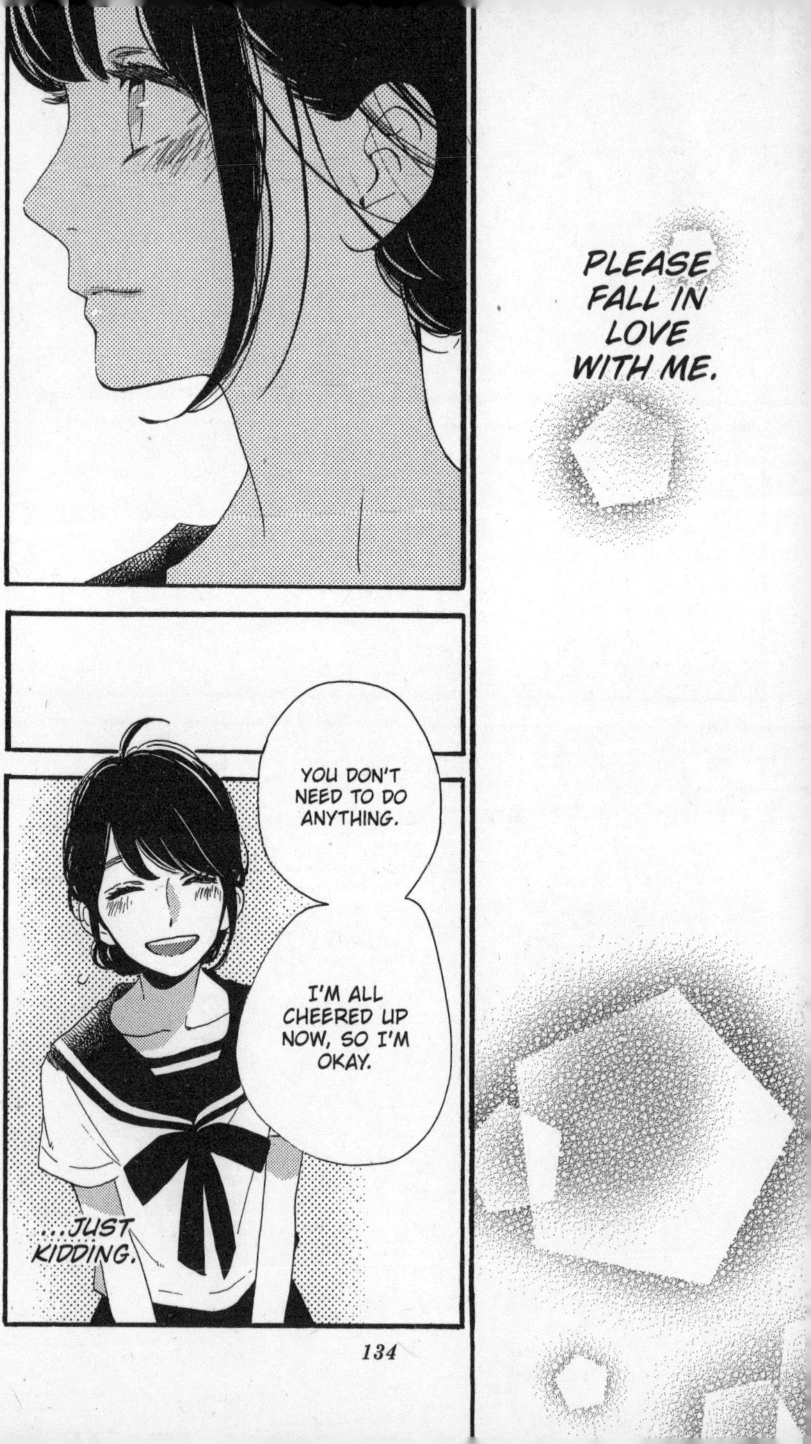
PLEASE FALL IN LOVE WITH ME.
YOU DON'T NEED TO DO ANYTHING.
I'M ALL CHEERED UP NOW, SO I'M OKAY.
...JUST KIDDING.

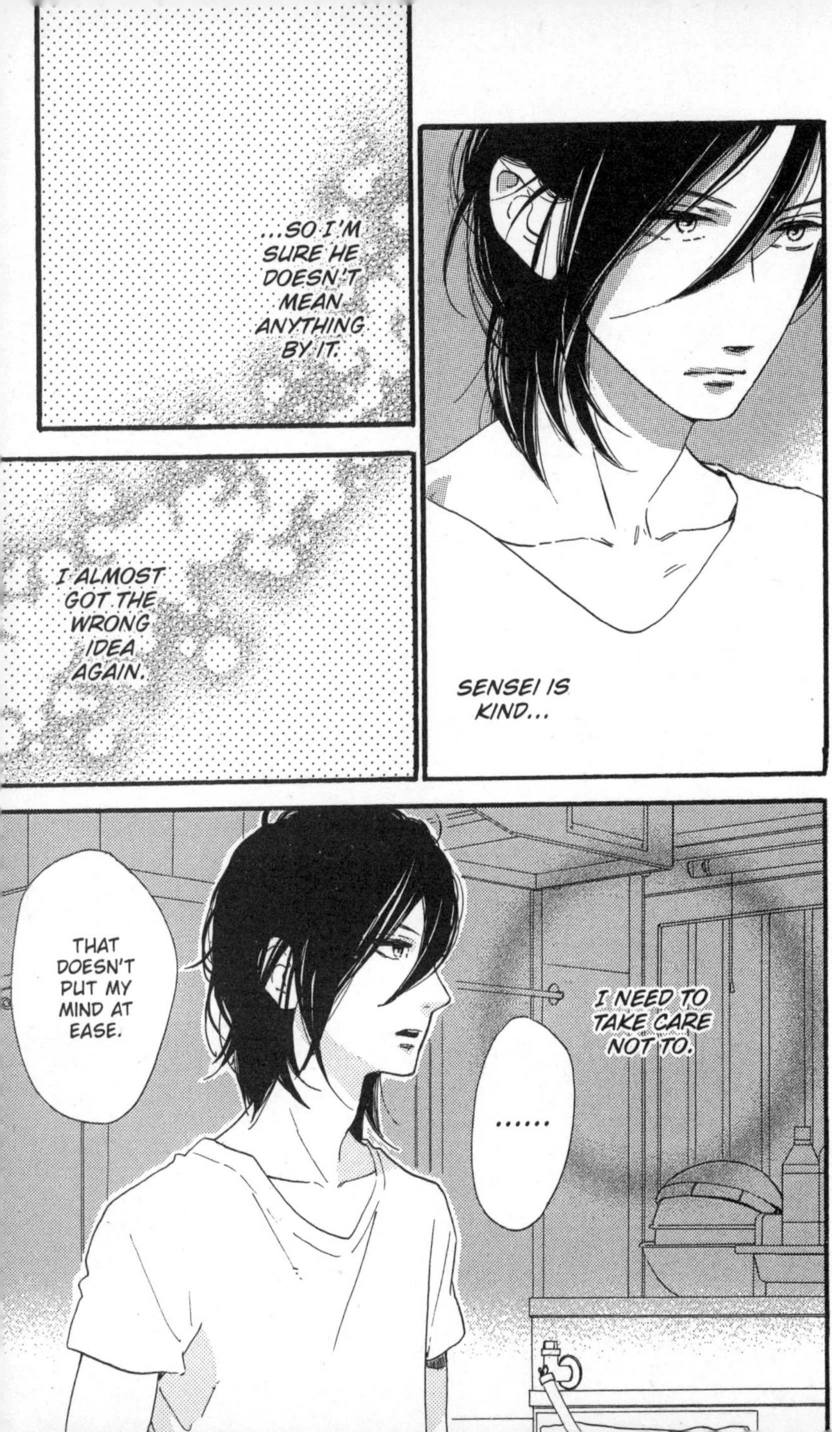
SENSEI IS KIND...
...SO I'M SURE HE DOESN'T MEAN ANYTHING BY IT.
I ALMOST GOT THE WRONG IDEA AGAIN.
I NEED TO TAKE CARE NOT TO.
......
THAT DOESN'T PUT MY MIND AT EASE.

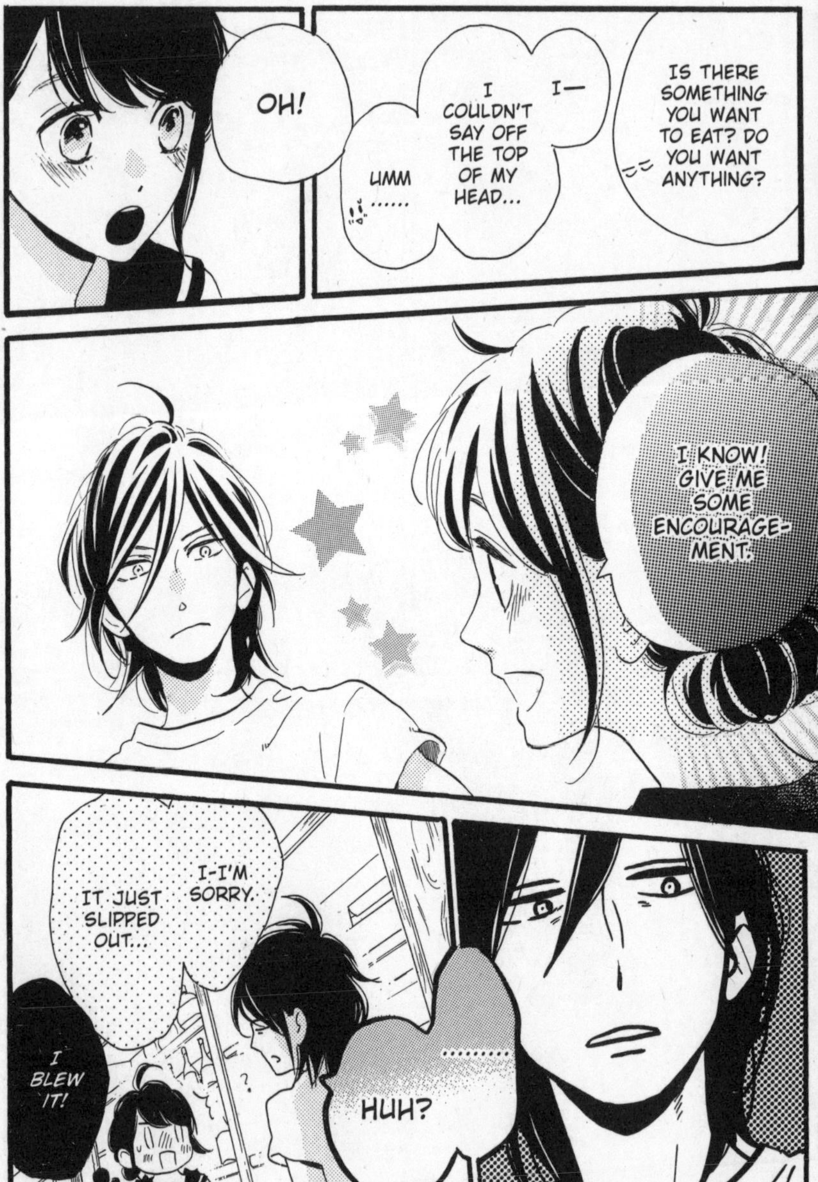
IS THERE SOMETHING YOU WANT TO EAT? DO YOU WANT ANYTHING?
I—
I COULDN'T SAY OFF THE TOP OF MY HEAD...
UMM ......
OH!
I KNOW! GIVE ME SOME ENCOURAGE-MENT.
....
HUH?
I-I'M SORRY.
IT JUST SLIPPED OUT...
I BLEW IT!

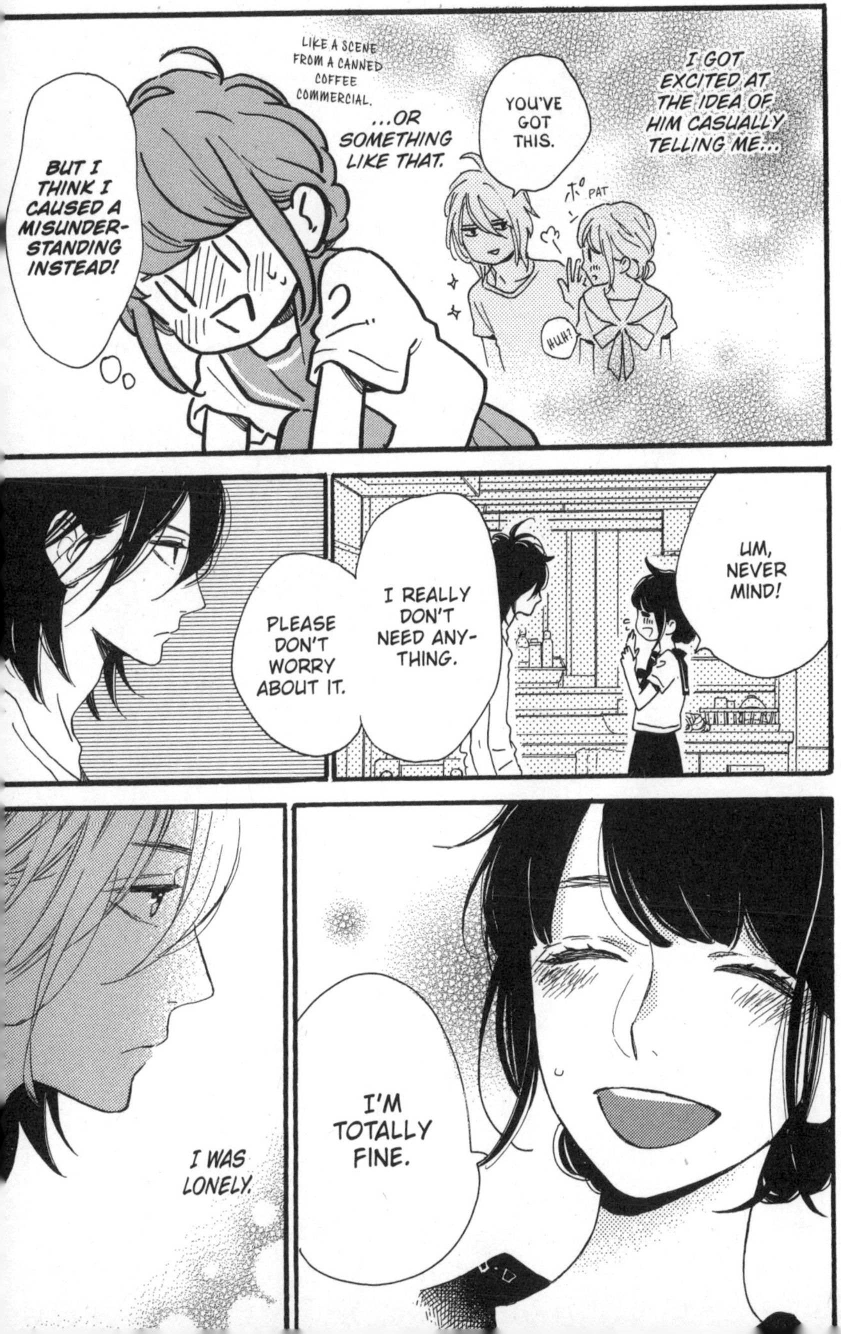
I GOT EXCITED AT THE IDEA OF HIM CASUALLY TELLING ME...
YOU'VE GOT THIS.
PAT
HUH?
...OR SOMETHING LIKE THAT.
LIKE A SCENE FROM A CANNED COFFEE COMMERCIAL.
BUT I THINK I CAUSED A MISUNDERSTANDING INSTEAD!
UM, NEVER MIND!
I REALLY DON'T NEED ANYTHING.
PLEASE DON'T WORRY ABOUT IT.
I'M TOTALLY FINE.
I WAS LONELY.

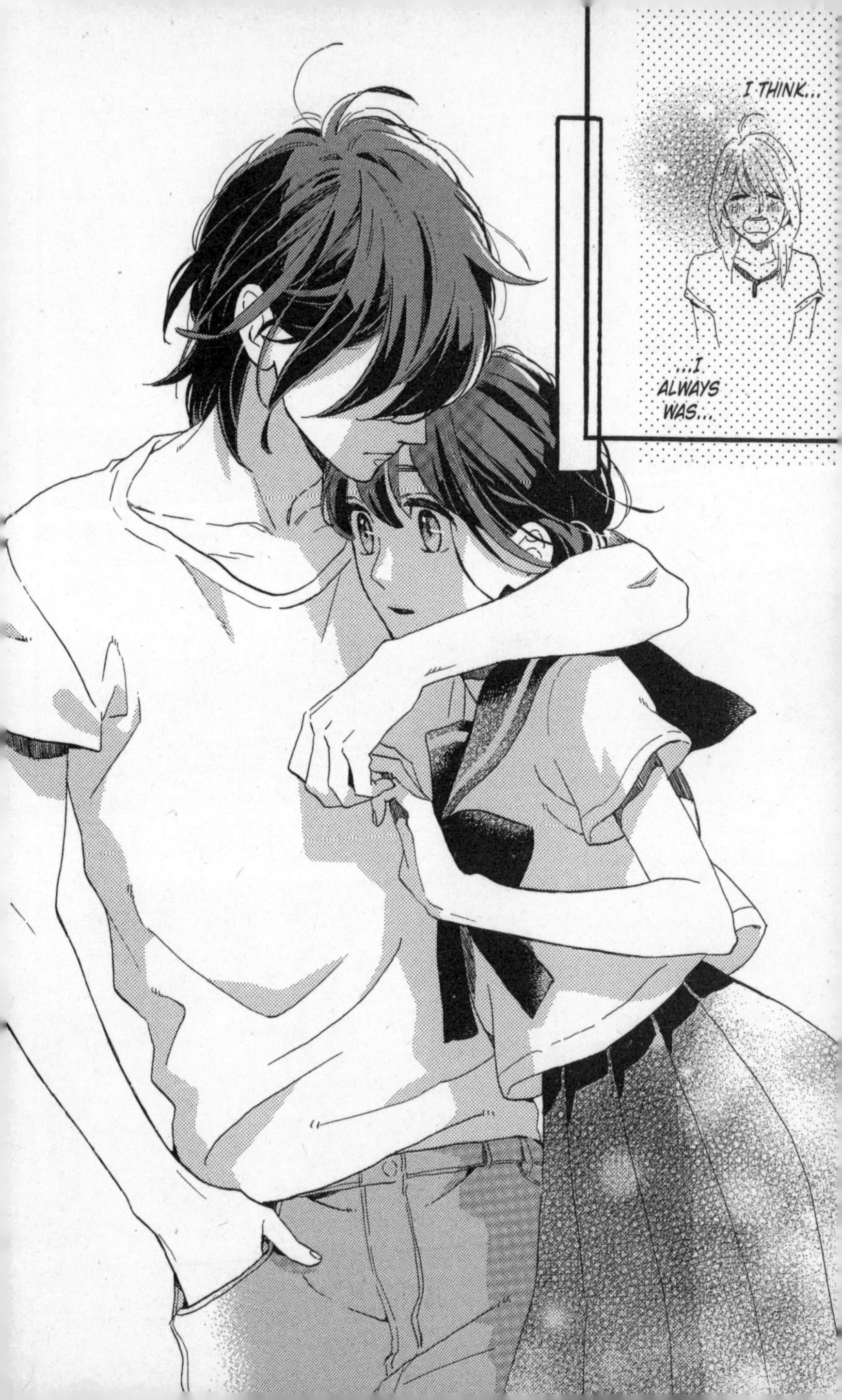
I THINK...
...I ALWAYS WAS...

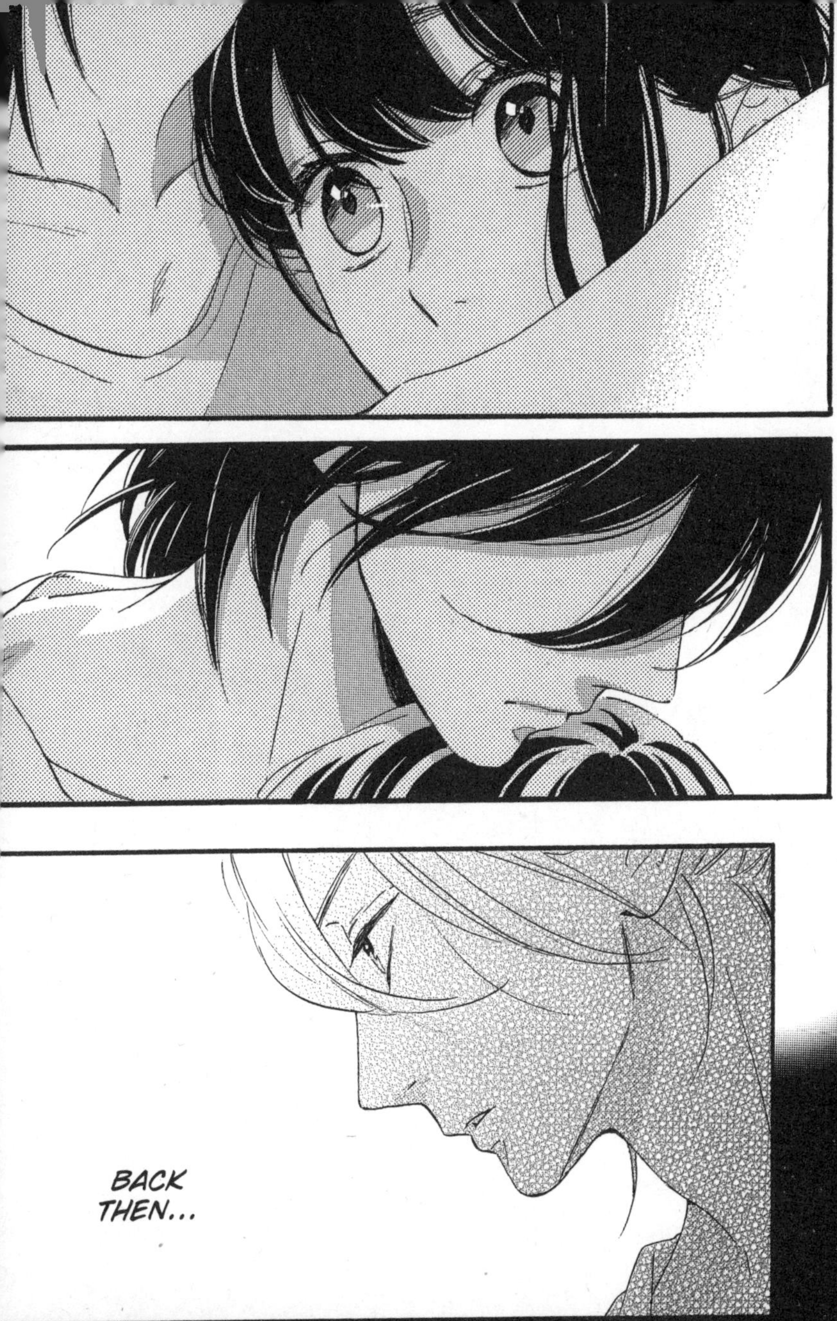
BACK THEN...

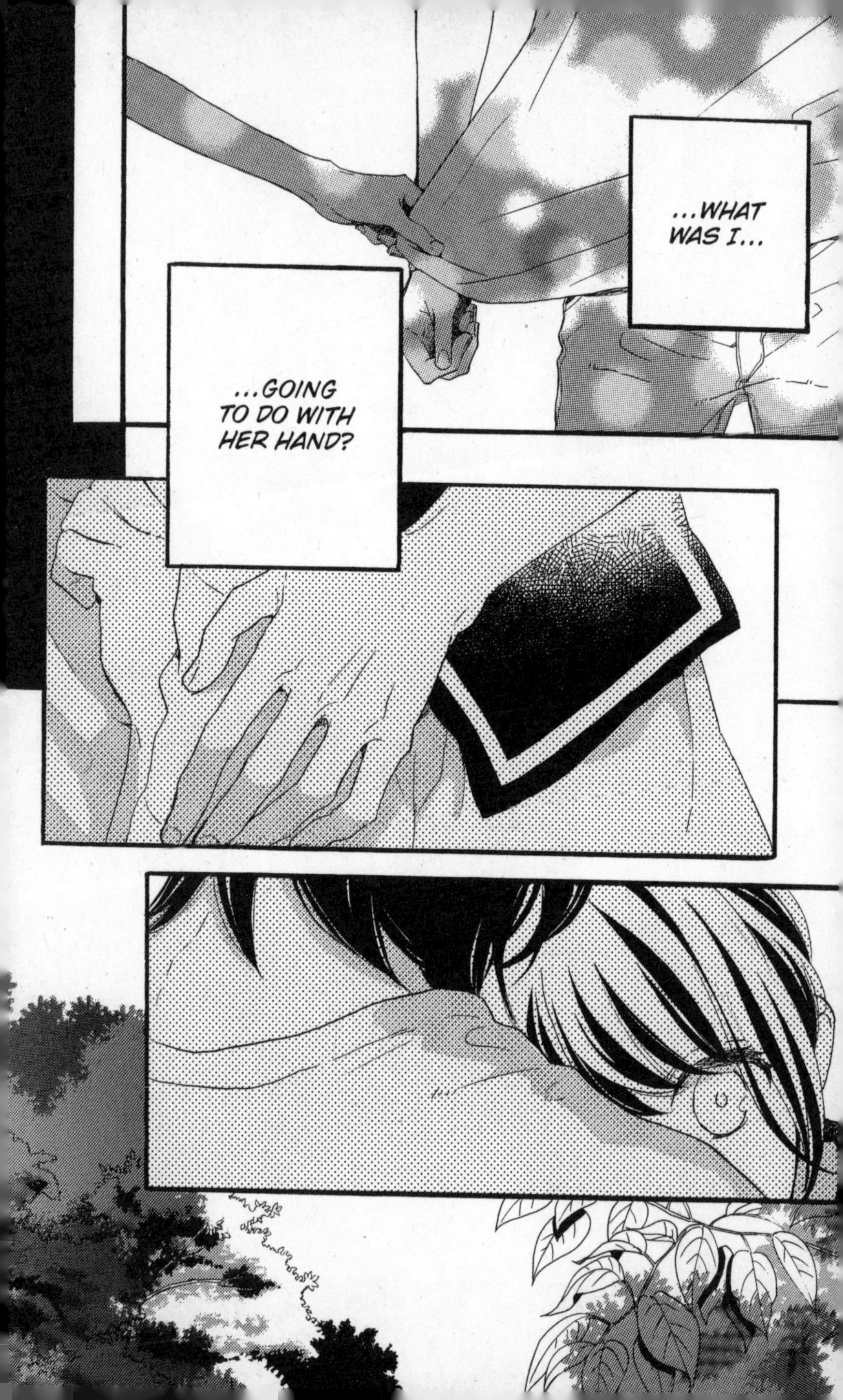
...WHAT WAS I...
...GOING TO DO WITH HER HAND?

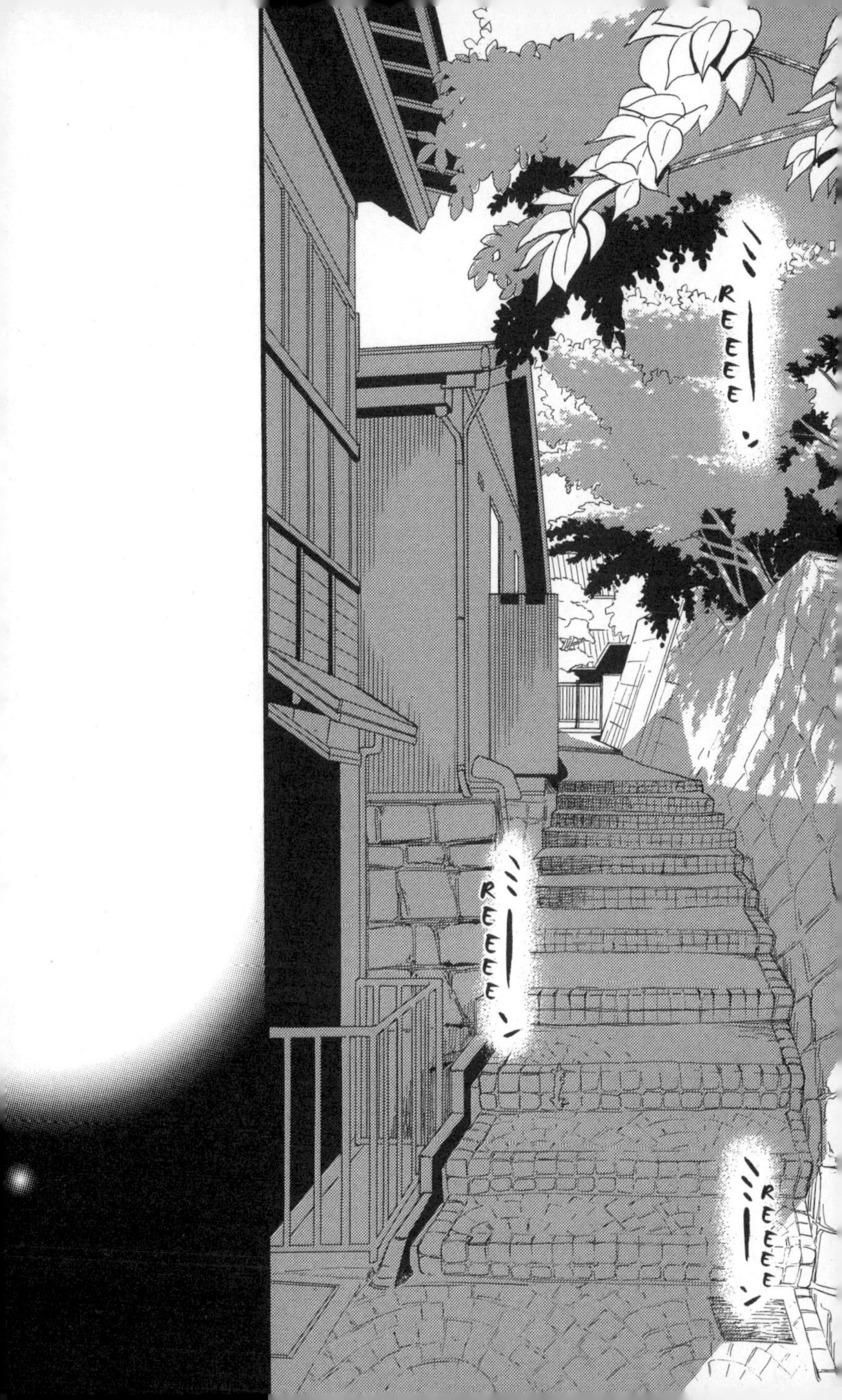
REEEE
REEEE
REEEE

ALL
STRETCHED
OUT

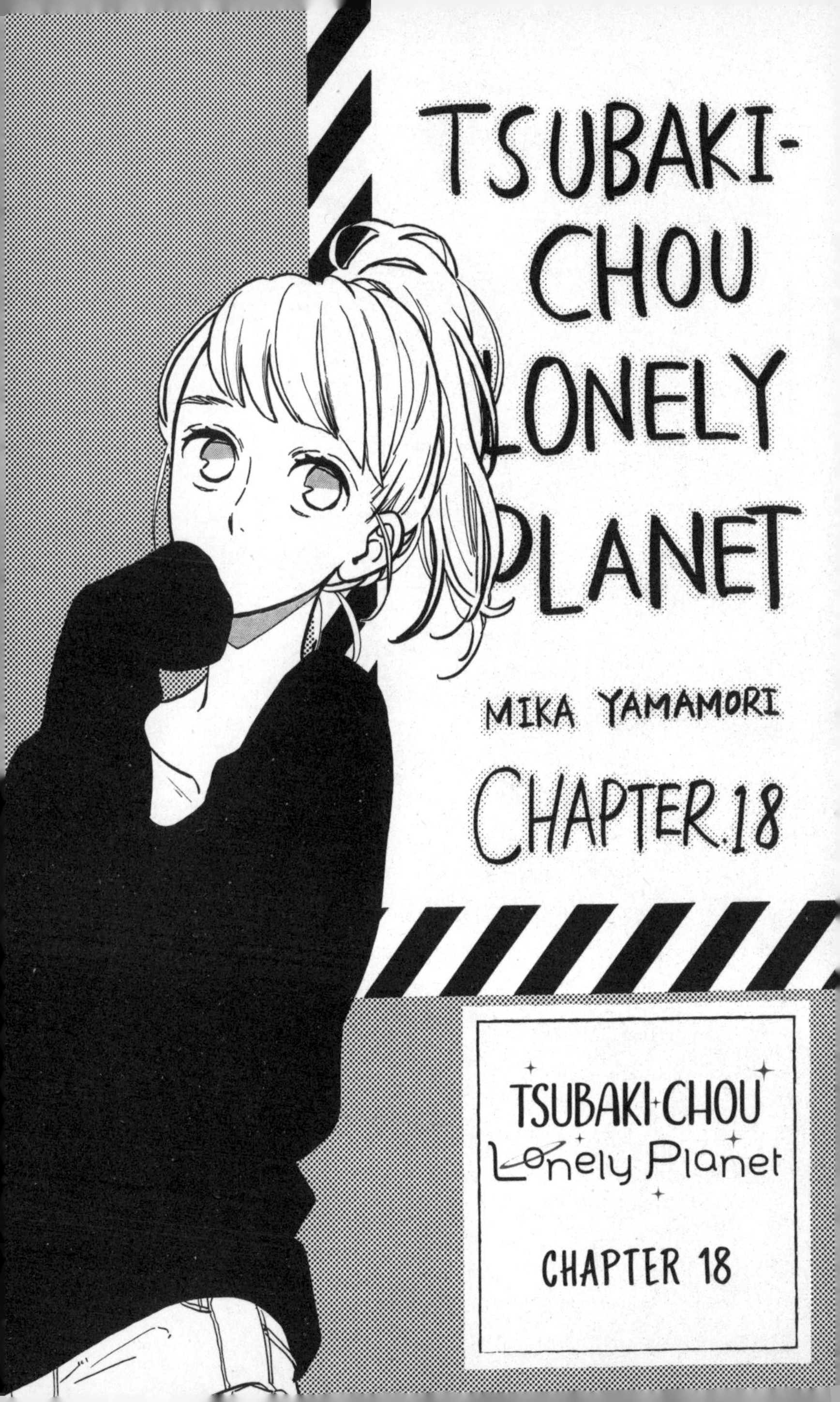
TSUBAKI-CHOU LONELY PLANET
MIKA YAMAMORI
CHAPTER.18
TSUBAKI-CHOU Lonely Planet
CHAPTER 18

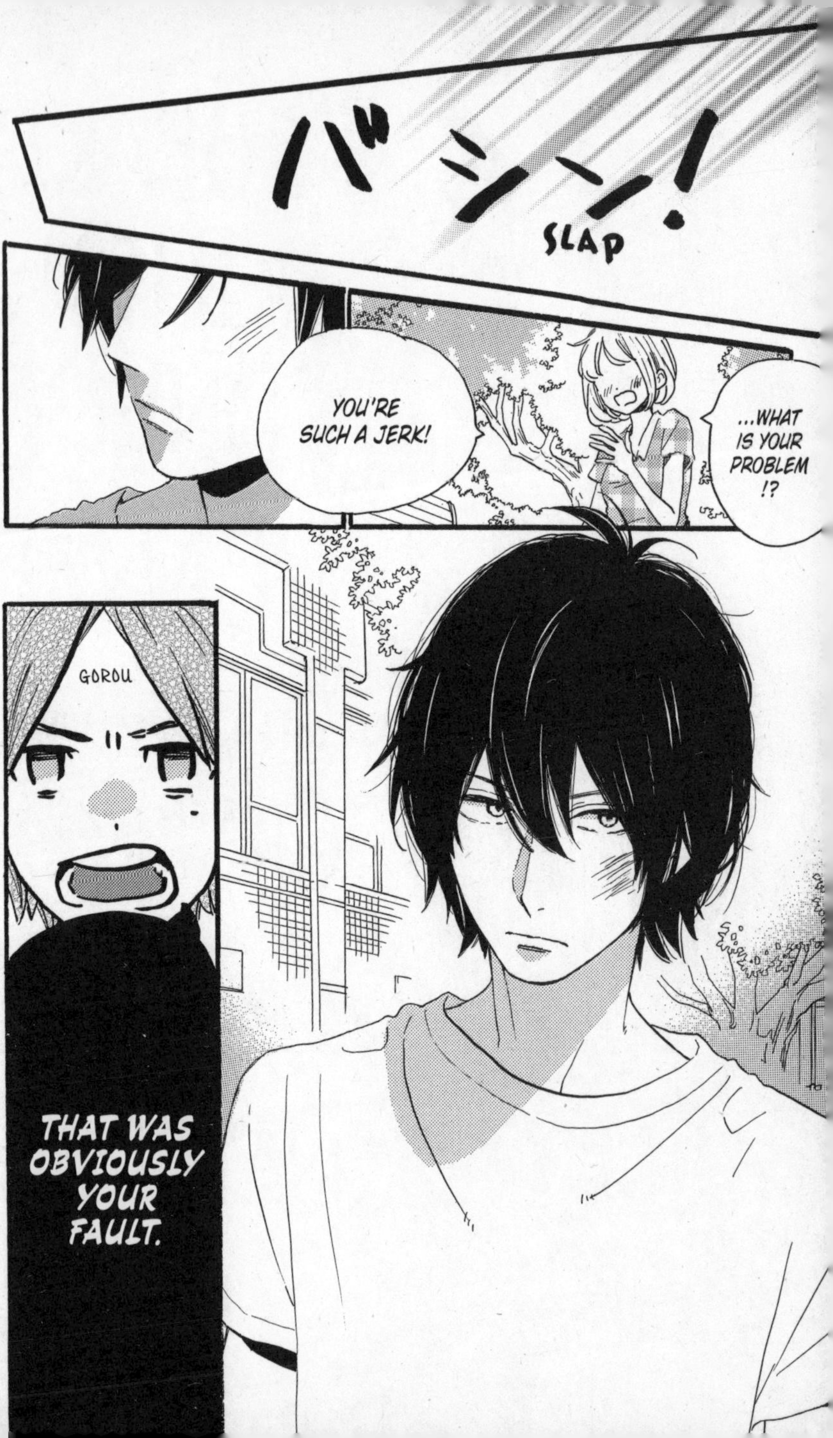
バシーン!
SLAP
...WHAT IS YOUR PROBLEM !?
YOU'RE SUCH A JERK!
GOROU
THAT WAS OBVIOUSLY YOUR FAULT.

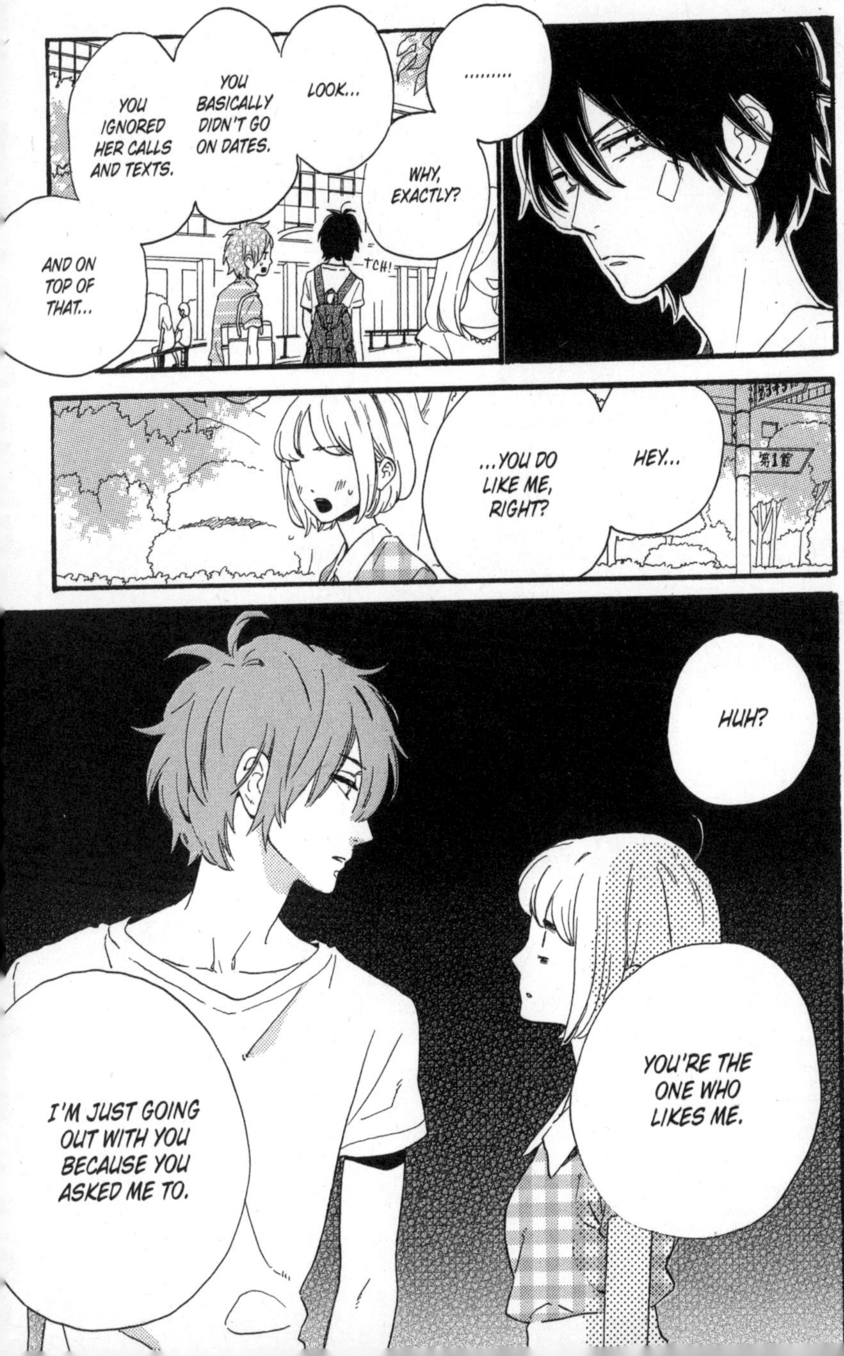
LOOK...
WHY, EXACTLY?
YOU BASICALLY DIDN'T GO ON DATES.
YOU IGNORED HER CALLS AND TEXTS.
AND ON TOP OF THAT...
TCH!
....
HEY...
...YOU DO LIKE ME, RIGHT?
第1館
HUH?
YOU'RE THE ONE WHO LIKES ME.
I'M JUST GOING OUT WITH YOU BECAUSE YOU ASKED ME TO.

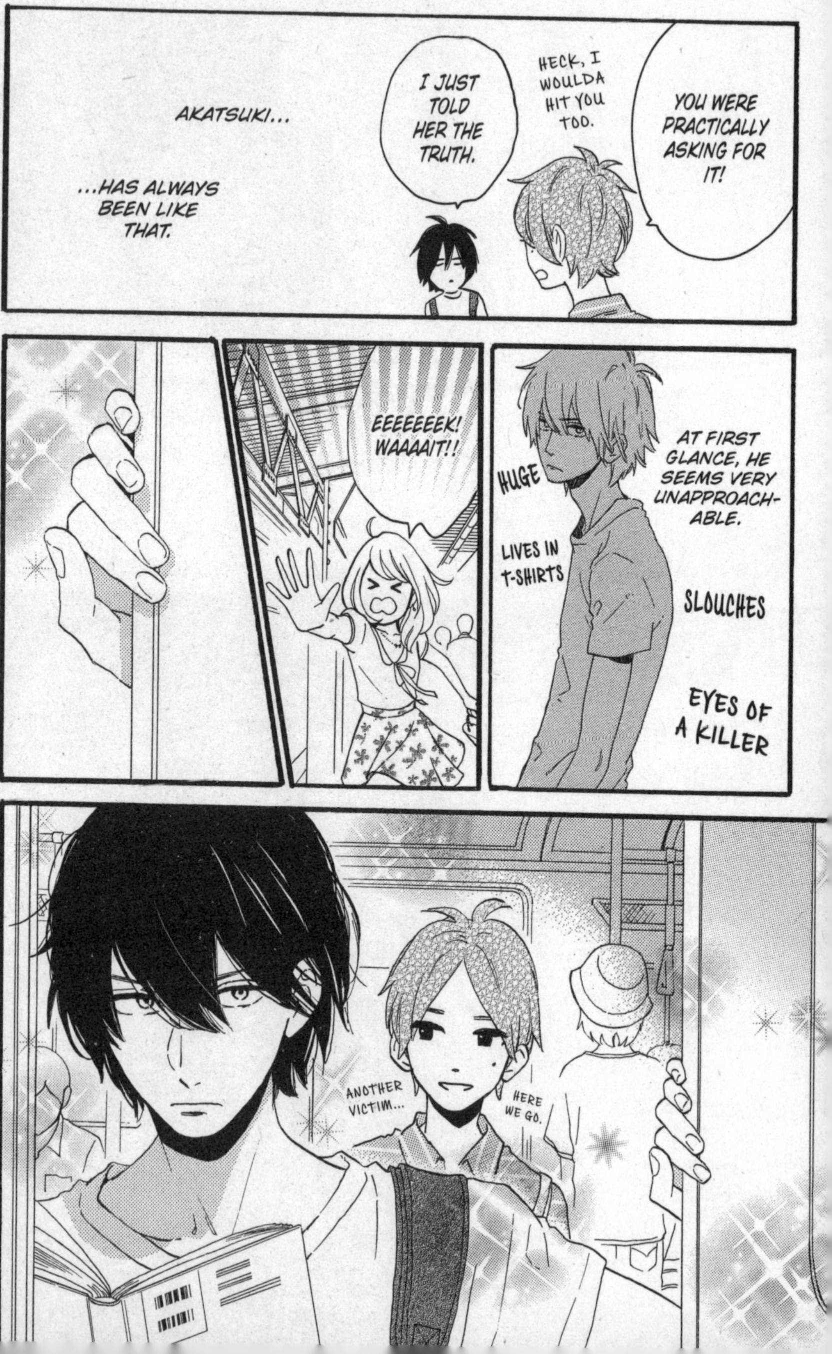
YOU WERE PRACTICALLY ASKING FOR IT!
HECK, I WOULDA HIT YOU TOO.
I JUST TOLD HER THE TRUTH.
AKATSUKI...
...HAS ALWAYS BEEN LIKE THAT.
AT FIRST GLANCE, HE SEEMS VERY UNAPPROACH-ABLE.
HUGE
LIVES IN T-SHIRTS
SLOUCHES
EYES OF A KILLER
EEEEEEEK! WAAAAIT!!
HERE WE GO.
ANOTHER VICTIM...

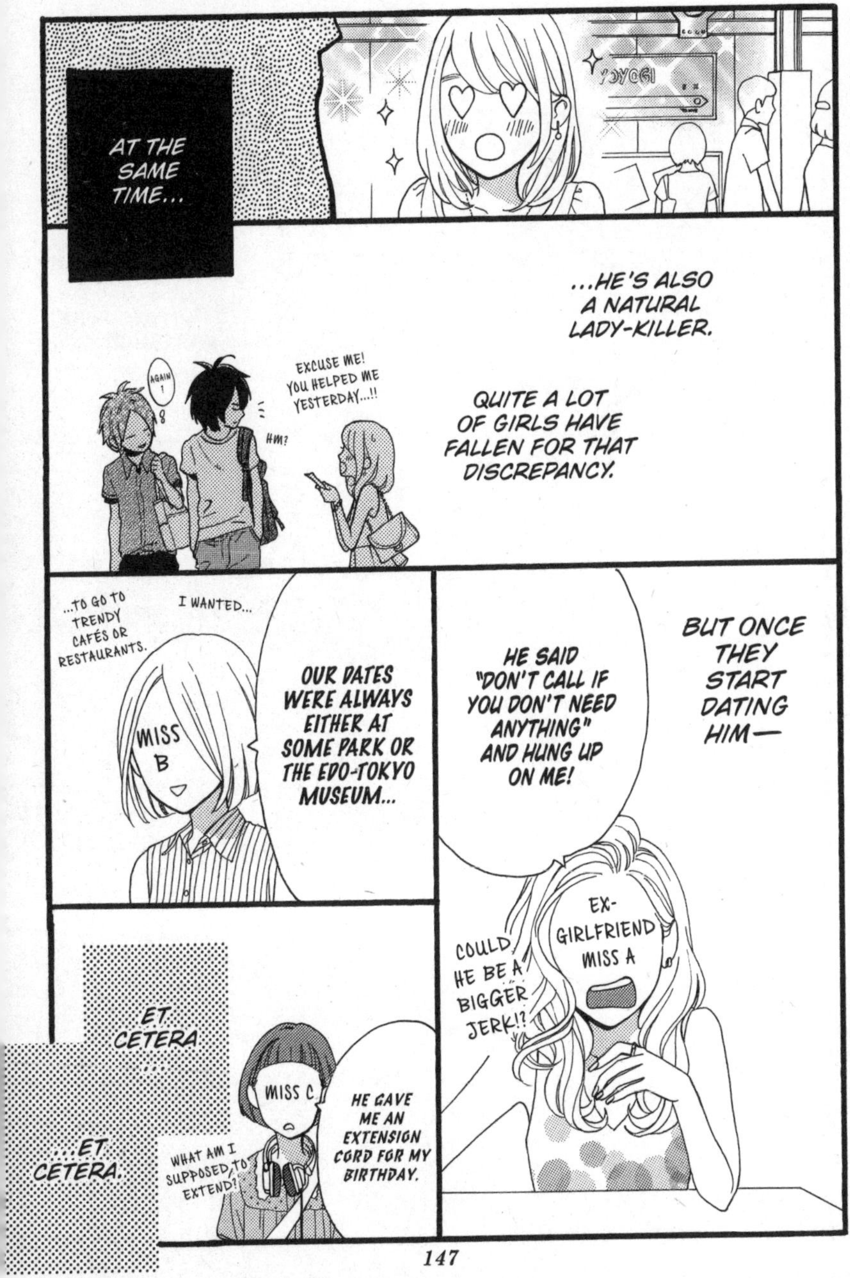
AT THE SAME TIME...
...HE'S ALSO A NATURAL LADY-KILLER.
QUITE A LOT OF GIRLS HAVE FALLEN FOR THAT DISCREPANCY.
EXCUSE ME! YOU HELPED ME YESTERDAY...!!
HM?
AGAIN!
BUT ONCE THEY START DATING HIM—
HE SAID "DON'T CALL IF YOU DON'T NEED ANYTHING" AND HUNG UP ON ME!
EX-GIRLFRIEND MISS A
COULD HE BE A BIGGER JERK!?
OUR DATES WERE ALWAYS EITHER AT SOME PARK OR THE EDO-TOKYO MUSEUM...
I WANTED...
...TO GO TO TRENDY CAFÉS OR RESTAURANTS.
MISS B
HE GAVE ME AN EXTENSION CORD FOR MY BIRTHDAY.
MISS C
WHAT AM I SUPPOSED TO EXTEND?
ET CETERA...
...ET CETERA.

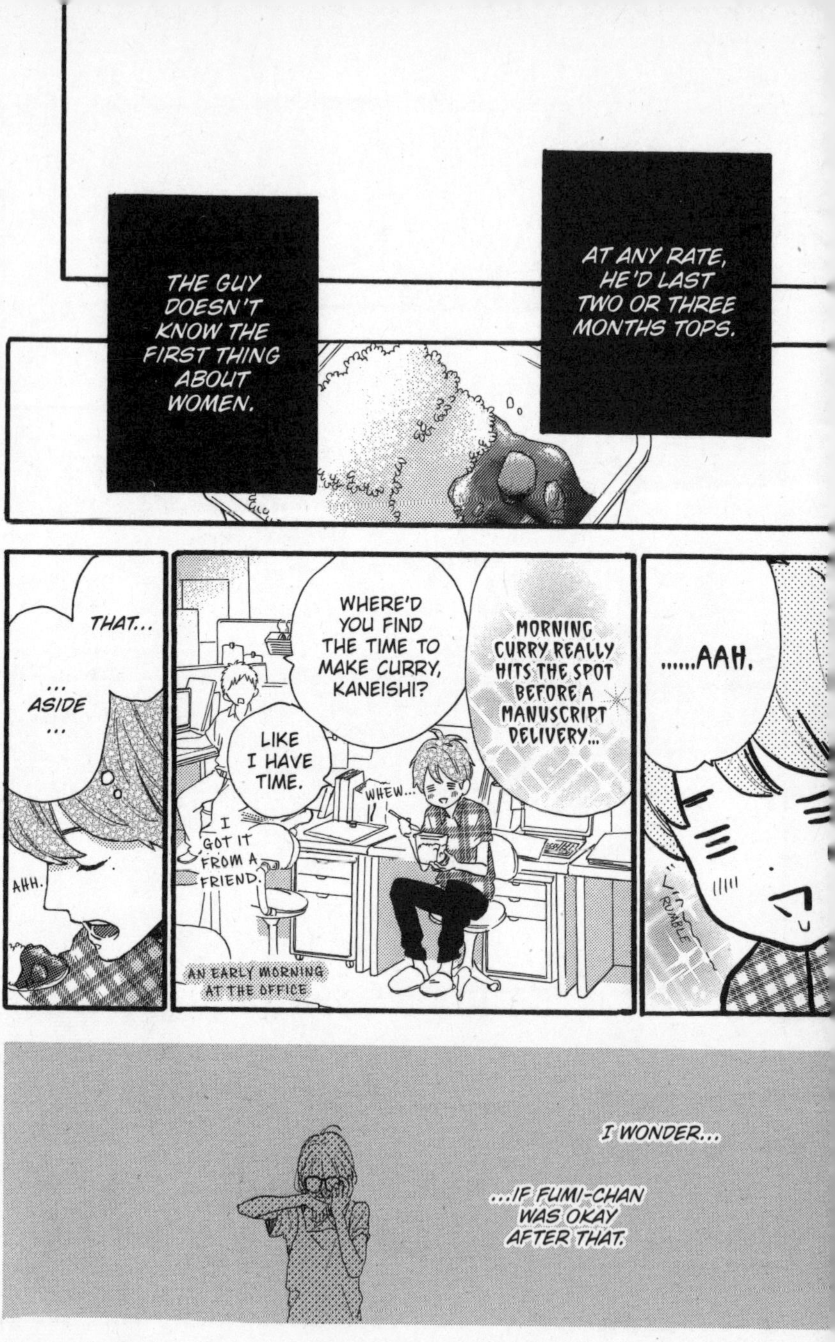
AT ANY RATE, HE'D LAST TWO OR THREE MONTHS TOPS.
THE GUY DOESN'T KNOW THE FIRST THING ABOUT WOMEN.
......AAH.
RUMBLE
MORNING CURRY REALLY HITS THE SPOT BEFORE A MANUSCRIPT DELIVERY...
WHERE'D YOU FIND THE TIME TO MAKE CURRY, KANEISHI?
LIKE I HAVE TIME.
WHEW...
I GOT IT FROM A FRIEND.
AN EARLY MORNING AT THE OFFICE
THAT...
...ASIDE...
AHH.
I WONDER...
...IF FUMI-CHAN WAS OKAY AFTER THAT.

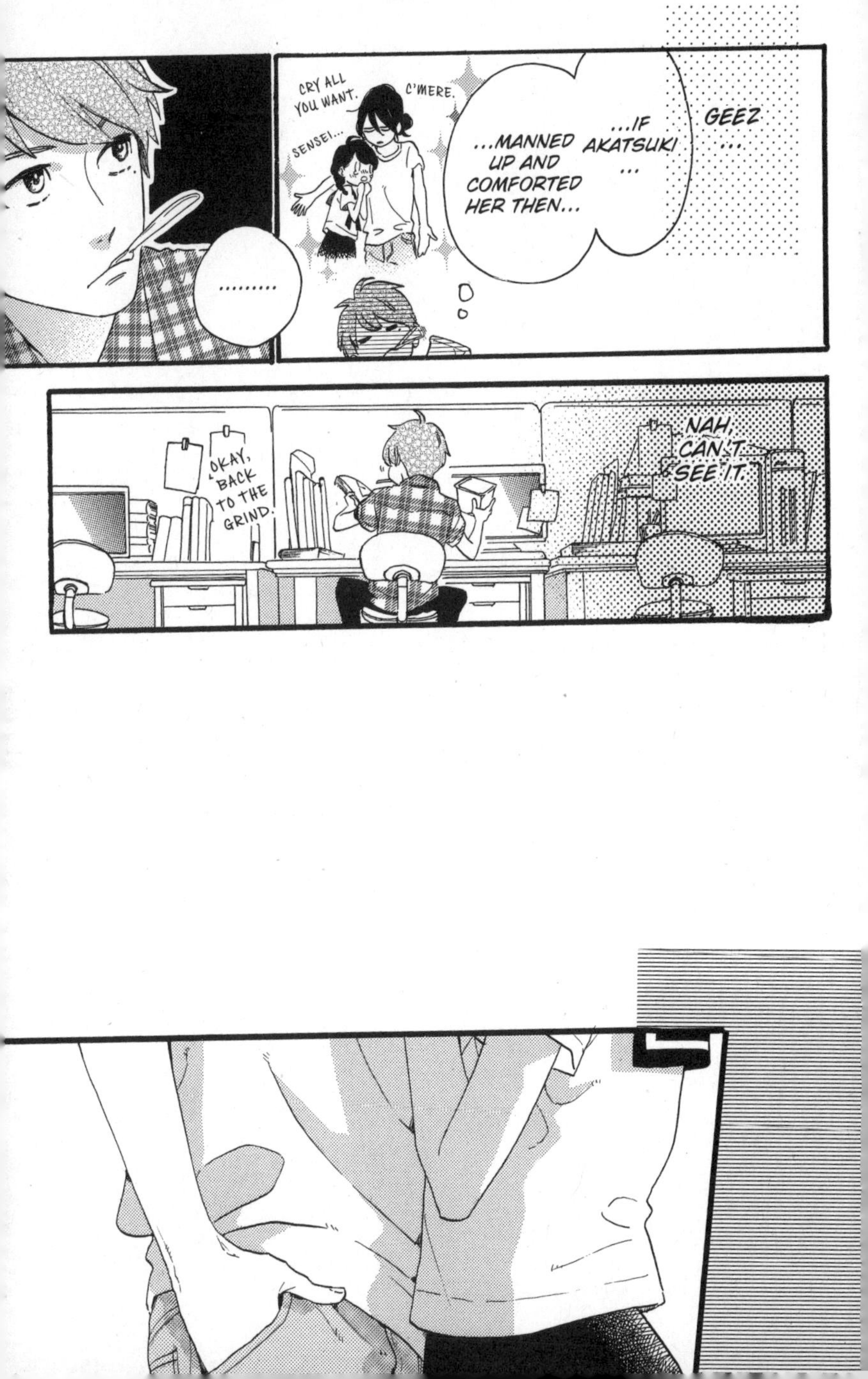
GEEZ...
...IF AKATSUKI...
...MANNED UP AND COMFORTED HER THEN...
C'MERE.
CRY ALL YOU WANT.
SENSEI...
....
NAH, CAN'T SEE IT.
OKAY, BACK TO THE GRIND.

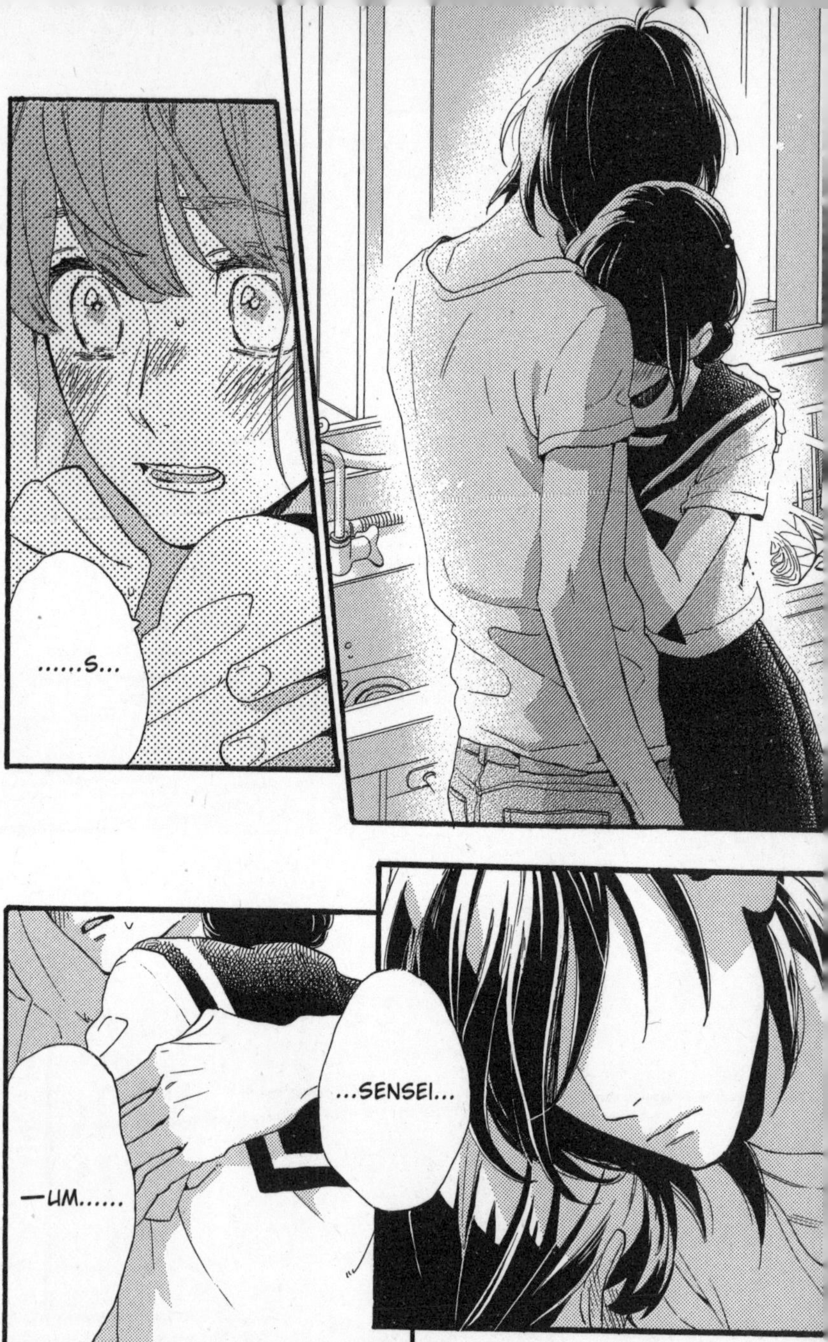
......S...
...SENSEI...
—UM......

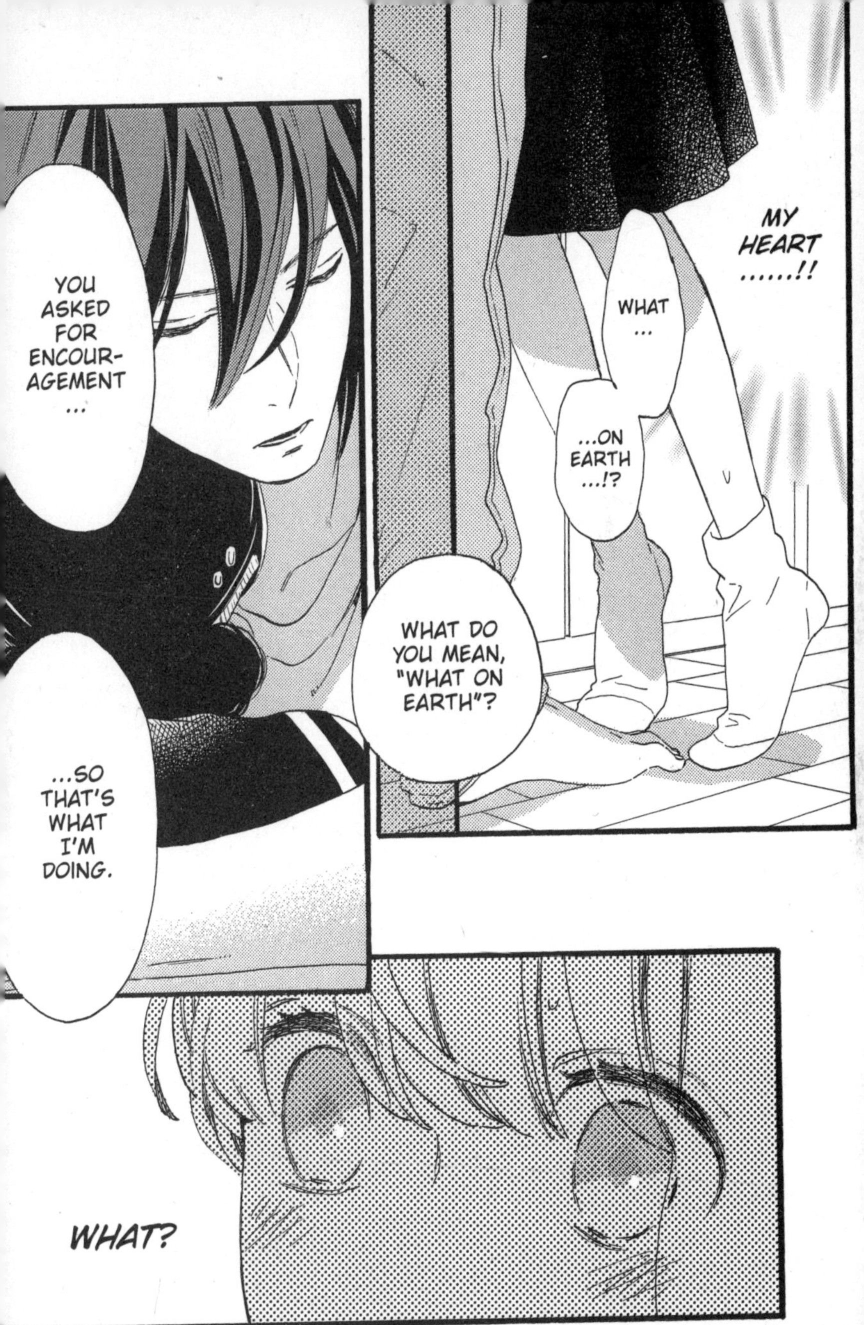
MY HEART ......!!
WHAT ...
...ON EARTH ...!?
WHAT DO YOU MEAN, "WHAT ON EARTH"?
YOU ASKED FOR ENCOURAGEMENT ...
...SO THAT'S WHAT I'M DOING.
WHAT?

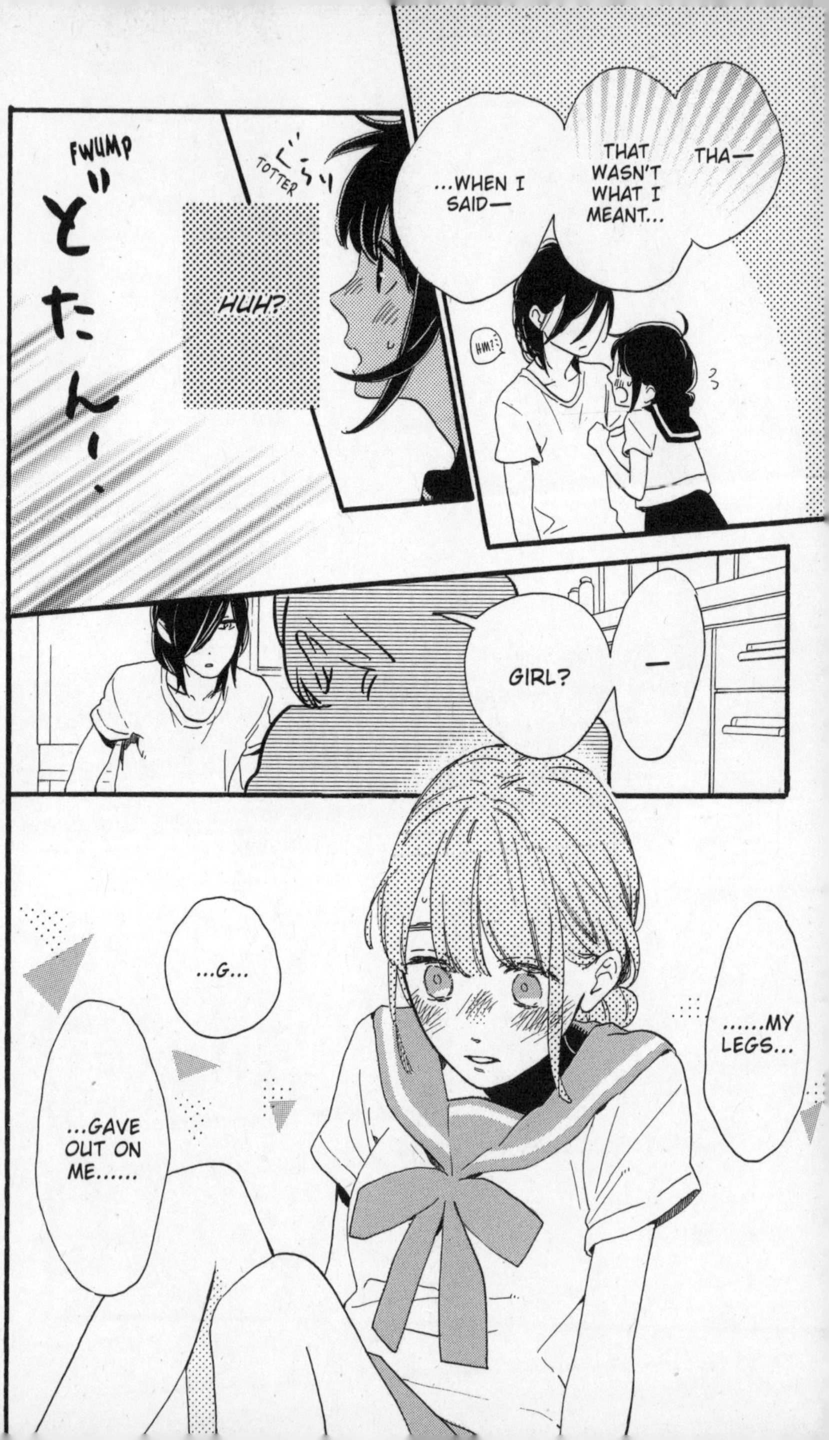
THA—
THAT WASN'T WHAT I MEANT...
...WHEN I SAID—
HM?
ぐらり
TOTTER
HUH?
FWUMP
どたん
—
GIRL?
......MY LEGS...
...G...
...GAVE OUT ON ME......

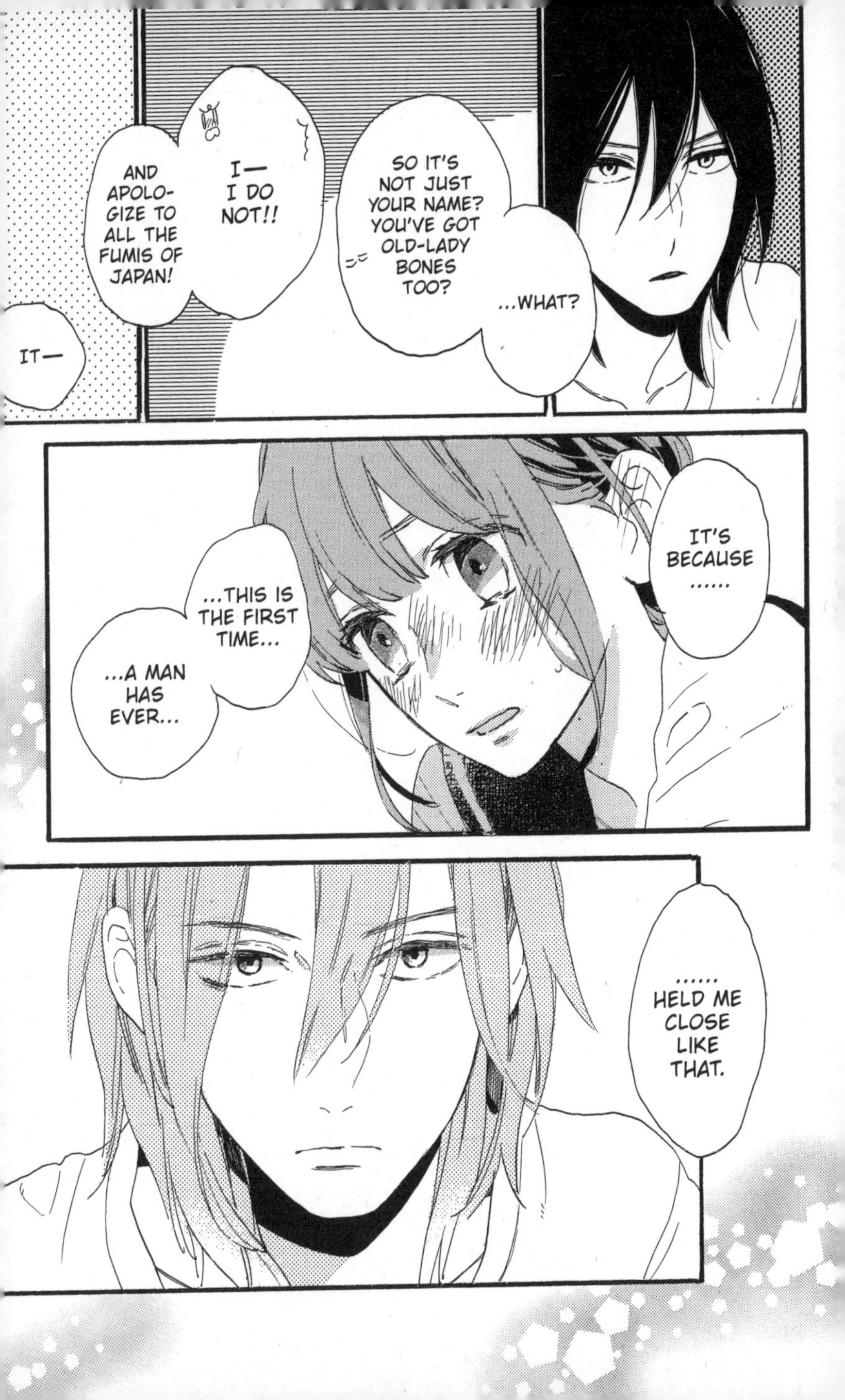
...WHAT?
SO IT'S NOT JUST YOUR NAME? YOU'VE GOT OLD-LADY BONES TOO?
I— I DO NOT!!
AND APOLO-GIZE TO ALL THE FUMIS OF JAPAN!
IT—
IT'S BECAUSE ......
...THIS IS THE FIRST TIME...
...A MAN HAS EVER...
...... HELD ME CLOSE LIKE THAT.

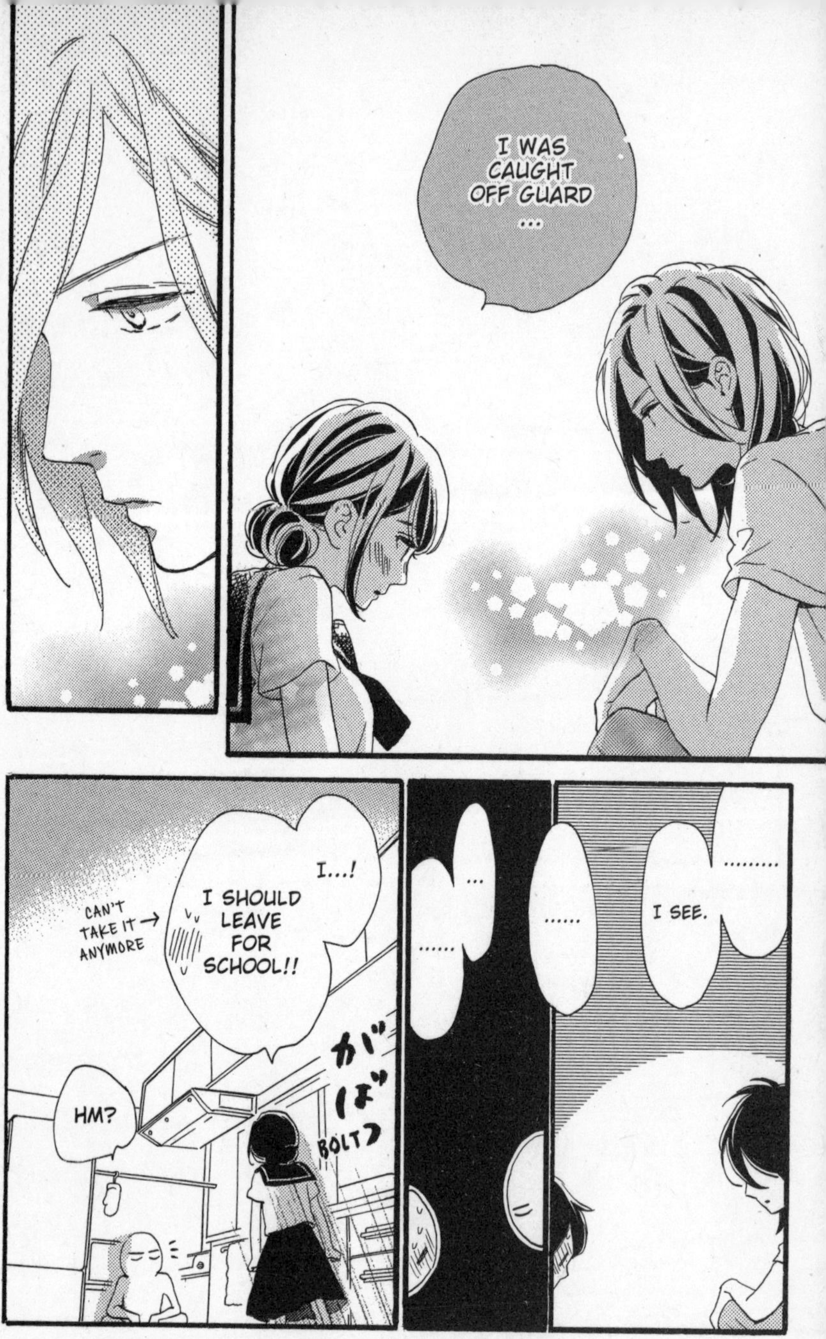
I WAS CAUGHT OFF GUARD ...
....
I SEE.
......
...
......
I...! I SHOULD LEAVE FOR SCHOOL!!
CAN'T TAKE IT → ANYMORE
がばっ
BOLT
HM?

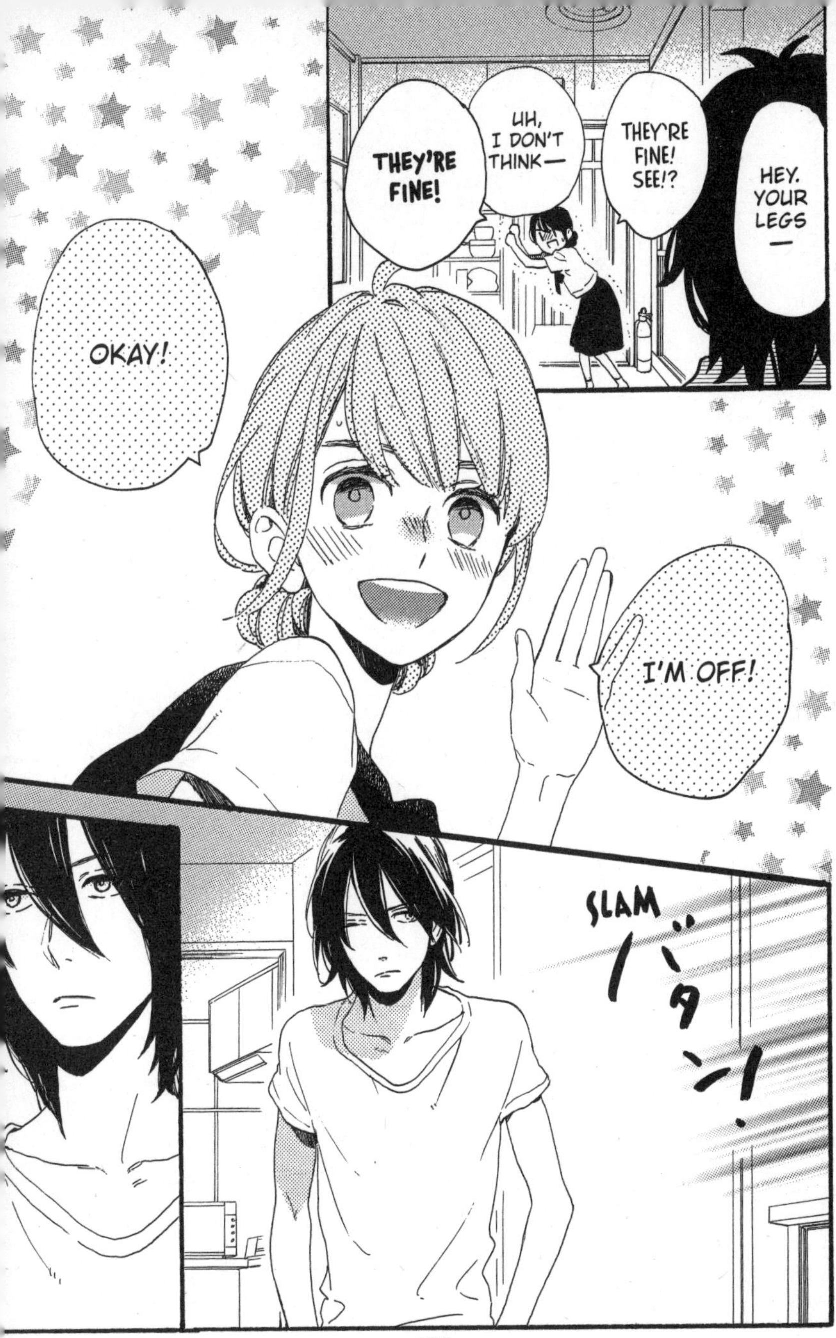
HEY. YOUR LEGS—
THEY'RE FINE! SEE!?
UH, I DON'T THINK—
THEY'RE FINE!
OKAY!
I'M OFF!
SLAM
バタン!

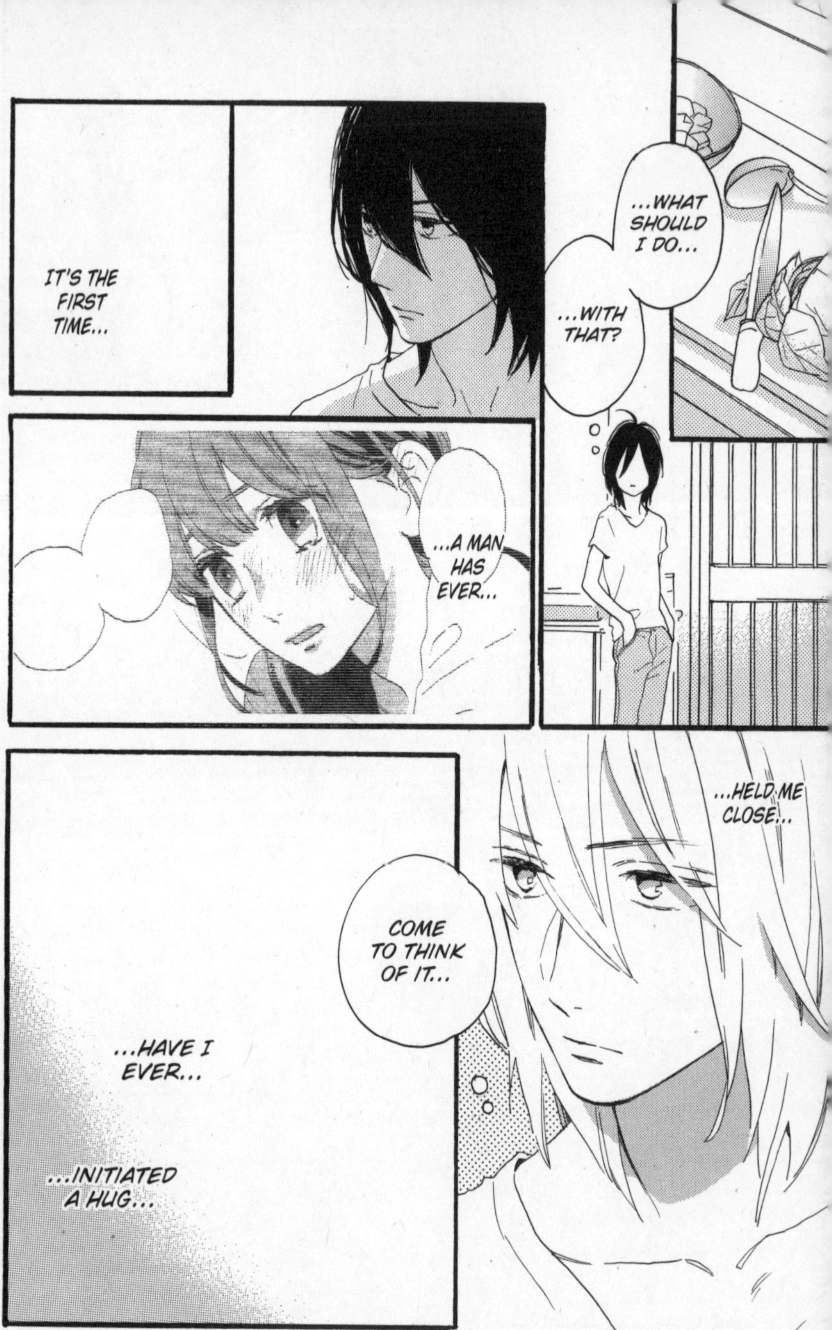
...WHAT SHOULD I DO...
...WITH THAT?
IT'S THE FIRST TIME...
...A MAN HAS EVER...
...HELD ME CLOSE...
COME TO THINK OF IT...
...HAVE I EVER...
...INITIATED A HUG...

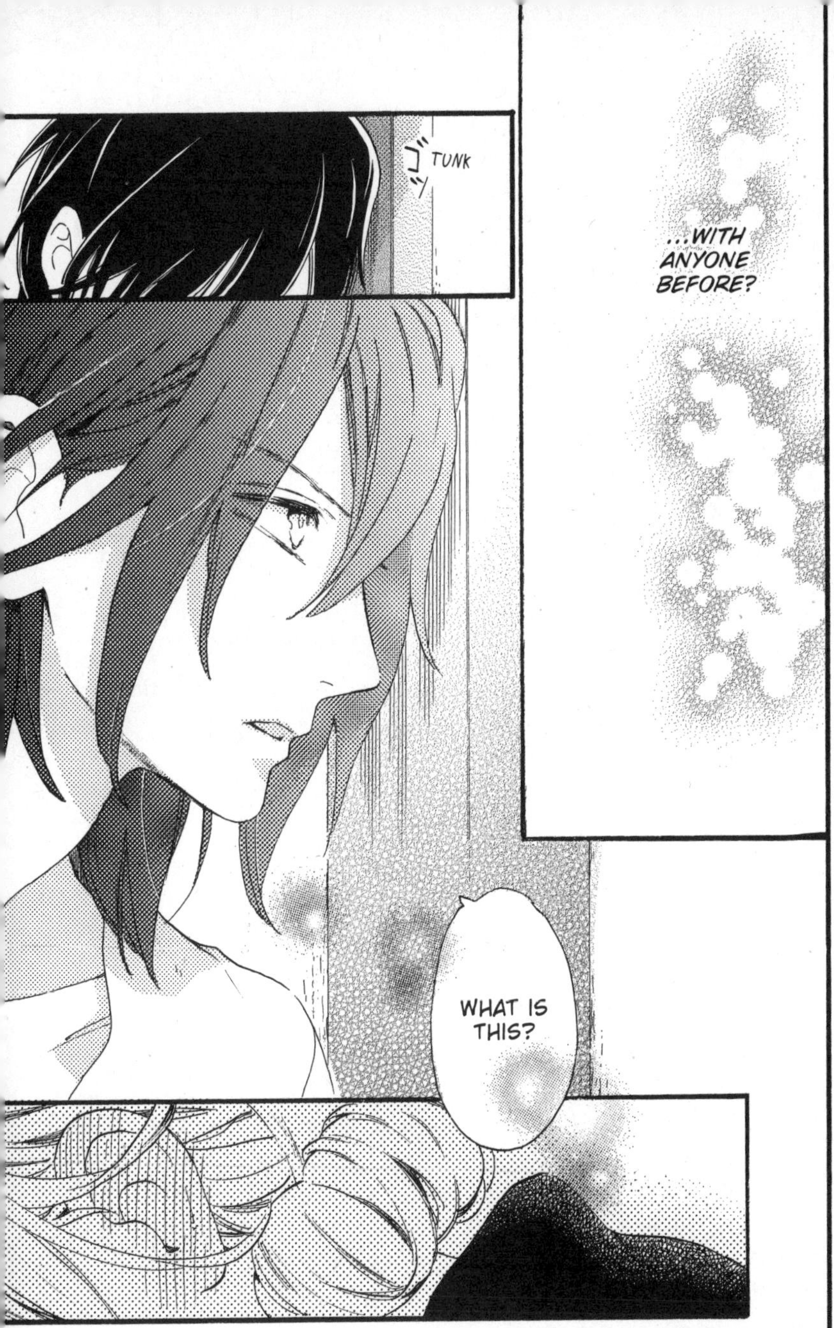
...WITH ANYONE BEFORE?
TUNK
WHAT IS THIS?

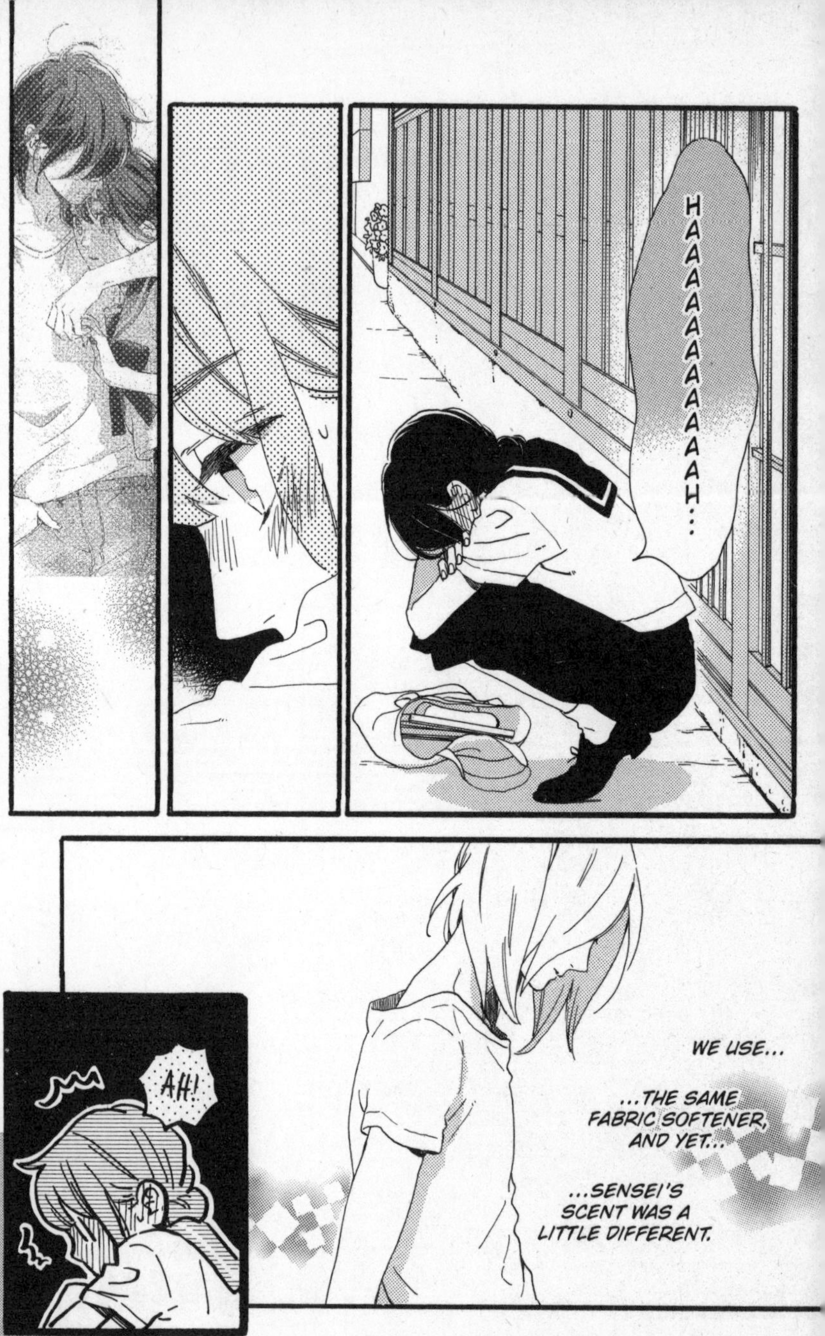
HAAAAAAAAAAAH...
WE USE...
...THE SAME FABRIC SOFTENER, AND YET...
...SENSEI'S SCENT WAS A LITTLE DIFFERENT.
AH!

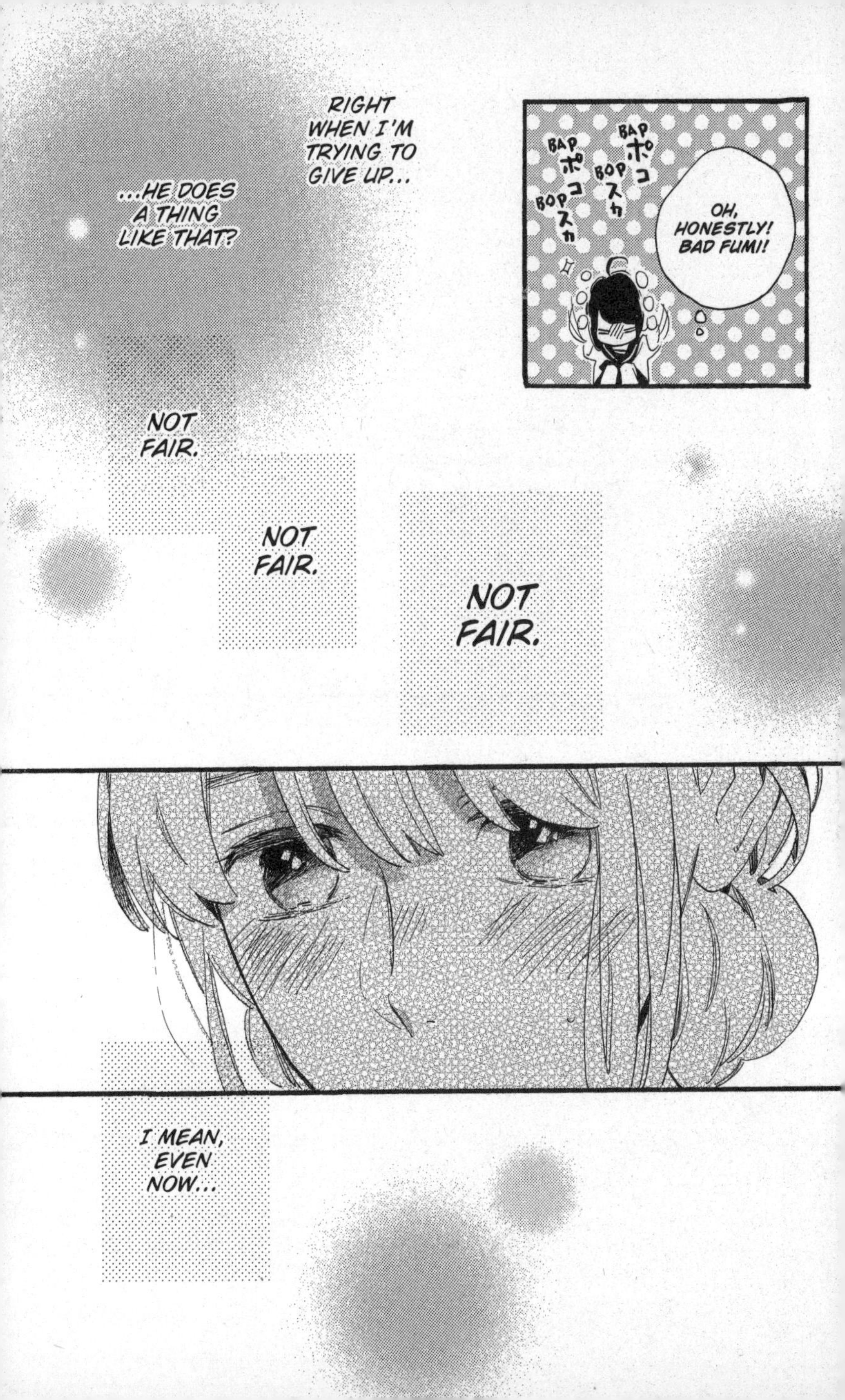
BAP ポコ
BOP スカ
BAP ポコ
BOP スカ
OH, HONESTLY! BAD FUMI!
RIGHT WHEN I'M TRYING TO GIVE UP...
...HE DOES A THING LIKE THAT?
NOT FAIR.
NOT FAIR.
NOT FAIR.
I MEAN, EVEN NOW...

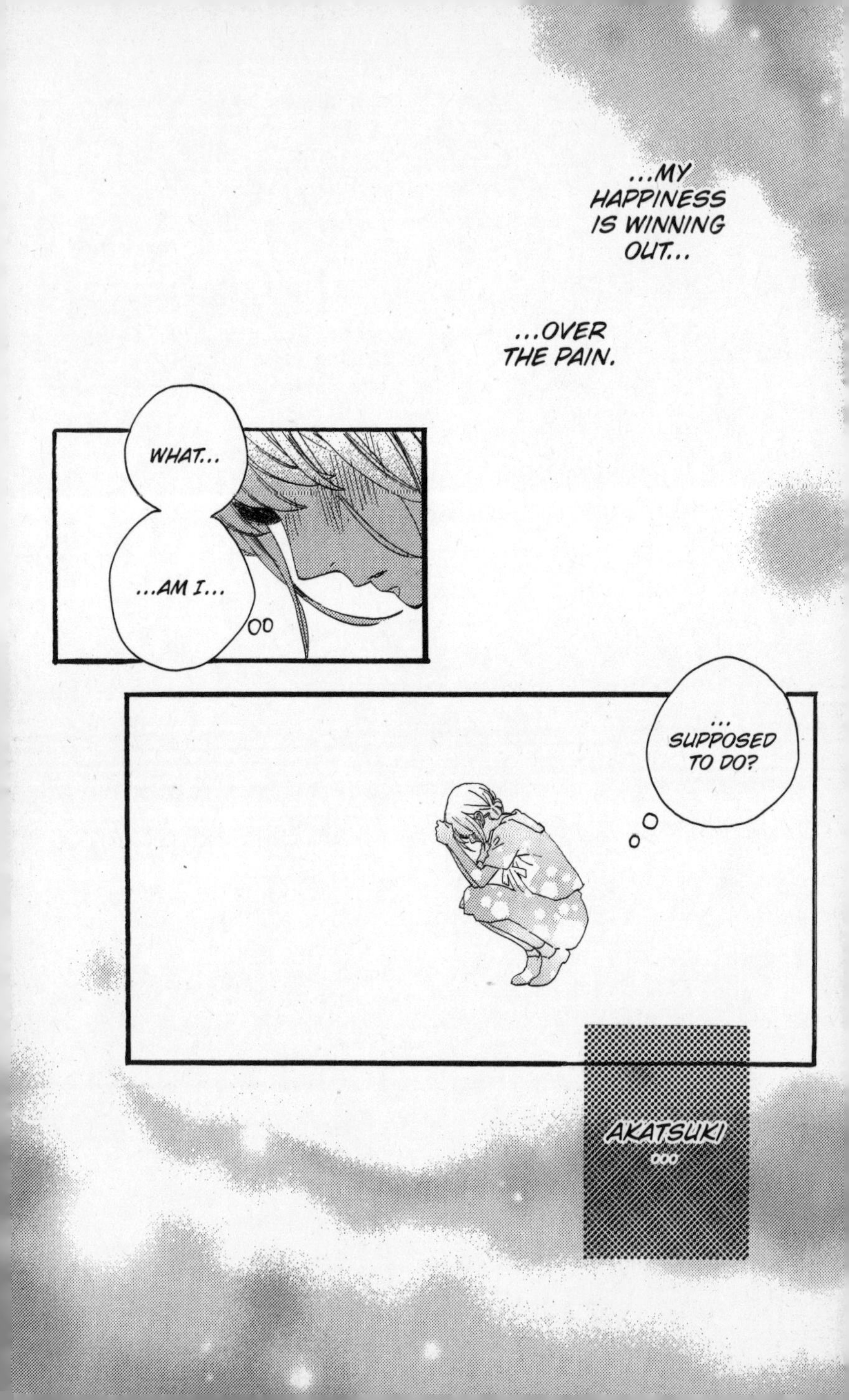
...MY HAPPINESS IS WINNING OUT...
...OVER THE PAIN.
WHAT...
...AM I...
...SUPPOSED TO DO?
AKATSUKI...

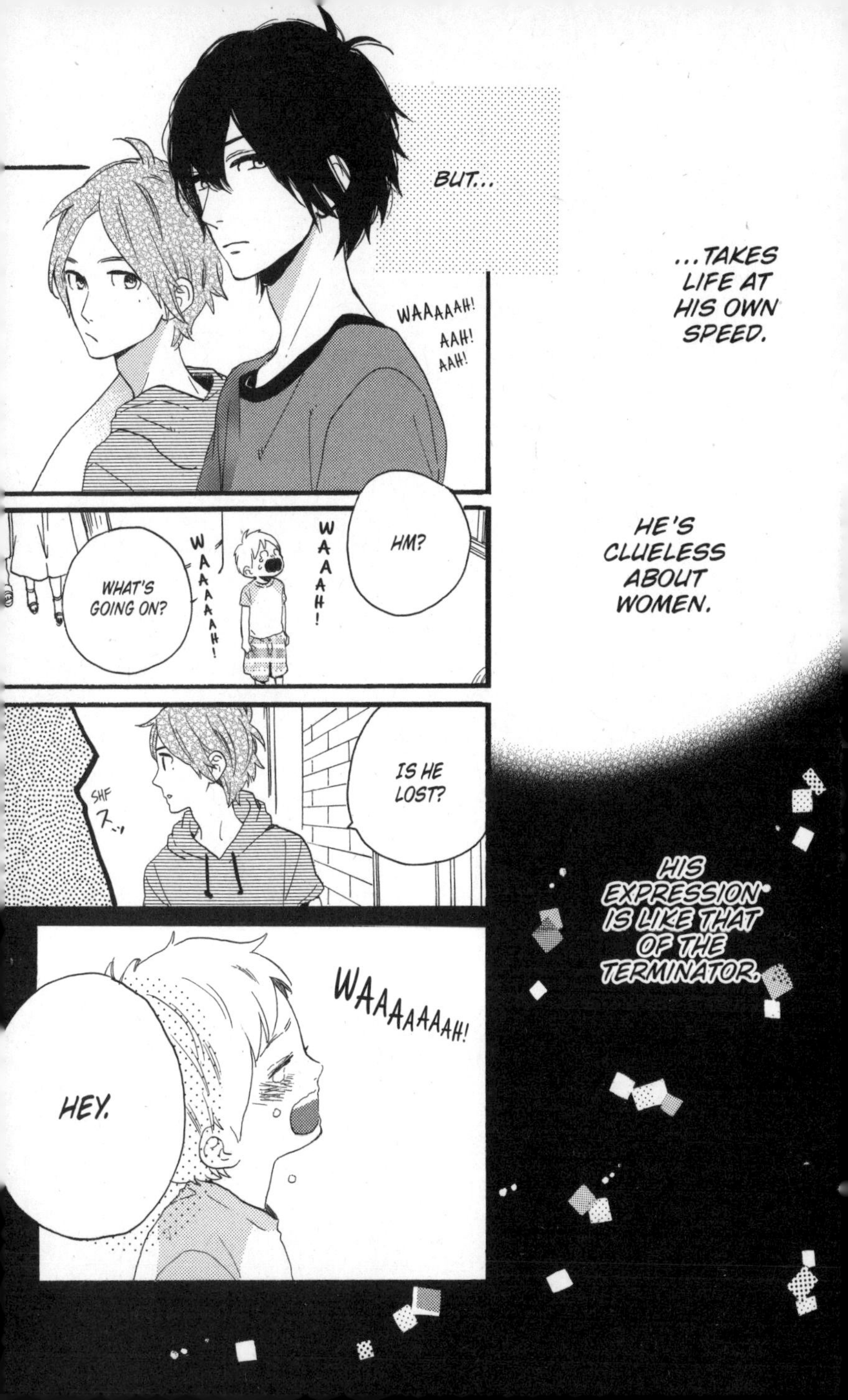
BUT...
...TAKES LIFE AT HIS OWN SPEED.
WAAAAAH!
AAH!
AAH!
HE'S CLUELESS ABOUT WOMEN.
HM?
WAAAAH!
WAAAAAAH!
WHAT'S GOING ON?
IS HE LOST?
SHF
HIS EXPRESSION IS LIKE THAT OF THE TERMINATOR.
WAAAAAAAH!
HEY.

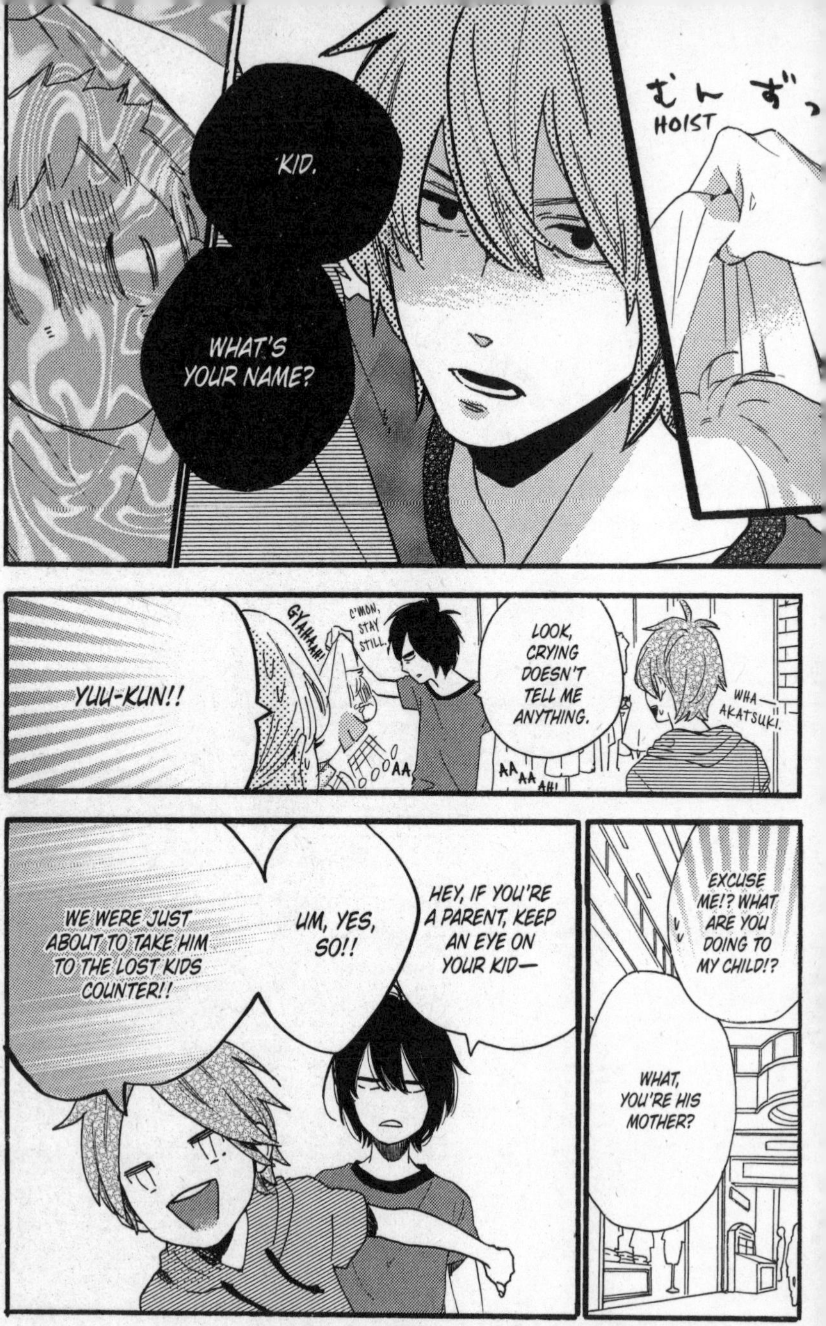
むんずっ
HOIST
KID.
WHAT'S YOUR NAME?
WHA— AKATSUKI.
LOOK, CRYING DOESN'T TELL ME ANYTHING.
AA AA AH!
C'MON, STAY STILL.
GYAHAAH!
OOOAA
YUU-KUN!!
EXCUSE ME!? WHAT ARE YOU DOING TO MY CHILD!?
WHAT, YOU'RE HIS MOTHER?
HEY, IF YOU'RE A PARENT, KEEP AN EYE ON YOUR KID—
UM, YES, SO!!
WE WERE JUST ABOUT TO TAKE HIM TO THE LOST KIDS COUNTER!!

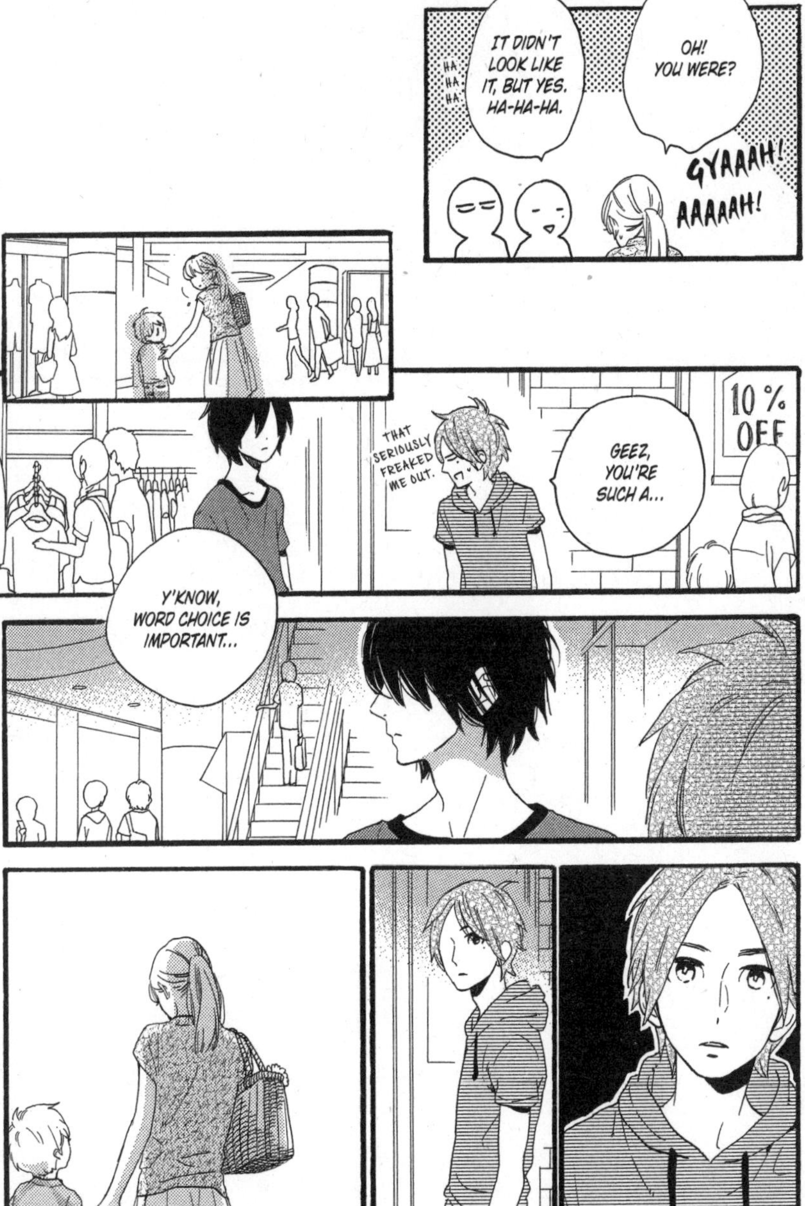
OH! YOU WERE?
IT DIDN'T LOOK LIKE IT, BUT YES. HA-HA-HA.
HA HA HA
GYAAAH! AAAAAH!
10 % OFF
GEEZ, YOU'RE SUCH A...
THAT SERIOUSLY FREAKED ME OUT.
Y'KNOW, WORD CHOICE IS IMPORTANT...

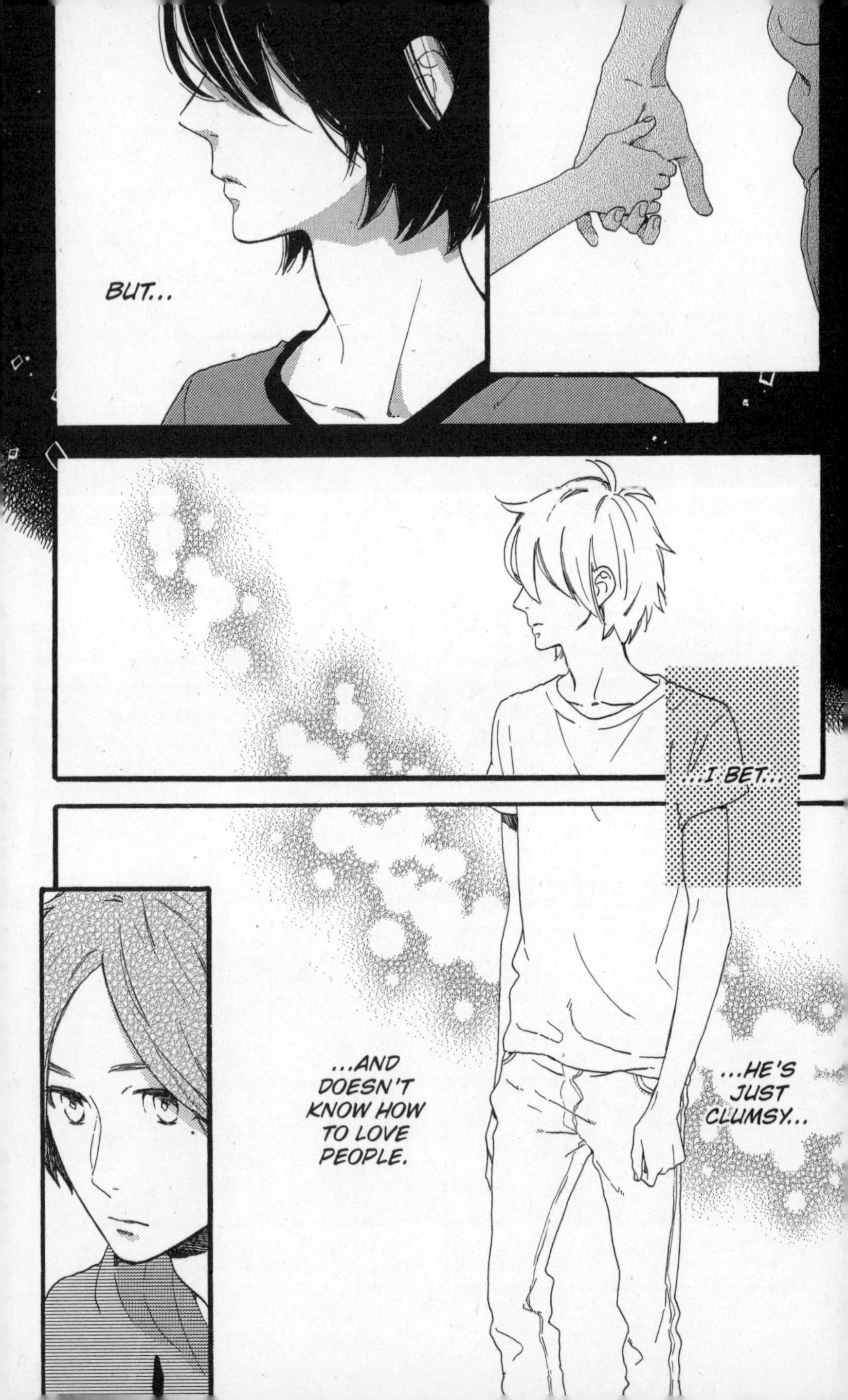
BUT...
...I BET...
...HE'S JUST CLUMSY...
...AND DOESN'T KNOW HOW TO LOVE PEOPLE.

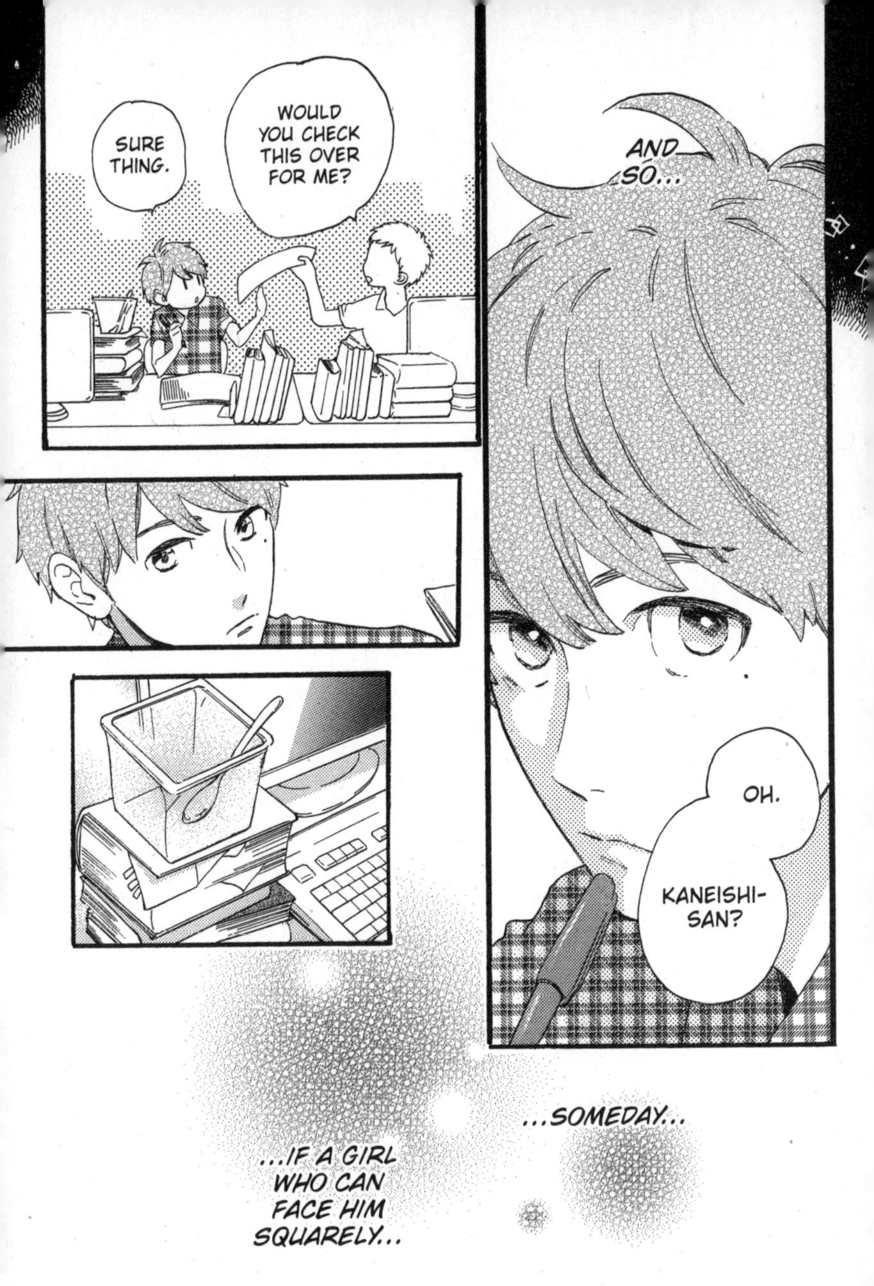
AND SO...
OH.
KANEISHI-SAN?
WOULD YOU CHECK THIS OVER FOR ME?
SURE THING.
...SOMEDAY...
...IF A GIRL WHO CAN FACE HIM SQUARELY...

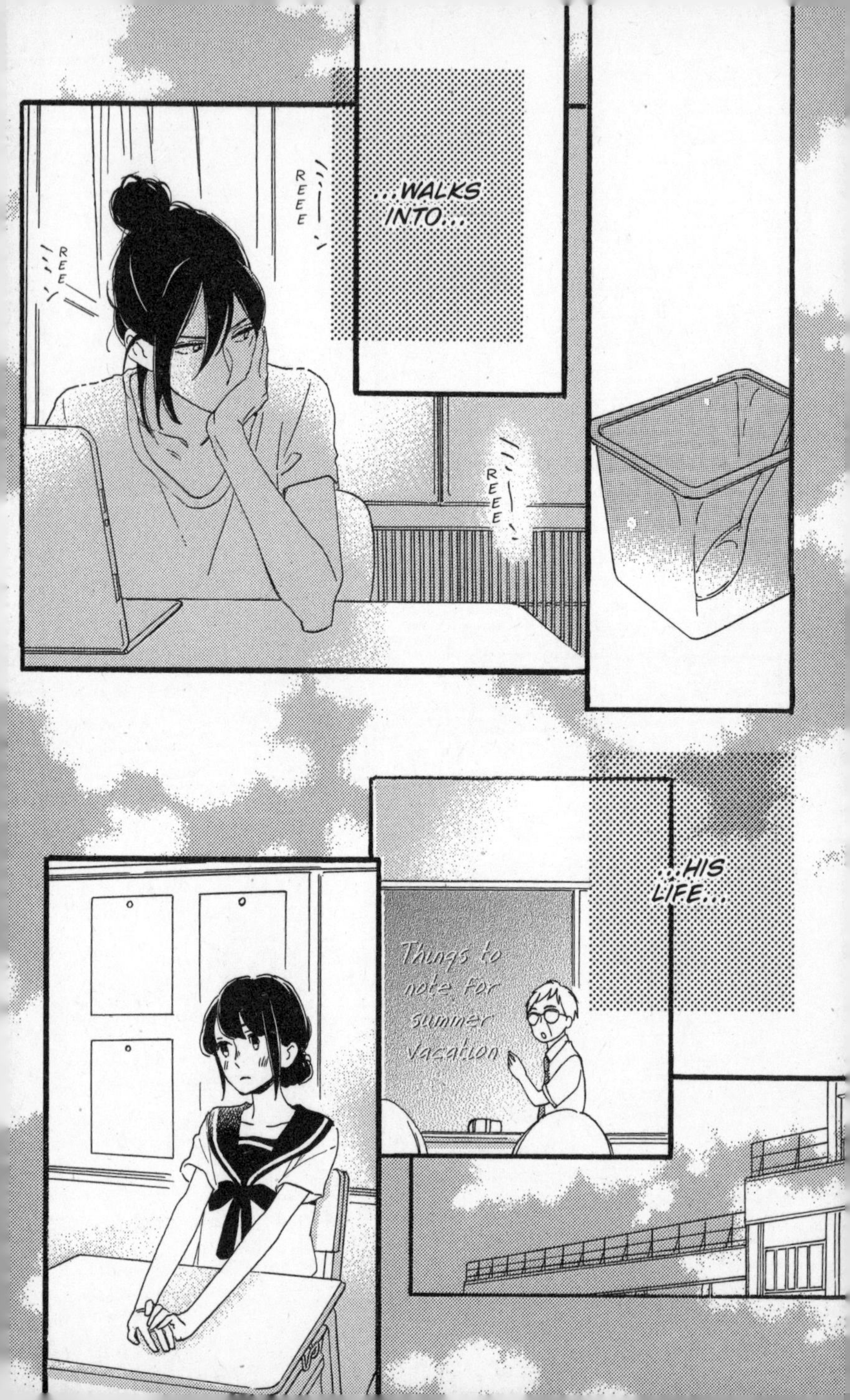
...WALKS INTO...
REEE
REEE
REE
...HIS LIFE...
Things to note for summer vacation

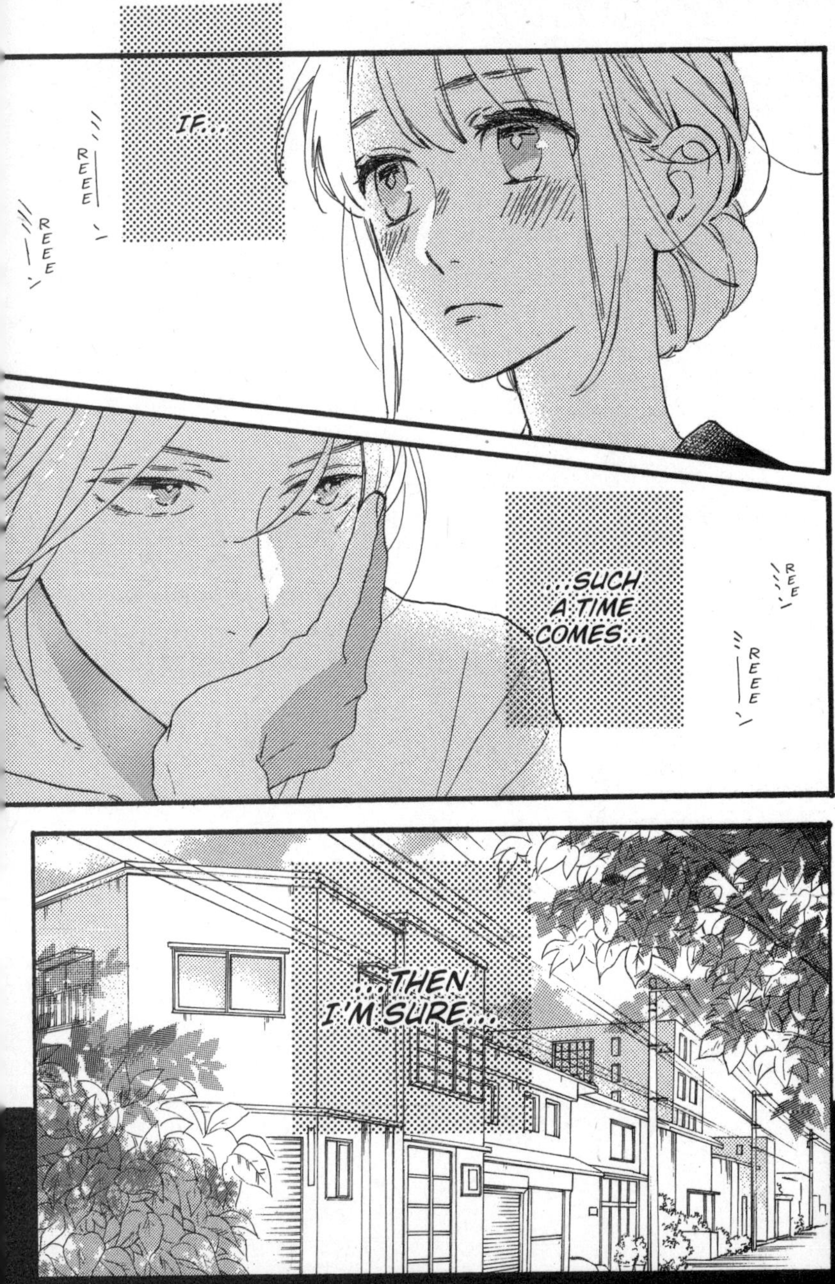
IF...
REEE
REEE
...SUCH A TIME COMES...
REE
REEE
...THEN I'M SURE...

<TO BE CONTINUED>

GOROMARU
POSE
IN SECRET.

Afterword.

So what did you think of *tsubaki-chou*, Volume 3? Volume 4 should be out soon, so please keep an eye out for it!

Special Thanx.

My editor, N-sama
The *Margaret* editorial department
The designer
Everyone at the printer
Kame-chan, Nozomu Yuu-sama, Eriko Umeno-sama, Arika Nijino-sama, Tirol Takahashi-sama, and all my readers.

Let's meet again in Volume 4!

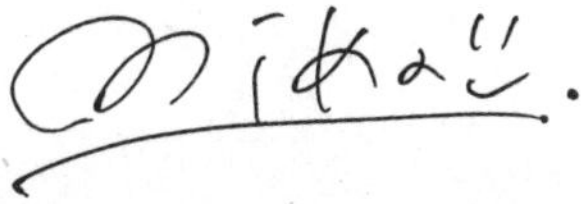

SUMMER VACATION! IN OTHER WORDS—

PREVIEW OF NEXT VOLUME

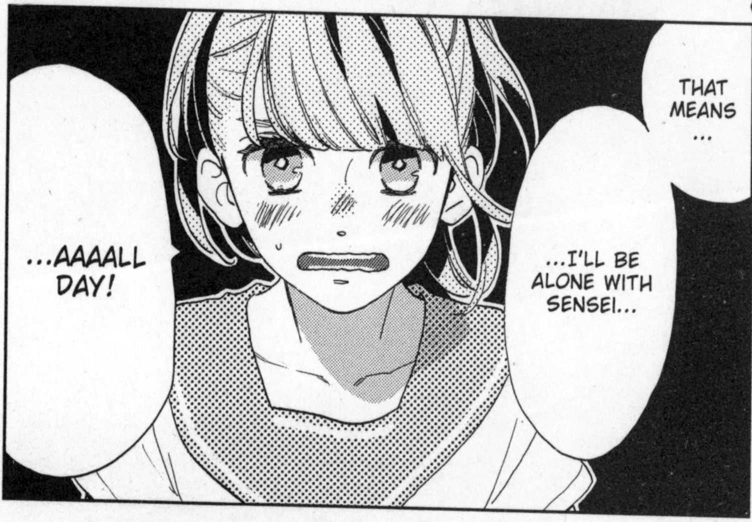
THAT MEANS ...
...I'LL BE ALONE WITH SENSEI...
...AAAALL DAY!

TOGETHER ALL DAY LONG!!

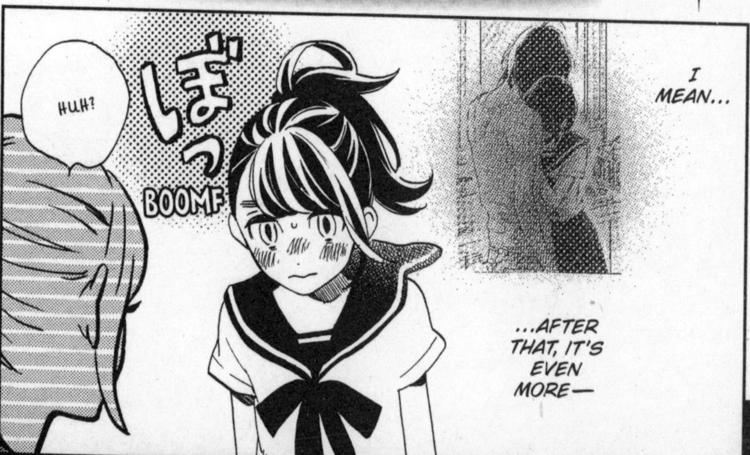
I MEAN...
...AFTER THAT, IT'S EVEN MORE—
ぼっ
BOOMF
HUH?

AND JUST AS SHE'S WONDERING WHAT TO DO...

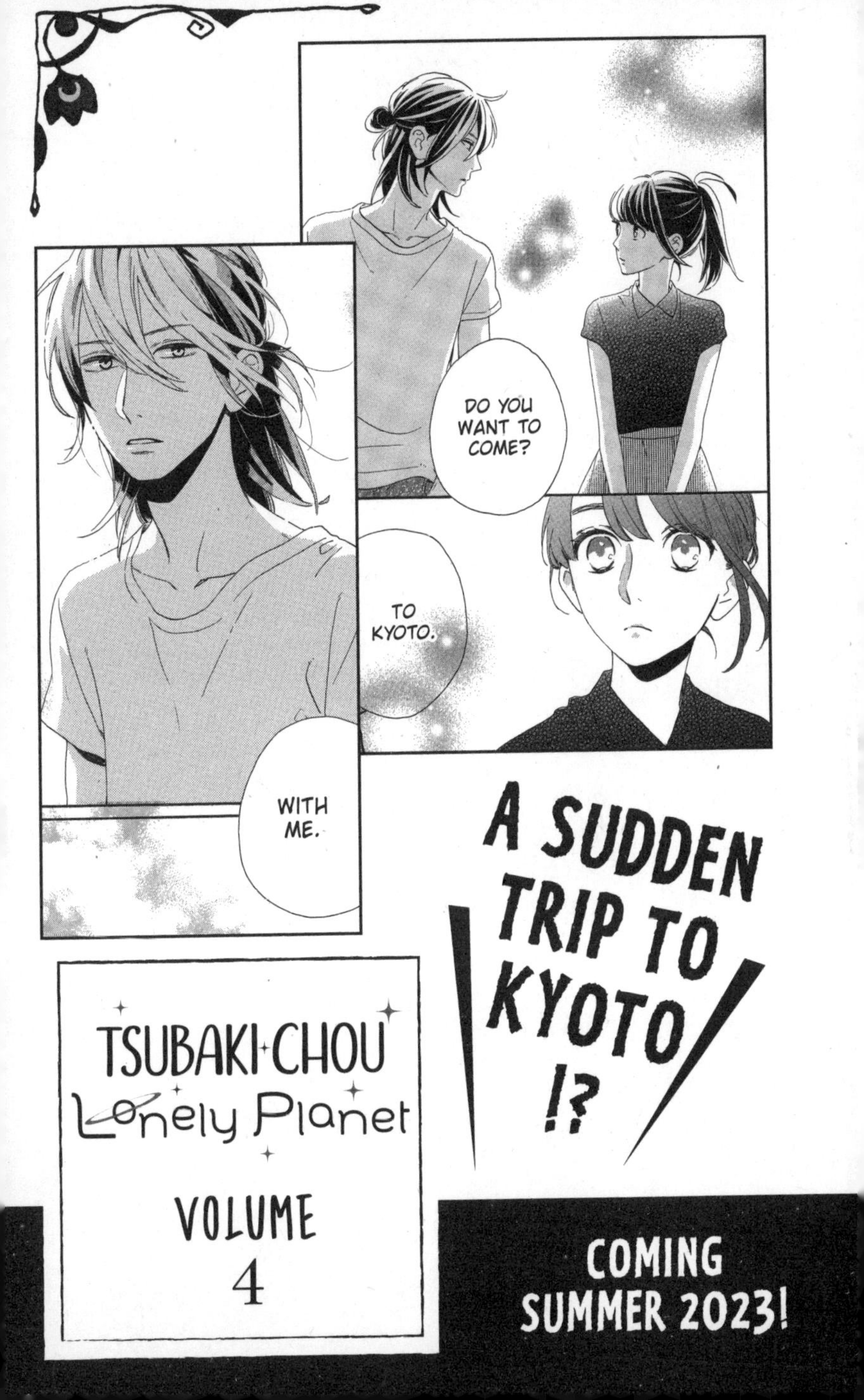
DO YOU WANT TO COME?
TO KYOTO.
WITH ME.
A SUDDEN TRIP TO KYOTO !?
TSUBAKI-CHOU Lonely Planet
VOLUME 4
COMING SUMMER 2023!

TRANSLATION NOTES

-san: The Japanese equivalent of Mr./Mrs./Miss. If a situation calls for politeness, this is the fail-safe honorific.

-kun: Used most often when referring to boys, this indicates affection or familiarity. Occasionally used by older men among their peers, but it may also be used by anyone referring to a person of lower standing.

-chan: An affectionate honorific indicating familiarity used mostly in reference to girls; also used in reference to cute persons or animals regardless of gender.

-sensei: A respectful term for teachers, artists, or high-level professionals.

No honorific: Indicates familiarity or closeness; if used without permission or reason, addressing someone in this manner would be interpreted as an insult or disrespectful.

General

Tsubaki: means "camellia," so the neighborhood's name translates to "town of camellias" or "Camellia Place."

PAGE 0010

Dorayaki: These are a type of Japanese sweet. There are several variations, but the most common version consists of sweetened red bean paste sandwiched between two sweet pancakes.

Sasakama: Short for *sasakamaboko*, or fish paste cakes formed into the shape of bamboo leaves. They're a popular souvenir from the city of Sendai.

PAGE 014

Restaurant Kameyoshi: This is possibly a reference to a similarly named restaurant located in the neighborhood of Shibuya.

PAGE 015

Myoga: It is Japanese ginger and belongs to the same family as the ginger used in Western cooking. However, while the ginger commonly sold in the U.S. is the whole, powdered, or shredded root

of the plant, only the buds and flowers of the *myoga* plant are used in cooking.

PAGE 016

Suigei sake: *Suigei* means "drunken whale." Youdou Yamauchi (also known as Toyoshige Yamauchi, 1827 – 1872) was a feudal lord of the Tosa Domain in Shikoku near the end of the Edo period. He loved liquor, women, and poetry, and referred to himself as "the drunken lord of the whales' domain."

"The drunken lord of the domain of whales. When tipsy, an imperialist. Once sober, a shogunate supporter.": This is a famous real-life jab directed at Yamauchi, who was pretty indecisive politically. The saying is attributed to the imperial loyalist faction.

Shogunate: While Japan did have an emperor during the Edo period, the *shogun* was the one who was truly in power. The fall of the *shogunate* marked the end of the period, and in the subsequent Meiji period, power was restored to the emperor.

PAGE 071

Keema curry: A type of Indian curry made with minced meat.

PAGE 129

Ghost Story of Yotsuya: Commonly known as *Yotsuya Kaidan* in Japanese, it is an extremely famous horror story that began as an 1825 *Kabuki* play. One of the main characters is the vengeful ghost of a woman named Oiwa,

who becomes hysterical and accidentally
kills herself when her face is disfigured
by a poisoned facial cream given to
her by a love rival. The disfiguration
is especially prominent around
the character's eyes, which is why
Akatsuki makes this association.

PAGE 168
Goromaru: Ayumu Goromaru is a
Japanese rugby player who is often
photographed in this pose.

PAGE 169
Magaret: The *manga* magazine released
by publishing company Shueisha. It
focuses primarily on *shoujo manga*,
which is *manga* geared towards a
younger female demographic, such
as *Tsubaki-chou Lonely Planet*.

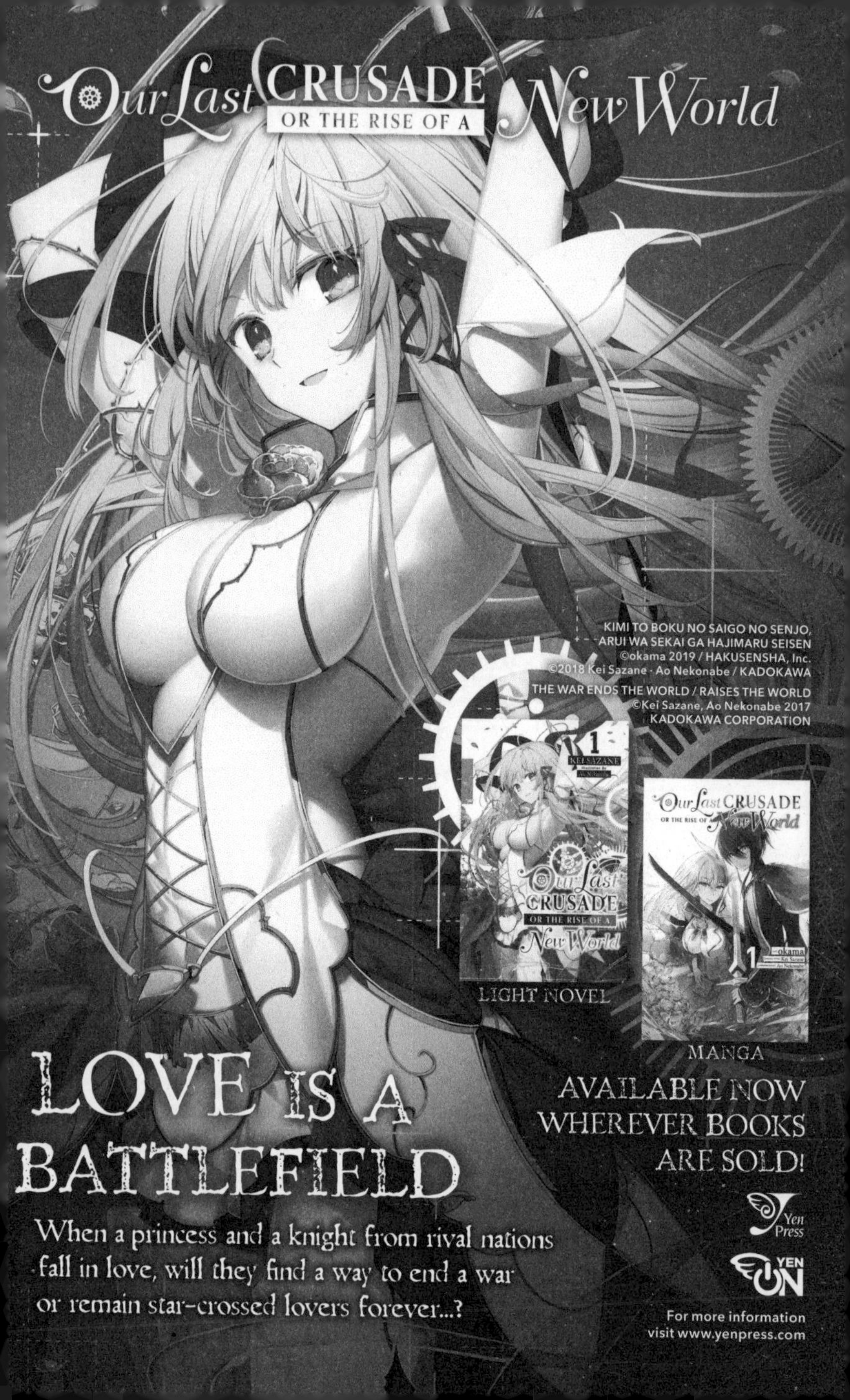
Our Last CRUSADE OR THE RISE OF A New World
KIMI TO BOKU NO SAIGO NO SENJO, ARUI WA SEKAI GA HAJIMARU SEISEN ©okama 2019 / HAKUSENSHA, Inc. ©2018 Kei Sazane · Ao Nekonabe / KADOKAWA
THE WAR ENDS THE WORLD / RAISES THE WORLD ©Kei Sazane, Ao Nekonabe 2017 KADOKAWA CORPORATION
LIGHT NOVEL
MANGA
LOVE IS A BATTLEFIELD
When a princess and a knight from rival nations fall in love, will they find a way to end a war or remain star-crossed lovers forever...?
AVAILABLE NOW WHEREVER BOOKS ARE SOLD!
Yen Press
YEN ON
For more information visit www.yenpress.com

TSUBAKI·CHOU Lonely Planet

3

MIKA YAMAMORI

Translation: Taylor Engel ✦ Lettering: Lys Blakeslee

TSUBAKI-CHOU LONELY PLANET Vol. 3
© 2015 by Mika Yamamori
All rights reserved. First published in Japan in 2015 by SHUEISHA, Inc.
English translation rights arranged with SHUEISHA, Inc.
through Tuttle-Mori Agency, Inc.

English translation © 2023 by Yen Press, LLC

Yen Press
150 West 30th Street, 19th Floor
New York, NY 10001

Visit us at yenpress.com
facebook.com/yenpress
twitter.com/yenpress
yenpress.tumblr.com
instagram.com/yenpress

First Yen Press Edition: April 2023
Edited by Yen Press Editorial: Won Young Seo, JuYoun Lee
Designed by Yen Press Design: Eddy Mingki

Yen Press is an imprint of Yen Press, LLC.
The Yen Press name and logo are trademarks of Yen Press, LLC.

Library of Congress Control Number: 2022936178

ISBNs: 978-1-9753-4624-9 (paperback)
978-1-9753-4625-6 (ebook)

10 9 8 7 6 5 4 3 2 1

LSC-C

Printed in the United States of America